THE GOSPEL'S POWER AND MESSAGE

Recovering the Gospel

❧

The Gospel's Power and Message

The Gospel Call and True Conversion

Gospel Assurance and Warnings

THE GOSPEL'S POWER AND MESSAGE

PAUL WASHER

Reformation Heritage Books
Grand Rapids, Michigan

The Gospel's Power and Message
© 2012 Paul Washer

Published by
Reformation Heritage Books
3070 29th St. SE
Grand Rapids, MI 49512
616-977-0889
e-mail: orders@heritagebooks.org
website: www.heritagebooks.org

Printed in the United States of America
22 23 24 25 26 27/14 13 12 11 10 9 8

Library of Congress Cataloging-in-Publication Data

Washer, Paul, 1961-
  The Gospel's power and message / Paul Washer.
    pages cm. — (Recovering the Gospel)
  ISBN 978-1-60178-195-6 (pbk. : alk. paper) 1. Christian life. 2. Salvation—
Biblical teaching. 3. Evangelistic work. I. Title.
  BV4501.3.W374 2012
  230—dc23
                              2012035293

*For additional Reformed literature, request a free book list from Reformation Heritage
Books at the above address.*

Contents

Series Preface: Recovering the Gospel

The gospel of Jesus Christ is the greatest of all treasures given to the church and the individual Christian. It is not *a* message among many but *the* message above them all. It is the power of God for salvation and the greatest revelation of the manifold wisdom of God to men and angels.[1] It is for this reason that the apostle Paul gave the gospel the first place in his preaching, endeavored with all his might to proclaim it clearly, and even pronounced a curse upon all those who would pervert its truth.[2]

Each generation of Christians is a steward of the gospel message, and through the power of the Holy Spirit, God calls upon us to guard this treasure that has been entrusted to us.[3] If we are to be faithful stewards, we must be absorbed in the study of the gospel, take great pains to understand its truths, and pledge ourselves to guard its contents.[4] In doing so, we will ensure salvation both for ourselves and for those who hear us.[5]

This stewardship drives me to write these books. I have little desire for the hard work of writing, and there is certainly no lack of Christian books, but I have put the following collection of sermons in written form for the same reason that I preached them: to be free from their burden. Like Jeremiah, if I do not speak forth this message, "then…in my heart [it becomes] like a burning fire shut up in my bones; and I was weary of holding it back, and I could not."[6] As the apostle Paul exclaimed, "Woe is me if I do not preach the gospel!"[7]

---

1. Romans 1:16; Ephesians 3:10
2. 1 Corinthians 15:3; Colossians 4:4; Galatians 1:8–9
3. 2 Timothy 1:14
4. 1 Timothy 4:15
5. 1 Timothy 4:16
6. Jeremiah 20:9
7. 1 Corinthians 9:16

As is commonly known, the word *gospel* comes from the Greek word *euangélion*, which is properly translated "good news." In one sense, every page of Scripture contains the gospel, but in another sense, the gos-pel refers to a very specific message—the salvation accomplished for a fallen people through the life, death, resurrection, and ascension of Jesus Christ, the Son of God.

In accordance with the Father's good pleasure, the eternal Son, who is equal with the Father and is the exact representation of His nature, willingly left the glory of heaven, was conceived by the Holy Spirit in the womb of a virgin, and was born the God-man: Jesus of Nazareth.[8] As a man, He walked on this earth in perfect obedience to the law of God.[9] In the fullness of time, men rejected and crucified Him. On the cross, He bore man's sin, suffered God's wrath, and died in man's place.[10] On the third day, God raised Him from the dead. This resurrection is the divine declaration that the Father has accepted His Son's death as a sacrifice for sin. Jesus paid the penalty for man's disobedience, satisfied the demands of justice, and appeased the wrath of God.[11] Forty days after the resurrection, the Son of God ascended into the heavens, sat down at the right hand of the Father, and was given glory, honor, and dominion over all.[12] There, in the presence of God, He represents His people and makes requests to God on their behalf.[13] All who acknowledge their sinful, helpless state and throw themselves upon Christ, God will fully pardon, declare righteous, and reconcile unto Himself.[14] This is the gospel of God and of Jesus Christ, His Son.

One of the greatest crimes committed by this present Christian generation is its neglect of the gospel, and it is from this neglect that all our other maladies spring forth. The lost world is not so much gospel hardened as it is gospel ignorant because many of those who proclaim the gospel are also ignorant of its most basic truths. The essential themes that make up the very core of the gospel—the justice of God, the radical depravity of man, the blood atonement, the nature of true conversion,

---

8. Acts 2:23; Hebrews 1:3; Philippians 2:6–7; Luke 1:35
9. Hebrews 4:15
10. 1 Peter 2:24; 3:18; Isaiah 53:10
11. Luke 24:6; Romans 1:4; Romans 4:25
12. Hebrews 1:3; Matthew 28:18; Daniel 7:13–14
13. Luke 24:51; Philippians 2:9–11; Hebrews 1:3; Hebrews 7:25
14. Mark 1:15; Romans 10:9; Philippians 3:3

and the biblical basis of assurance—are absent from too many pulpits. Churches reduce the gospel message to a few creedal statements, teach that conversion is a mere human decision, and pronounce assurance of salvation over anyone who prays the sinner's prayer.

The result of this gospel reductionism has been far-reaching. First, it further hardens the hearts of the unconverted. Few modern-day "converts" ever make their way into the fellowship of the church, and those who do often fall away or have lives marked by habitual carnality. Untold millions walk our streets and sit in our pews unchanged by the true gospel of Jesus Christ, and yet they are convinced of their salvation because one time in their life they raised a hand at an evangelistic campaign or repeated a prayer. This false sense of security creates a great barrier that often insulates such individuals from ever hearing the true gospel.

Secondly, such a gospel deforms the church from a spiritual body of regenerated believers into a gathering of carnal men who profess to know God, but by their deeds they deny Him.[15] With the preaching of the true gospel, men come to the church without gospel entertainment, special activities, or the promise of benefits beyond those offered by the gospel. Those who come do so because they desire Christ and are hungry for biblical truth, heartfelt worship, and opportunities for service. When the church proclaims a lesser gospel, it fills up with carnal men who share little interest in the things of God, and the maintenance of such men is a heavy burden upon the church.[16] The church then tones down the radical demands of the gospel to a convenient morality, and true devotion to Christ gives way to activities designed to meet the felt needs of its members. The church becomes activity-driven rather than Christ-centered, and it carefully filters or repackages the truth so as not to offend the carnal majority. The church lays aside the great truths of Scripture and orthodox Christianity, and pragmatism (i.e., whatever keeps the church going and growing) becomes the rule of the day.

Thirdly, such a gospel reduces evangelism and missions to little more than a humanistic endeavor driven by clever marketing strategies based upon a careful study of the latest trends in culture. After years of witnessing the impotence of an unbiblical gospel, many evangelicals seem convinced that the gospel will not work and that man has somehow

---

15. Titus 1:16
16. 1 Corinthians 2:14

become too complex a being to be saved and transformed by such a simple and scandalous message. There is now more emphasis on understanding our fallen culture and its fads than on understanding and proclaiming the only message that has the power to save it. As a result, the gospel is constantly being repackaged to fit what contemporary culture deems most relevant. We have forgotten that the true gospel is always relevant to every culture because it is God's eternal word to every man.

Fourthly, such a gospel brings reproach to the name of God. Through the proclamation of a lesser gospel, the carnal and unconverted come into the fellowship of the church, and through the almost total neglect of biblical church discipline, they are allowed to stay without correction or reproof. This soils the purity and reputation of the church and blasphemes the name of God among the unbelieving.[17] In the end, God is not glorified, the church is not edified, the unconverted church member is not saved, and the church has little or no witness to the unbelieving world.

It does not become us as ministers or laymen to stand so near and do nothing when we see "the glorious gospel of our blessed God" replaced by a gospel of lesser glory.[18] As stewards of this trust, we have a duty to recover the one true gospel and proclaim it boldly and clearly to all. We would do well to pay heed to the words of Charles Haddon Spurgeon:

> In these days, I feel bound to go over the elementary truths of the gospel repeatedly. In peaceful times, we may feel free to make excursions into interesting districts of truth which lie far afield; but now we must stay at home, and guard the hearts and homes of the church by defending the first principles of the faith. In this age, there have risen up in the church itself men who speak perverse things. There be many that trouble us with their philosophies and novel interpretations, whereby they deny the doctrines they profess to teach, and undermine the faith they are pledged to maintain. It is well that some of us, who know what we believe, and have no secret meanings for our words, should just put our foot down and maintain our standing, holding forth the word of life, and plainly declaring the foundation truths of the gospel of Jesus Christ.[19]

17. Romans 2:24
18. 1 Timothy 1:11
19. Charles H. Spurgeon, *The Metropolitan Tabernacle Pulpit* (repr., Pasadena, Tex.: Pilgrim Publications), 32:385.

Although the Recovering the Gospel series does not represent an entirely systematic presentation of the gospel, it does address most of the essential elements, especially those that are most neglected in contemporary Christianity. It is my hope that these words might be a guide to help you rediscover the gospel in all its beauty, scandal, and saving power. It is my prayer that such a rediscovery might transform your life, strengthen your proclamation, and bring the greatest glory to God.

Your brother,
Paul David Washer

PART ONE

An Apostolic Introduction

Moreover, brethren, I declare to you the gospel which I preached to you, which also you received and in which you stand, by which also you are saved, if you hold fast that word which I preached to you—unless you believed in vain. For I delivered to you first of all that which I also received: that Christ died for our sins according to the Scriptures, and that He was buried, and that He rose again the third day according to the Scriptures.

—1 Corinthians 15:1–4

CHAPTER ONE

A Gospel to Know and Make Known

Moreover, brethren, I declare to you the gospel which I preached to you.
—1 Corinthians 15:1

A writer or preacher would be hard-pressed to produce a better introduction to the gospel of Jesus Christ than the apostle Paul gives to the church in Corinth.[1] In these few lines, he provides enough truth to live on for a lifetime and to bring us home to glory. Only the Holy Spirit could enable a man to say so much, so clearly, and in so few words.

KNOWING THE GOSPEL

In this small portion of Scripture, we find a truth that all of us must rediscover. The gospel is not merely an introductory message to Christianity—it is *the* message of Christianity, and the believer would do well to give his life in the pursuit of knowing its glory and making its glory known. There are many things to be known in this world and countless truths to be investigated within the realm of Christianity itself; nevertheless, the glorious gospel of our blessed God and His Son Jesus Christ ranks high above them all.[2] It is the message of our salvation, the means of our progress toward sanctification, and the pristine fountain from which flows every pure and right motivation for the Christian life. The believer who has comprehended something of its content and character will never lack in zeal nor be so impoverished that he seeks to draw strength from broken, waterless cisterns hewn by the hands of men.[3]

---

1. 1 Corinthians 15:1–4
2. 1 Timothy 1:11
3. Jeremiah 2:13; 14:3

First Corinthians 15:1 explains that the apostle had already preached the gospel to the church in Corinth. In fact, he was their father in the faith![4] Yet he sees the greatest need to continue teaching the gospel to them—not only to remind them of its essential ingredients, but also to expand their knowledge of it. At their conversion, they had only just begun a journey of discovery that would encompass their entire life and carry on through the endless ages of eternity, discovering the glories of God revealed in the gospel of Jesus Christ.

As preachers and congregants, we would be wise to see the gospel anew through the eyes of this ancient apostle and to esteem it worthy of a lifetime of careful investigation. For though we may have already lived many years in the faith; though we may possess the intellect of Edwards and the insight of Spurgeon; though we may have memorized every biblical text concerning the gospel; and though we may have digested every publication from the early church fathers, the Reformers, the Puritans, and up through the scholars of this present age, we can be assured that we have not yet even reached the foothills of this Everest that we call the gospel. Even after an eternity of eternities the same will be said of us!

We live in a world that offers us an almost infinite number of possibilities, and countless options vie for our attention. The same may be said of Christianity and the broad range of theological themes that a student might pursue. There is an almost infinite number of biblical truths that a man might spend a lifetime examining. However, one theme rises above them all and is foundational to the understanding of all other biblical truth: the gospel of Jesus Christ. Through this singular message, God's power manifests itself most in the church and in the life of the individual believer.

As we look through the annals of Christian history, we see men and women of unusual passion for God and His kingdom. We long to be like them, and we wonder how they came to have such enduring fire. After a careful consideration of their lives, doctrine, and ministries, we find that they differed in many things, but there was one common denominator among them: they had all caught a glimpse of the glory of the gospel, and its beauty kindled their passion and drove them on. Their lives and legacies prove that genuine and enduring passion comes from an ever-increasing, ever-deepening understanding of what God has done for His

---

4. 1 Corinthians 4:15

people in the person and work of Jesus Christ. For such knowledge there is no substitute!

In days gone by, the Christian gospel was often referred to as the *evangel*, from the Latin word *evangelium*, meaning gospel or good news. It is for this reason that believers are often referred to as evangelicals. We are Christians because we find our identity, life, and purpose in Christ. We are evangelical because we believe the gospel and esteem it as the great central truth of God's revelation to men. It is not a foreword, a byword, or an afterthought; it is not merely the introductory class to Christianity; it is the entire course of study. It is the story of our lives, the unfathomable riches we seek to explore, and the message we live to proclaim. For this reason, we are most Christian and most evangelical when the gospel of Jesus Christ is our one hope, our one boast, and our one magnificent obsession.

Today, evangelicals design so many conferences, especially for our youth, with the intention of exciting the believer's passion through fellowship, music, eloquent speakers, emotional stories, and impassioned pleas. Yet whatever excitement they create often quickly vanishes. In the end, these experiences build little fires in little hearts that burn out in a few days.

We have forgotten that genuine, enduring passion is born out of one's knowledge of the truth, and specifically the truth of the gospel. The more you know or comprehend its beauty, the more its power will apprehend you. One glimpse of the gospel will move the truly regenerate heart to follow. Every greater glimpse will quicken its pace until it is running recklessly toward the prize.[5] The truly Christian heart cannot resist such beauty. This is the great need of the day! It is what we have lost and what we must regain—a passion for knowing the gospel and an equal passion for making the gospel known.

MAKING THE GOSPEL KNOWN

The apostle Paul was one of the greatest human instruments of the kingdom of God in the history of humanity and the story of redemption. He was responsible for the spread of the gospel throughout the entire Roman Empire during a time of almost unequaled persecution, and he is

---

5. Philippians 3:13–14

an outstanding example of what it means to be a Christian minister. Yet he accomplished all of this through the simple proclamation of the most scandalous message ever to reach the ears of men. Paul was an exceptionally gifted man, especially with regard to his intellect and zeal. Yet he himself taught us that the power of his ministry did not lie in his gifting, but in the faithful proclamation of the gospel. In his first letter to the Corinthians, Paul writes his great disclaimer: "For Christ did not send me to baptize, but to preach the gospel, not with wisdom of words, lest the cross of Christ should be made of no effect.... For Jews request a sign, and Greeks seek after wisdom; but we preach Christ crucified, to the Jews a stumbling block and to the Greeks foolishness, but to those who are called, both Jews and Greeks, Christ the power of God and the wisdom of God."[6]

The apostle Paul was, above everything else, a preacher. Like Jeremiah before him, he was constrained to preach. The gospel was like a burning fire shut up in his bones that he could not hold in.[7] To the Corinthians, he declared, "I believed, and therefore have I spoken,"[8] and also, "Woe is me if I do not preach the gospel!"[9] Such a high estimation of the gospel and the preaching of it cannot be feigned when it does not exist in the heart of the preacher, and it cannot be hidden when it does.

God calls all types of men to carry the burden of the gospel message. Some of them are more solemn and grave, while others are more lighthearted and jovial. Yet when the conversation turns to the gospel, a change comes upon a preacher's countenance, and it seems as though an entirely different person is standing before us. Eternity is etched across his face, the veil has been removed, and the glory of the gospel shines forth with an unfabricated passion. Such a man has little time for quaint stories, moral antidotes, or sharing thoughts from his heart. He has come to preach, and preach he must! He cannot rest until the people have heard from God. If Abraham's servant could not eat until he had delivered the message of his master Abraham,[10] how much less can the

---

6. 1 Corinthians 1:17, 22–24
7. Jeremiah 20:9
8. 2 Corinthians 4:13 KJV
9. 1 Corinthians 9:16
10. Genesis 24:33

gospel preacher stand at ease until he has delivered the gospel treasure entrusted to him![11]

Although few would disagree with what we have said so far, it seems that for the most part, such impassioned preaching has gone out of style. Many would say it lacks the refinement and sophistication that are necessary to be effective in this modern era. The postmodern man, who prefers a bit more humility and openness to other viewpoints, considers a passionate preacher who proclaims the truth boldly and unapologetically to be an obstacle. The majority argument is that we simply must change the way we preach because it *just looks foolish* to the world.

Such an attitude toward preaching is proof that we have lost our bearings in the evangelical community. It is God who has ordained the "foolishness of preaching" to be the instrument for bringing the saving message of the gospel to the world.[12] That is not to say that preaching should be foolish, illogical, or outlandish. However, Scripture is the standard for all preaching, not the contemporary opinions of a fallen and corrupt culture that is wise in its own eyes and that would rather have its ears tickled and its heart entertained than to hear the Word of the Lord.[13]

Everywhere the apostle Paul traveled, he preached the gospel, and we would do well to follow his example. Although the gospel may be shared through many mediums, there is no medium so ordained by God as that of preaching. Therefore, those who are constantly seeking innovative means to communicate the gospel to a new generation of seekers would do well to begin and end their search in the Scriptures. Those who would send out thousands of questionnaires asking the unconverted what they would desire most in a worship service should realize that ten thousand unanimous opinions of carnal men do not carry the authority of one jot or tittle of God's Word.[14] We must understand that there is a great gulf of irreconcilable differences between what God has ordained in the Scriptures and what our present carnal culture desires.

We should not be amazed that carnal men both inside and outside the church desire drama, music, and media in the place of gospel preaching and biblical exposition. Until God regenerates a man's heart, that man

---

11. Galatians 2:7; 1 Thessalonians 2:4; 1 Timothy 1:11; 6:20; 2 Timothy 1:14; Titus 1:3
12. 1 Corinthians 1:21
13. Romans 1:22; 2 Timothy 4:3
14. Matthew 5:18

will address the gospel in the same way the demons of the Gadarenes addressed the Lord Jesus Christ: "What have we to do with You?"[15] The carnal man can have no true interest or appreciation in the gospel apart from the regenerating work of the Holy Spirit, and yet this miracle takes place in the heart of a man through the gospel preaching which he at first disdains. Therefore, we must preach to carnal men the very message they do not want to hear, and the Spirit must work! Apart from this, sinners can no more see beauty in the gospel than a swine can find beauty in pearls, or a dog can show reverence toward sanctified meat, or a blind man can appreciate a Rembrandt.[16] Preachers do no service to carnal men by giving them the very things their fallen hearts desire, but preachers do serve men by putting true food before them until, by the miraculous work of the Holy Spirit, they recognize it for what it is and they taste and see that the Lord is good.[17]

Before we conclude this brief discussion of gospel preaching, we must address one final issue. Some theorize that our present culture cannot tolerate the type of preaching that was so effective during the great awakenings and revivals of the past. The preaching of Jonathan Edwards, George Whitefield, Charles Spurgeon, and other like-minded preachers would be ridiculed, lampooned, and laughed to scorn by modern man. Yet this theory fails to take into account that in their day, men ridiculed and lampooned these preachers! True gospel preaching will always be foolishness to every culture. Any attempt to remove the offense and make preaching "appropriate" diminishes the power of the gospel. It also defeats the purpose for which God chose preaching as the means of saving men—that men's hope might not rest in refinement, eloquence, or worldly wisdom, but in the power of God.[18]

We live in a culture bound by sin like bands of iron. Moral stories, quaint maxims, and life lessons shared from the heart of a beloved pulpiteer or spiritual life coach have no real power against such darkness. We need preachers of the gospel of Jesus Christ who know the Scriptures, and by God's grace face any culture with the cry, "Thus saith the Lord!"

---

15. Matthew 8:29
16. Matthew 7:6
17. Isaiah 55:1–2; Psalm 34:8
18. 1 Corinthians 1:27–30

CHAPTER TWO

A Gospel to Be Received

Which also you received and in which you stand.
—1 Corinthians 15:1

Since the gospel is *the* message from God to man, we would suppose that it should evoke some sort of reaction and demand some kind of response. From our text, we learn that upon hearing the gospel, the church in Corinth both received it in a manner appropriate to its great worth and made it the foundation upon which they stood before God. If we are to be right with God, we must do the same.

RECEIVING THE GOSPEL

For men to be saved, they must, by God's grace, receive the gospel. Yet what does that mean? There is nothing extraordinary about the word *received* in English or biblical Greek, but in the context of the gospel, it becomes quite extraordinary—one of the most radical words in Scripture.

First, when two things are contrary or diametrically opposed to one another, to receive the one is to reject the other. Since there is no affinity or friendship between the gospel and the world, to receive the gospel is to reject the world. This demonstrates just how radical the act of receiving the gospel can be. To receive and follow the gospel call is to reject all that can be seen with the eye and held in the hand in exchange for what cannot be seen.[1] It is to reject personal autonomy and the right to self-government in order to enslave oneself to a Messiah who died two thousand years ago as an enemy of the state and a blasphemer. It is to reject the majority and its views in order to join oneself to a berated and

---

1. Hebrews 11:1, 7, 27; 1 Peter 1:8

seemingly insignificant minority called the church. It is to risk everything in this one and only life in the belief that this impaled prophet is
the Son of God and the Savior of the world. To receive the gospel is not
merely to pray a prayer asking Jesus to come into one's heart, but it is to
put away the world and embrace the fullness of the claims of Christ.

Secondly, a man who receives the gospel trusts exclusively in the person and work of Jesus Christ as the only way of right standing before
God. It is a common maxim that to trust in anything exclusively is dangerous, or at best, a very unwise thing to do. Our society considers a
man careless if he does not have a backup plan or an alternative escape
route, if he has not diversified his investments, if he has put all his eggs
in the same basket, or if he has burned bridges behind him. Yet this is the
very thing that the man who receives Jesus Christ must do. The Christian
faith is exclusive. To receive Christ truly is to throw off every other hope
in everything but Christ alone. It is for this reason that the apostle Paul
declared that the Christian is of all men most to be pitied if Christ is a
hoax.[2] If He is not the Savior, then the Christian is lost, for he has no other
plan or confidence. By faith, he has declared, "My Lord, in Thee I trust. If
Thou art unable or unwilling to save me, then I will find my place in hell.
I will make for myself no other preparation!"

A genuine receiving of the gospel not only involves a disdain for and
turning from sin but also a disdain for and turning from any confidence
other than Christ, especially a confidence in self. It is for this reason that
a person who is truly converted will become almost nauseous at even
the slightest suggestion that his right standing before God might be the
product of his own virtue or merit. Although his new life in Christ pro-
duces good works, he has cast off all hope in good works as a means of
salvation and trusts exclusively in the person and perfect work of Christ.

Thirdly, to receive the gospel is to open or expose one's life to the
lordship of Jesus Christ. Modern-day evangelism often teaches men that
they should make Jesus the Lord of their lives. It would be better to tell
them that Jesus *is* the Lord of their lives whether they presently bow
their knee to Him in love or they clench their fist at Him in hatred. The
Scriptures declare that God has made this Jesus whom we crucified both
Lord and Christ.[3] He has installed His King upon His holy mountain and

---

2. 1 Corinthians 15:19
3. Acts 2:36

scoffs at those who would rebel against Him.[4] God does not call men to make Jesus Lord (as though they had such power), but to live in absolute submission to the Lord He has made. Therefore, the man who desires to receive the benefits of the gospel must first decide if he is willing to turn over all autonomy and self-government to the Lord of the gospel.

As gospel preachers, we must be very careful to explain the terms of this transaction clearly and not minimize or gloss over them so that they are virtually indiscernible. We must recognize that we have not been honest until we have explained to seekers that receiving Christ is the most sensible yet dangerous thing they could ever do. After all, like C. S. Lewis's Aslan in *The Lion, the Witch, and the Wardrobe,* He is not a tame lion, and He certainly is not safe. He has the right to ask anything of those who confess His lordship. The same Jesus who beckons the weary to Himself may also ask everything of them, even sending them forth to lose their lives for His sake in this dark and fallen world.[5] Those who do not understand the danger of the gospel call have heard it only faintly. Yet those who hear and, by grace, respond to it in spite of the danger have done a very sensible thing. What could be more reasonable than to follow the omnipotent Creator and Sustainer of the universe, who has loved His people with an eternal love, redeemed them with His own blood, and demonstrated an uncompromising commitment to every promise He has made to them?[6] Yet even if He were not this way and all this goodness was not in Him, it would still be most sensible to follow Him, for who can resist His will?[7] It is for these reasons and countless more that the apostle urges us to "present your bodies a living sacrifice, holy, acceptable to God," and calls it our spiritual or "reasonable" service of worship.[8]

Fourthly, to receive the gospel is to receive an entirely different view of reality where Christ is the epicenter of all things. It is for this reason that theologians refer to salvation and the Christian life as Christocentric. He becomes the center of our universe, the source, the purpose, the goal, and the motivation of all that we are and do. When a man receives the gospel, his entire life begins to be lived out in a different context, and

---

4. Psalm 2:4–6

5. Matthew 11:28; 10:16, 39

6. Colossians 1:15–17; Hebrews 1:3; Jeremiah 31:3; Revelation 5:9; Hebrews 13:5; 2 Timothy 2:13; 2 Corinthians 1:20; Matthew 28:20

7. Romans 9:19; 2 Chronicles 20:6; Job 9:12; Daniel 4:35

8. Romans 12:1

that context is Christ. Although the outward signs at the moment of true conversion may be less than dramatic, the gradual effects will be monumental. Like a pebble cast in the center of a lake, the ripple effect of the gospel will eventually reach the full circumference of the believer's life and touch every shore. The true convert does not receive the gospel as an addition to his previous life, but in exchange for it. To receive one is to lose the other. This is the clear teaching of Jesus: "For whoever desires to save his life will lose it, but whoever loses his life for My sake will find it."[9]

Finally, to receive the gospel is to take Christ as the very source and sustenance of one's life. Christ cannot be received as a part of one's life or as an addition to all the other good things that one already possesses without Him. He is not some minor accessory that dresses up our life and makes it better. In receiving the gospel, He becomes our life.[10]

There are few things more blasphemous than a preacher who compliments the unbeliever on the wonderful life he has made for himself, extolling all that he has achieved, and then adding that he lacks one thing: he needs Jesus to make it all complete. This was not the attitude of the apostle Paul, who counted even the most splendid things in his previous life to be dung in comparison to Christ.[11] We should never present Christ to the unbeliever as the cherry on top of an already wonderful life. The unbeliever must see that he has no life, and that all his personal achievements prior to Christ are monuments to his own vanity: made of sand and quickly passing.

Jesus taught, "Most assuredly, I say to you, unless you eat the flesh of the Son of Man and drink His blood, you have no life in you."[12] The meaning of this "hard saying" is that Christ must become the very sustenance of our lives and not merely a condiment or complement.[13]

For the believer, Jesus is the Manna that comes down from heaven, the Rock that gushes forth living water in the midst of a desert, and the Vine in which he remains, from which he receives life and fruitfulness.[14] The believer who has truly partaken of Christ ceases to spend himself

---

9. Matthew 16:25
10. Colossians 3:4
11. Philippians 3:7–8
12. John 6:53
13. John 6:60
14. John 6:31–35, 41, 47–51, 58; 1 Corinthians 10:4; John 15:5–6

for what is not bread and cannot satisfy, and continues to seek the bread which comes down out of heaven, so that he may eat of it and not die.[15]

It should be the cry of the gospel preacher not only that men should repent but also that they should receive. The preacher must not only expose and denounce the unsatisfying fodder of this present age, he also must point men to the only store where true food can be found. He must join David in his admonition to all men: "Oh, taste and see that the LORD is good."[16] Furthermore, he must warn all men that the evidence that a person has truly and savingly tasted of Christ is that he goes on tasting, he goes on finding satisfaction in Christ, and he cannot bear the thought of ever being separated from Him.

STANDING IN THE GOSPEL

From our text, we not only learn that we are to receive the gospel but also that we are to stand in it! Paul writes, "I declare to you the gospel which I preached to you, which also you received and in which you stand." This simple declaration communicates two distinct yet related truths. The first has to do with the believer's position before God because of the gospel, and the second has to do with the believer's conviction or resolution regarding the gospel. Both of these truths have far-reaching implications for the believer's life. The former is a great foundation stone upon which the Christian's faith must rest: he is able to stand before God *in* Christ and the gospel. The latter is a powerful agent in shaping the Christian's life: he has made his stand *upon* the gospel and will not be moved.

A foundational truth of biblical Christianity is that the believer has a right standing before God in the gospel—in Christ alone. The psalms of David confront us with man's greatest dilemma: "Who may ascend into the hill of the LORD? Or who may stand in His holy place? He who has clean hands and a pure heart, who has not lifted up his soul to an idol, nor sworn deceitfully."[17] Any man who entertains even the remotest possibility that there is a personal and moral God must tremble at David's question. Unless he is an imbecile or his conscience has been seared beyond use, he must recognize that he does not possess the necessary

---

15. Isaiah 55:2; John 6:50
16. Psalm 34:8
17. Psalm 24:3–4

qualifications to stand approved before the Judge of all the earth.[18] The Scriptures tell us that if he looks within, he will find that his heart is more deceitful than all else and is wicked beyond comprehension.[19] If he turns to consider his own mind, he will find that there are wicked thoughts lodged within.[20] If he listens intently to his speech, he will become aware that it is full of deceit, cursing, and bitterness.[21] If he gazes upon his hands, he will see that they are stained with the residue of countless misdeeds. If in desperation he seeks to cover his shame by dressing himself in his most righteous deeds, he will find that he is clothed in the filthy rot of a leper.[22] Although he washes himself with lye and uses much soap, the stain of his iniquity remains.[23] Everywhere he turns, he finds himself accused, condemned, and without hope.

It is in this moment of absolute helplessness and final resignation that the illumined and regenerate sinner looks to Christ and finds his hope in Him. Turning from self-righteousness, he believes and is justified by grace alone through faith alone.[24] From that moment on, he bears the twin marks of a Christian: he glories in Christ Jesus and puts no confidence in the flesh.[25] He has entered into that great company of saints who believed God and it was reckoned to them as righteousness.[26] He has cast himself upon Christ and clings to Him with a strength multiplied by the terror of what would have befallen him if he had been left to fend for himself. He stands upon Christ alone and will not venture from Him. He is convinced that he can ascend into the hill of the Lord and stand in His holy place only by virtue of the person and merit of Christ. To paraphrase the old hymn writer: "His hope is built on nothing less than Jesus' blood and righteousness. He dare not trust the sweetest frame, but wholly lean on Jesus' name. On Christ the solid Rock he stands, all other ground is sinking sand; all other ground is sinking sand."[27]

18. Psalms 14:1; 53:1
19. Jeremiah 17:9
20. Jeremiah 4:14
21. Romans 3:13–14
22. Isaiah 64:6
23. Jeremiah 2:22
24. Ephesians 2:8–9
25. Philippians 3:3
26. Genesis 15:6; Galatians 3:6
27. Adapted from "The Solid Rock" by Edward Mote.

The Christian faith promises right standing before God through Christ alone. This being true, we must be resolute in holding to the gospel and standing upon it. It is helpful to note that the word *stand* is from the Greek verb *hístemi*, the common term used to denote the physical act of standing. However, in the New Testament, it is often used to denote conviction, resoluteness, steadfastness, firmness, and the quality of being unwavering and immovable. In his discussion on spiritual warfare, Paul uses the term three times to exhort the believers to "stand against the wiles of the devil."[28] From a related verb, we understand that believers are to "stand firm" in the Lord, in the faith, in the grace of God, and in the apostolic traditions.[29]

Above all things, the believer must stand firm in the gospel and not be moved away from it. If this foundation stone is removed, then the entire building falls with it. It is for this reason that the apostle Paul gave one of his strongest rebukes to the church in Galatia: "I marvel that you are turning away so soon from Him who called you in the grace of Christ, to a different gospel, which is not another; but there are some who trouble you and want to pervert the gospel of Christ. But even if we, or an angel from heaven, preach any other gospel to you than what we have preached to you, let him be accursed. As we have said before, so now I say again, if anyone preaches any other gospel to you than what you have received, let him be accursed."[30]

Every word and doctrine of the Scriptures is important; however, some doctrines carry greater weight than others do. Our eternal salvation does not depend upon some nuance in ecclesiology or eschatology, but it does depend entirely upon the gospel.[31] Throughout this earthly pilgrimage, the most thoughtful and mature Christian may change his opinion regarding many minor tenets of the faith; however he must not, he will not move away from the essentials of the gospel.[32] The man, woman, youth, or child who has truly received the gospel will stand upon it, and in their standing they prove that they have truly received it.

---

28. Ephesians 6:11, 13, 14

29. The related verb is *stéko*, the late present tense, from the present perfect *estéka*, from *hístemi*. Philippians 4:1; 1 Thessalonians 3:8; 1 Corinthians 16:13; 1 Peter 5:12; 2 Thessalonians 2:15.

30. Galatians 1:6–9

31. *Ecclesiology* refers to the study of the church, and *eschatology* refers to the study of the consummation, or last things.

32. Colossians 1:22–23

We live in a world that is hostile to the gospel of Jesus Christ and holds it in contempt. Furthermore, this world is under the power of the evil one, who opposes the gospel above all other doctrines and would eradicate it from the universe if he could.[33] In fact, the devil would gladly lay a Bible in the hands of every man and promote obedience to every command if in exchange we would give him the gospel. Yet without the gospel, the entire system of Christian belief falls to nothing.

As believers, we must not only receive the gospel but also stand firm in it. We must not be ignorant of the devil's schemes so that he takes us unaware.[34] When would-be saviors seek to steal our trust from Christ, we must not let them woo us away! When legalists seek to supplement our trust in Christ, we must not give in to them. When self-appointed prophets seek to repackage the gospel to make it more relevant or appealing to culture, we must not follow them. When the accuser points to our sin and mocks our hope of glory, we must point to the gospel and stand upon it. When his accusations turn to flattery and he points to our piety as worthy of reward, we must denounce him with the pledge: "But God forbid that I should boast except in the cross of our Lord Jesus Christ, by whom the world has been crucified to me, and I to the world."[35]

---

33. 1 John 5:19
34. 2 Corinthians 2:11
35. Galatians 6:14

CHAPTER THREE

A Gospel by Which We Are Saved

By which also you are saved, if you hold fast that word which I preached to you—unless you believed in vain.

—1 Corinthians 15:2

Each doctrine within the Christian faith must be held in a balance. We are in great danger of error whenever we overemphasize the importance of one truth to the demise or neglect of others. However, it is impossible to overstate or overemphasize the preeminence of the gospel. We cannot become too extreme with the gospel. This truth is seen in the fact that the gospel is the greatest revelation of God to man, and it is the only message by which men might be saved. Consequently, it is also the one message we must hold onto tenaciously. Although even the most minor departure from biblical truth is dangerous, we may misunderstand many things without putting our eternal destinies in jeopardy. However, to be wrong about the gospel is to be wrong about everything! Not giving the gospel preeminence is to misunderstand it altogether!

A GOSPEL THAT SAVES

In our text, the phrase, *you are saved* is translated from a present tense verb which describes both a "present process and a future reality."[1] It may be translated: "by which you are being saved." It is important not to forget that the Scriptures describe salvation in three tenses—past, present, and future. To ignore any one of these tenses or aspects of salvation will cause us to have a skewed or unhealthy view of salvation as a whole. In the past, God saved the believer from the condemnation of sin.

---

1. David E. Garland, *1 Corinthians*, Baker Exegetical Commentary on the New Testament (Grand Rapids: Baker Academic, 2003), 682.

This occurred at the moment of conversion, when the Christian believed God's testimony concerning the gospel and it was reckoned to him as righteousness.[2] Scripture commonly refers to this as justification.[3]

In the present, the believer is being saved from the power of sin. This is a gradual process known throughout the New Testament as progressive sanctification. The believer is God's workmanship, and God is working in him both to will and to work according to His good pleasure.[4] Through the Word and the Spirit, trials and tribulations, blessing and discipline, God is transforming the believer and bringing the whole of his or her life into conformity to the image of Jesus Christ.[5]

In the future, the believer will be saved completely and eternally from the power and presence of sin. This final stage is commonly known as glorification and is as certain as the others because He who began a good work will perfect it.[6] As the apostle Paul declares in what has come to be known as the golden chain of salvation: "And we know that all things work together for good to those who love God, to those who are the called according to His purpose. For whom He foreknew, He also predestined to be conformed to the image of His Son, that He might be the firstborn among many brethren. Moreover whom He predestined, these He also called; whom He called, these He also justified; and whom He justified, these He also glorified."[7]

We live in a day in which the temporal and the trivial are exalted to a prominence they should not be given among God's people. We desire these momentary pleasures as though they were actually worthy of such affection. However, we must hold to a singular truth: the greatest promise of the gospel is salvation. All other promises and all other benefits pale in comparison to this one thing: the gospel is the power of God for salvation, and whoever will call upon the name of the Lord will be saved.[8]

According to the apostle Peter, salvation is the very outcome or goal of the believer's faith.[9] It is the purpose behind all that Christ has done

---

2. Romans 4:20–22
3. Romans 5:1
4. Ephesians 2:10; Philippians 2:13
5. Romans 8:29
6. Philippians 1:6
7. Romans 8:28–30
8. Romans 1:16; 10:13
9. 1 Peter 1:9

for His people, and it ought to be the believer's great longing and the goal toward which he strives. God can give no greater gift and the believer can have no greater hope or motivation than that of final salvation through the gospel of Jesus Christ.

When we realize what we were before Christ and what we deserved in that state, it further magnifies the enormity of the gospel for us. We were sinners by nature and deed, and we were corrupt to the point of depravity. We were lawbreakers and criminals without excuse or plea before the bar of God's justice.[10] We deserved nothing less than death and eternal condemnation, but now the blood of God's own Son saves us. While we were helpless sinners and enemies of God, Christ died for the ungodly.[11] Through Him, we who were far off have now been brought near.[12] In Him, we have redemption through His blood, and the forgiveness of our trespasses, according to the riches of His grace.[13] We are saved from our sin, reconciled to God, and brought into fellowship with Him as sons! What more could we desire, or what more do we need? Is not the gift of salvation through the blood of God's own Son enough to fill our hearts to overflowing for an eternity of eternities? Is it not enough to motivate us to live for Him who died? What need do we have of other promises? Will we live for Him with great zeal because He promises us not only salvation but also healing, ease of life, wealth, and honor? What are any of these things compared to the gift of salvation and of knowing Him? Away with those who would seek to coax us to devotion by promising us things other than Jesus Christ. If everyone you have ever loved was taken from you, and your body lay rotting on a dung heap, and your name was slandered by friend and enemy alike, you should still find all the devotion you need to love, praise, and serve Him in this one thing: He shed His own blood for your soul. This one holy passion fuels pure and undefiled religion.

Why is it then that the promise of eternal salvation alone no longer seems to have as much power to attract men to Christ? Why is modern man more interested in how the gospel can help him in this present life? First, it is because preachers are no longer preaching about the certainty

---

10. Ephesians 2:1–3; Romans 3:10–19
11. Romans 5:6–10
12. Ephesians 2:13
13. Ephesians 1:7

of judgment and the dangers of hell. When preachers teach these things biblically and clearly, men begin to see that their greatest need is to be saved from eternal condemnation, and the more "practical" needs of this present age become trivial in comparison. Secondly, we must understand that the great majority of men on the street and in the pew are carnal, and carnally minded men cherish this world above the next. They have little interest in the things of God and eternity.[14] Most would sooner attend a conference on self-esteem and self-realization than listen to one sermon on sanctification, without which no one will see the Lord.[15] Many would cross land and sea to find their best life now, but they would not walk across the street to attend a series of meetings on the infinite worth of Christ or the sufferings of Calvary!

Although it is true that the gospel can and often does improve one's station and condition in life, as stewards of the gospel, we must shun the temptation to attract hearers and congregants with any promise or prop other than Jesus Christ and eternal life. Although it would be beyond radical in this modern age of evangelism, we would do well to cry out to the masses, "Jesus Christ promises you two things: an eternal salvation in which to hope and a cross on which to die.[16] The Spirit and the bride say, 'Come.'"[17]

HOLDING FAST THE GOSPEL

The doctrine of the perseverance of the saints is one of the most precious truths to the believer who understands it.[18] It is the greatest comfort and encouragement to know that He who began a good work in us will finish it.[19] However, this doctrine has been grossly perverted, becoming the chief instrument of false assurance for countless individuals who are yet unconverted and still in their sin. This is a "hard saying" but is true nonetheless.

---

14. Romans 8:5

15. Hebrews 12:14

16. This call did not originate with the author, but he heard these words many years ago while attending a series of meetings held by Leonard Ravenhill.

17. Revelation 22:17

18. The Abstract of Principles, the first confession Baptists officially endorsed, describes the doctrine of perseverance: "Those whom God hath accepted in the Beloved, and sanctified by His Spirit, will never totally nor finally fall away from the state of grace, but shall certainly persevere to the end."

19. Philippians 1:6

In the text at the beginning of the chapter, the apostle Paul writes, "You are saved, *if* you hold fast that word." The word *if* introduces a conditional clause that we must not ignore and we cannot remove. The logic is clear: a person is saved *if* he holds fast the gospel, but *if* he does not hold fast, he is not saved. This is not a denial of the doctrine of perseverance but rather an explanation of it. None of those who truly believe unto salvation will ever be lost to eternal destruction. The grace and power of the God who saved them will also keep them until that final day. However, the evidence that they have truly believed is that they continue in the things of God and do not turn away from Him. Although they will still struggle against the flesh and be subject to many failings, the full course of their life will reveal a definite and notable progress in both faith and godliness. Their perseverance does not save them or make them objects of grace, but it reveals that they are objects of grace who are truly saved by faith. To put it plainly, the proof or validation of genuine conversion is that the one who professes faith in Christ perseveres in that faith and grows in sanctification throughout the full course of his life. If a person professes faith in Christ and yet falls away or makes no progress in godliness, it does not mean that he has lost his salvation. It reveals that he was never truly converted.

This truth runs throughout the full course of the Scripture's teaching on salvation. Jesus taught that the one who endured in his faith until the end would be saved.[20] In the parable of the sower, He explained that though many would seem to embrace the gospel of the kingdom, most would fall away because of affliction, persecution, the worries of the world, and the deceitfulness of wealth.[21] The apostle John, referring to those who had left the church in Ephesus, wrote, "They went out from us, but they were not of us; for if they had been of us, they would have continued with us; but they went out that they might be made manifest, that none of them were of us."[22]

It is important to note once again that these Scriptures are not a denial of the believer's security in Christ. The truly regenerate child of God will continue in the faith until the end because of the faithfulness and power of the One who began a good work in him.[23] However, these

---

20. Matthew 24:13
21. Matthew 13:21–22
22. 1 John 2:19
23. Philippians 1:6

warnings have an important function in the Christian faith and should not be ignored. They help us to discern the difference between true and false conversion, and they function as a warning for the believer to apply all diligence in making his calling and election sure.[24]

These warnings are especially relevant in light of the present state of evangelicalism in the West, and they have tremendous and far-reaching implications for many who profess faith in Christ. There are many who believe they are saved and thoroughly Christian because they once prayed a prayer and asked Jesus to come into their hearts. However, they did not continue on in the faith. They never came out of the world, or if they did, they quickly returned. They possess no practical reality of the fear of the Lord. There is no fragrance of divine grace in their lives. They show no outward evidence of inward transformation. There is not even a hint of the divine discipline that God provides to all His children.[25] Yet they stand assured of their salvation because of one decision in their past and their belief that their prayer was truly sincere. No matter how popular such a belief may be, it has no biblical grounds.

It is true that conversion happens at a specific moment in time when men pass from death to life through faith in Jesus Christ.[26] However, biblical assurance that a person has passed from death to life finds a basis not merely upon an examination of the moment of conversion but also upon an examination of his or her life from that moment on. In the midst of great carnality, the apostle Paul did not ask the Corinthians to reevaluate their conversion experience in the past, but he admonished them to examine their lives in the present.[27]

We would do well to follow Paul's lead in the counseling of supposed converts. They must know—and we must teach them—that the evidence of a genuine saving work of God in the past is the continuation of that work into the present and until that final day. We are saved *if* we hold fast to the word that was preached to us. We can have little or no assurance of salvation if such is not the case. This one simple biblical truth, if properly preached with conviction and compassion, would demolish the false assurance of countless multitudes in the pew and result in the salvation of many.

---

24. 2 Peter 1:5–10
25. Hebrews 12:8
26. John 5:24
27. 2 Corinthians 13:5

Oh, that God would raise up men who understand that false assurance is one of the great maladies of the age and the blight that all but ruins the testimony of the church. When will we realize that one of the greatest mission fields in the West is the pews of our churches every Sunday morning? When will we acknowledge that our superficial treatment of the gospel, our ignorance of the nature of true conversion, and our refusal to practice compassionate church discipline led to this great and deadly deception?

CHAPTER FOUR

A Gospel of First Importance

For I delivered to you first of all that which I also received.

—1 Corinthians 15:3

There is no word or truth of greater importance than the gospel of Jesus Christ. The Scriptures are full of many messages, the least among them being more valuable than the combined wealth of the world and more important than the greatest thoughts ever formed in the mind of man. If the very dust of Scripture is more precious than gold, how can we calculate the worth or importance of the gospel?[1] Even within the Scriptures themselves, the gospel message has no equal. The story of creation, though lined with splendor, bows before the message of the cross. The law of Moses and the words of the prophets point away from themselves to this singular message of redemption. Even the second coming, though full of wonder, stands in the shadows of the gospel. It is no exaggeration to say that the gospel of Jesus Christ is the one great and essential message, the acropolis of the Christian faith, and the foundation of the believer's hope.[2]

There is nothing more important, nothing more useful, and nothing more necessary for the promotion of the glory and kingdom of God! Borrowing from the language of Proverbs, we may rightly say of the gospel: "For her proceeds are better than the profits of silver, and her gain than fine gold. She is more precious than rubies, and all the things you may desire cannot compare with her."[3]

---

1. Job 28:6
2. *Acropolis* is from the Greek words *akro* meaning "high" and *polis* meaning "city." The gospel is the high point of the Christian faith, its fortified city.
3. Proverbs 3:14–15

This being true, comprehending the gospel should be our magnificent obsession. It is an impossible task but is worth every ounce of effort spent—for there we find all the riches of God and every true joy for the believer. It is worth shutting ourselves away from every lesser endeavor and inferior pleasure so that we might sound the depths of God's grace revealed in this one message. Job 28:1–9 contains a beautiful illustration of such a passion:

> Surely there is a mine for silver, and a place where gold is refined. Iron is taken from the earth, and copper is smelted from ore. Man puts an end to darkness, and searches every recess for ore in the darkness and the shadow of death. He breaks open a shaft away from people; in places forgotten by feet. They hang far away from men; they swing to and fro. As for the earth, from it comes bread, but underneath it is turned up as by fire; its stones are the source of sapphires, and it contains gold dust. That path no bird knows, nor has the falcon's eye seen it. The proud lions have not trodden it, nor has the fierce lion passed over it. He puts his hand on the flint; he overturns the mountains at the roots.

Even in the ancient world of Job, there were men who were willing to push themselves to the farthest limit, to deprive themselves of surface life, to burrow through solid rock in gloom and deep shadow, to risk life and limb, and to leave no stone unturned in their search for the treasures of this earth. How much more should we who have been enlightened by the Holy Spirit and tasted the good Word of God and the powers of the age to come be willing to leave off the things of lesser glory to pursue the glories of God in the gospel of Jesus Christ?[4] Why, then, is a true passion for the gospel so scarce among God's people?

A WATERED-DOWN GOSPEL

First, we must understand that the gospel that "was once for all delivered to the saints" has passed through many revisions and reductions in recent generations.[5] When we consider the Scriptures, we quickly note a great difference in content and quality between the apostolic gospel and our more contemporary version. Even when we read the gospel preaching of the Reformers, the Puritans, Edwards, Whitefield, Spurgeon, and

---

4. Hebrews 6:4–5
5. Jude v. 3

even those as recent as Martyn Lloyd-Jones, we quickly realize that today we barely have the bones of the proclamation of the beautiful gospel they expounded and reduced it down to a few spiritual laws and a "Romans Road."[6] We have made it a simple, easy-to-understand creedal statement that amputates much of its original beauty and leaves little glory to be admired or further investigated.

It is true that God has a plan, that we are sinners, and that Christ died and rose again that we might be saved by faith, but memorizing these statements does not mean that we know or understand the gospel. We must not leave such precious stones unturned! Lesser animals can learn to mimic and repeat, but we must search the Scriptures and discover the meaning of these things. Like miners, we must be willing to push ourselves to the farthest limit, deprive ourselves of temporal joys, and burrow through countless hours of study and prayer in order to gain the prize of the knowledge of the gospel. Otherwise, we will always be a people dull of heart because of the ignorance that is in us.[7] We must turn our eyes to the rock from which we were hewn.[8] We must seek to rediscover the gospel of old, to be recaptured by it, and to preach it with passion like people who know their God and understand what He has done for them![9]

A LOW VIEW OF THE GOSPEL

A second reason that God's people lack passion for the gospel today is that many see it to be little more than Christianity 101, or the baby step taken into the faith that is quickly mastered and left behind for deeper things. Yet nothing could be further from the truth. The gospel is the "deep thing" of Christianity! Eschatology and the book of Revelation will become clear at the second coming, but we will never master or fully comprehend the glory of God in the gospel of Jesus Christ. Anyone who thinks that he knows the gospel well enough to leave it behind and go on to greater things would do well to follow the admonition of the apostle Paul: "If anyone thinks that he knows anything, he knows nothing yet as

6. 1 Timothy 1:11
7. Ephesians 4:18
8. Isaiah 51:1
9. Daniel 11:32

he ought to know."[10] If we had the power to call forth the greatest theologians and preachers of history, they would all testify that they were babes in the gospel during their earthly pilgrimage. They would join with the wise man of Proverbs who exclaimed, "Surely I am more stupid than any man, and do not have the understanding of a man. I neither learned wisdom nor have knowledge of the Holy One."[11]

We must understand that our journey into the gospel will last beyond our lifetime and into a thousand eternities. With each new truth discovered, the gospel's glory will capture us more and more until it consumes our thoughts and governs our will. You may wonder if there is anything worth pursuing, anything big enough to hold your attention. Take heart! The gospel is much more than what you may have been told, and it contains a glory that cannot be exhausted. In fact, we will spend eternity attempting to track down all the glory that is contained in this singular message, and after an eternity of eternities there will still be infinite glory yet unseen. The gospel will always be the thing into which the angels and the redeemed long to look![12] Remember this: you must always be growing in the gospel and your knowledge of it. It is not Christianity 101, but Christianity from A to Z. You have not mastered the gospel, nor will you master it, but it will master you!

A LACK OF INSTRUCTION IN THE GOSPEL

A third reason for a lack of passion for the gospel among God's people springs from a faulty and deadly assumption: we assume that God's people, even God's ministers, understand the gospel, and therefore we neglect to instruct them in the gospel, let alone make such instruction a priority. When a new convert comes forward to make his public profession, how much time is he then instructed in the gospel? Often, someone counsels him for a few minutes using a step-by-step gospel tract, and then he is placed into a discipleship class to learn the how-tos of the Christian life. How much instruction regarding the gospel does he hear from the pulpit? It is possible he could sit his entire life in the pew without ever hearing sermons dedicated to a proper and specific explanation of what was accomplished through Calvary and the empty tomb. If he senses the

---

10. 1 Corinthians 8:2
11. Proverbs 30:2–3
12. 1 Peter 1:12

call to ministry, how many classes in seminary will he attend that are solely dedicated to the content and application of the gospel? One would have to survey the curricula of many religious institutions before finding even one class specifically dedicated to such a purpose. Prior to the reign of the godly King Josiah, the law of God had been lost in the temple for many years.[13] Has the same thing occurred among us? Has the *evangel* been lost among evangelicals?

A NEGLECT OF THE GOSPEL IN PREACHING

A fourth and final reason for the lack of passion for the gospel in the pew is the lack of passion for the same in the pulpit. The minister of Christ is above all a minister of Christ's gospel. It is our great steward-ship, privilege, and burden.[14] Though we are earthen vessels, frail and broken, we carry the most precious treasure that heaven and earth has ever known.[15] God has set us apart to dwell in His presence. He calls us to use the greater part of our days searching out His mysteries and revealing them to others through the preached word. Yet many preach-ers today have been drawn away from their primary calling to know God and to make Him known. The study is barren, and the prayer closet is closed. The minister is no longer a man of God but a man of the people. The preacher's message is no longer, "Thus saith the Lord!" but he comes with a message born out of questionnaires and his supposed knowledge of the congregation's felt needs. He cannot say with the prophet Elijah, "As the LORD of hosts lives, before whom I stand," nor does he any longer stand before the people as one sent from God.[16]

We who minister in Christ's name are not called to be spiritual life coaches, facilitators, or motivational speakers—we are preachers! Just because the world mocks such a title, and just because there are countless charlatans who give them good reason to do so, this does not mean we should despise the mantle that Christ has placed upon us. We are preachers, and above all, we are gospel preachers. We must not be seduced by a lesser purpose merely because it has the world's approval. We must not be coaxed away from our chambers of study and prayer,

---

13. 2 Chronicles 34:14–21
14. 1 Corinthians 4:1; 1 Timothy 1:12; 1 Peter 1:12; 1 Corinthians 9:16
15. 2 Corinthians 4:7
16. 1 Kings 18:15; John 1:6

but we must discipline ourselves for the purpose of godliness.[17] We must be diligent to present ourselves approved to God as workmen who do not need to be ashamed, accurately handling the word of truth.[18] We must take pains with these things; we must be absorbed in them, so that our progress will be evident to all.[19] We must never neglect the spiritual gift within us, but give ourselves to the public reading of Scripture, to exhortation and teaching.[20]

Let us be like the apostles of old who declared in the face of many other valid needs, "It is not desirable that we should leave the word of God and serve tables...but we will give ourselves continually to prayer and to the ministry of the word."[21] Like the ancient miners of Job's day, we must push ourselves to the farthest limit, even deprive ourselves of surface life, to burrow through solid rock, in gloom and deep shadow, in order that we might discover the infinite treasures of the gospel of Jesus Christ and set them before God's people. This is the great and only means of setting fire to both the pulpit and the pew.

---

17. 1 Timothy 4:7–8
18. 2 Timothy 2:15
19. 1 Timothy 4:15
20. 1 Timothy 4:13–14
21. Acts 6:2, 4

CHAPTER FIVE

A Gospel Handed Down and Delivered

For I delivered to you...that which I also received: that Christ died for our sins according to the Scriptures, and that He was buried, and that He rose again the third day according to the Scriptures.

—1 Corinthians 15:3–4

In the above text, we learn two important truths about the gospel. First, it was not the result of human invention, but of men moved by the Holy Spirit.[1] Thus it bears the full authority of the Scripture as a God-breathed message.[2] Secondly, it was a message delivered once and for all to the saints, and each generation of Christians is responsible for handing it down unaltered to the generation that follows.[3]

A GOSPEL HANDED DOWN

When the apostle Paul writes that he "received" the gospel, he is making a claim to special revelation. He did not fabricate this message, nor was it borrowed from others. Rather, it came to him through an extraordinary revelation of Jesus Christ. In Galatians 1:11–12, Paul describes this experience in greater detail: "But I make known to you, brethren, that the gospel which was preached by me is not according to man. For I neither received it from man, nor was I taught it, but it came through the revelation of Jesus Christ."

Paul's purpose for relating this unique experience is to demonstrate that his gospel has a divine origin. He was not writing to exalt himself or to suggest that his gospel was somehow different from that given to the

---

1. 2 Peter 1:21
2. 2 Timothy 3:16
3. Jude v. 3

other apostles or to the church as a whole. In fact, he later relates in the same letter that he had submitted his gospel to those who were of high reputation in the church of Jerusalem, and they had neither corrected him nor contributed anything to his understanding.[4] Paul intends for all of this to demonstrate that there is only one true gospel. It was born in the heart of God and handed down to the church through the apostles. It is an eternal and immutable word that transcends both time and culture. It is not to be modified or adapted to please the palates of differing cultures or epochs, but it is to be held in the highest regard as absolute and immutable truth.

For this reason, we who have become recipients and stewards of the gospel should learn to handle it with great caution, even fear. Jude, the half brother of the Lord, exhorted us to contend earnestly for this gospel faith that was once and for all handed down to the saints, and the apostle Paul admonished us to guard it as an entrusted treasure.[5] He even went so far as to pronounce a curse upon any man or angel who would alter its contents for any reason: "But even if we, or an angel from heaven, preach any other gospel to you than what we have preached to you, let him be accursed. As we have said before, so now I say again, if anyone preaches any other gospel to you than what you have received, let him be accursed."[6]

Each generation of Christians must realize that an eternal gospel has been handed down to them.[7] As stewards, it is our charge to preserve that gospel without additions, subtractions, or any sort of modification. To alter the gospel in any way is to bring a curse upon ourselves and to hand down a corrupt gospel to the following generations. For this reason, the apostle Paul warned young Timothy to take pains with the truths entrusted to him, and Paul promised him that in doing so he would ensure salvation both for himself and for those who heard him.[8]

We who have received the gospel have a fearful obligation to deliver it in all its fullness and apostolic purity. This obligation is not only to God but also to our own generation and the generations to come. The apostle Paul declared to the church in Rome that he was a "debtor both to the

---

4. Galatians 2:1–10
5. Jude v. 3; 2 Timothy 1:14
6. Galatians 1:8–9
7. Revelation 14:6
8. 1 Timothy 4:15–16

Greeks, and to the Barbarians; both to the wise, and to the unwise."[9] In a similar fashion, we are also debtors to all men now living and to the countless generations of men who may still follow. To the degree that we are faithful to the gospel, we will be as lights shining in the darkness, and a source of blessing to the generations to come. To the degree that we are otherwise, we will be enemies of the cross of Christ, stumbling blocks in the midst of the kingdom, and guilty of shipwrecking the faith of many.[10] As ministers of the gospel, a trust has been placed upon us that is as terrible as it is wonderful. Who is sufficient for these things? Who is competent for such a task?[11]

Knowing the seriousness of our charge, let us be diligent to present ourselves approved of God as workmen who do not need to be ashamed because we accurately handle the word of truth.[12] Let us imitate Ezra the scribe, who "had prepared his heart to seek the Law of the LORD, and to do it, and to teach statutes and ordinances in Israel."[13] Let us follow the example of the godly priest whom God honored through the prophet Malachi: "He feared Me and was reverent before My name. The law of truth was in his mouth, and injustice was not found on his lips. He walked with Me in peace and equity, and turned many away from iniquity. For the lips of a priest should keep knowledge, and people should seek the law from his mouth; for he is the messenger of the LORD of hosts."[14]

There is something worse than holding our silence while the lost of this world run headlong into hell: the crime of preaching to a different gospel than the one passed down to the saints. For this reason, we must shun the gospel of contemporary evangelicalism, for it is a watered-down, culturally carved, truncated gospel that allows men to hold to a form of godliness while denying its power, to profess to know God while denying Him with their deeds, and to call Jesus "Lord, Lord," while not doing the Father's will.[15] Woe to us if we do not preach the gospel, but even greater woe is due us if we preach it incorrectly![16]

---

9. Romans 1:14 KJV
10. Philippians 3:18; Matthew 13:41; 1 Timothy 1:19
11. 2 Corinthians 2:16
12. 2 Timothy 2:15
13. Ezra 7:10
14. Malachi 2:5–7
15. 2 Timothy 3:5; Titus 1:16; Matthew 7:21
16. 1 Corinthians 9:16

A GOSPEL PROPERLY DELIVERED

The Old Testament law contains many prohibitions concerning mixtures of any sort.[17] When two types of anything mix together, their distinctions blur, and both of them are lost. The same may be said of the gospel. The gospel is everything in Christianity and in the Scriptures, but not everything in Christianity or the Scriptures is the gospel.[18] Physical healing, a sound marriage, and God's providential care, although founded upon and flowing from the gospel, are not the gospel.

It is a very dangerous thing for a minister to think that everything he preaches is the gospel of Jesus Christ, or that everything in his ministry could be called gospel ministry. The gospel is a very specific message in the Scriptures, and this text defines it clearly and concisely: "For I delivered to you…that which I also received: that Christ died for our sins according to the Scriptures, and that He was buried, and that He rose again the third day according to the Scriptures."[19]

In Paul's own words, we learn that the gospel of Jesus Christ rests upon two great pillars: His death and resurrection. The reference to His burial is important for two reasons. The first is that Scripture prophesied His death and the prophecy had to be fulfilled.[20] The second is that it validates or proves His death and lays the groundwork for His resurrection and ascension. He was buried because He really died, and since His death was real, so was His resurrection.

As we advance in this work, we will consider these great truths of the gospel, but for now we have only one goal: to demonstrate that we are required not only to proclaim these truths but also to explain them. When we preach or communicate the gospel in any form, we would do well to ask ourselves how much of its essential content we are actually conveying. Many can quote by heart the three facts of the gospel listed in our text: Christ died, was buried, and rose again. However, how many understand what these things mean? And why are they so rarely explained from the pulpit? Do we have such a low view of the gospel that we think it is not worthy of a detailed explanation? Or do we have such a superficial view of the gospel that we believe it requires no explanation?

---

17. Leviticus 19:19
18. In the sense that it is the great essential truth of Christianity and the Scriptures.
19. 1 Corinthians 15:3–4
20. Isaiah 53:9; Matthew 27:57–60

Perhaps we simply assume everyone understands the gospel and no explanation is needed.

COMPONENTS OF GOSPEL-CENTERED PREACHING

The power of words is in their meaning. It is not enough to quote certain gospel propositions by rote, but we must also work diligently to explain them. For this reason, the evangelist must also be a scribe, and the preacher must also be a teacher. Our bold proclamation of the death and resurrection of Christ must include a biblical, thoughtful, and clear explanation of exactly what these things mean! The following four applications provide proof of this need.

First, gospel preaching requires that we boldly proclaim to men that Christ died for their sins. Although there is no doubt that the Holy Spirit can use these five words to save the vilest man, there is no basis in Scripture for assuming that we should leave this extremely important truth without explanation.[21] Men cannot adequately understand the significance of Christ's death unless they also understand something of their own sin. Therefore, we must endeavor to make known to them not only the nature of sin and their own sinfulness, but we must also strive to teach them about the righteous character of God and His response to sin of every kind and magnitude. We must do this with a balance of straightforwardness and compassion, much in the same way that a good doctor seeks to explain the grievous nature of his patient's illness so that he might be moved to seek a cure without delay.[22] This groundwork, or "plowing of the human heart," is an absolute necessity in true gospel preaching. We should remember that it was only after the Lord's great proclamation of His own attributes that Moses "made haste and bowed his head toward the earth, and worshiped."[23] And it was only after God revealed the righteous requirements of the law to Paul that his sin was exposed, his self-righteousness destroyed, and he was converted.[24]

Secondly, gospel preaching requires that we tell men that Christ died according to the Scriptures. Although this is one of the most powerful

21. Romans 1:16; 1 Corinthians 2:2; 2 Timothy 2:15
22. 2 Timothy 2:25: "In humility correcting those who are in opposition, if God perhaps will grant them repentance, so that they may know the truth."
23. Exodus 34:8
24. Romans 7:9–11

declarations in the Scriptures, its impact upon the human heart increases exponentially as gospel preaching properly unfolds its truths and makes its implications known. Thus, we must labor with the Scriptures to explain to men the exact nature and implications of Christ's death. Christ died not only because of our sin but also because of God's character—He is just and cannot justify or pardon the wicked without first satisfying the demands of His justice against them.[25] Christ not only died, but He stood in the place of His people, bore their guilt, suffered God's wrath, and shed His blood.[26] Through His suffering, divine justice was satisfied and the wrath of God was appeased, that God might now be both just and the justifier of those who place their faith in Him.[27]

Almost every classical theological work on the cross of Christ identifies and explains these truths through such doctrines as atonement, penal substitution, imputation, propitiation, and expiation. These doctrines are not extravagant, unnecessary, or inaccessible, but they are the essential truths of the gospel. They can and must be preached to all men, believer and unbeliever alike. Those who would argue that they are too deep for the common person to understand are borrowing the language of the ancient popes who burned Bibles because they declared that the people of God were too ignorant to read them!

Thirdly, gospel preaching requires that we tell men that Christ was raised from the dead on the third day. However, for this proclamation to influence twenty-first-century man, we must also expound on the resurrection's significance and implications. We must proclaim to men that the resurrection was God's public vindication of Jesus' divine sonship, and it was the sign that He has accepted Christ's redemptive work on behalf of His people![28] We must explain how the resurrection lays the groundwork for Christ's ascension, and it is the evidence that God has made this same Jesus whom we crucified to be both Lord and Christ.[29] We must share that God has highly exalted Jesus and given Him a name that is above every name, so that at the name of Jesus every knee will bow and every tongue confess that He is Lord.[30] We must warn men that

---

25. Proverbs 17:15; Exodus 34:6–7; Romans 3:23–26
26. Hebrews 9:22
27. Isaiah 53:4–6, 10
28. Romans 1:4; 4:25
29. Acts 2:36
30. Philippians 2:6–11

the resurrection of Christ proves not only that the world has a Savior but also that the universe has a King who will reign until all His people have been gathered and His enemies have been made His footstool.[31] He is coming again and will judge the world in righteousness.[32] Therefore, all men, regardless of their station—pauper and king alike—must show discernment and pay homage to the Son, lest He become angry and they perish in the way. For His wrath may soon be kindled, yet blessed are all who take refuge in Him![33]

Finally, gospel preaching requires that we plead with men to come to Christ. However, our plea must be as biblical as our message. We must not reduce the great commands of repentance and faith to nothing more than the repetition of a sinner's prayer. Our hearers must understand repentance as a change of mind that encompasses not only the intellect but also the will and emotions. They must understand the nature of saving faith as "the substance of things hoped for, the evidence of things not seen," being fully assured that what God has promised in Jesus Christ, He is also able to perform.[34] Furthermore, we must instruct our hearers regarding the evidence of conversion. We must warn them that genuine repentance brings forth the fruit of repentance, and that faith without works is dead.[35] We must admonish them to examine themselves and test themselves to see if they are in the faith, and they must be diligent to make their calling and election sure.[36] We must not only preach to men a biblical gospel, for biblical invitation and proper instruction must also follow. We must not cast them out into eternity clutching to nothing more than a sinner's prayer, with only our feeble words of assurance ringing in their ears!

The brief explanations given above are mere fragments of the unsearchable gospel of Jesus Christ that we are responsible to proclaim to the nations. We must tell every creature what Christ has done, but we must also explain what it means and what they must do in response. Proclamations and the words that form them are important, but only to the degree that they are properly defined and applied. Such is the case with the gospel.

---

31. Luke 20:41–44; Acts 2:34–35; Hebrews 10:12–13
32. Acts 17:31
33. Psalm 2:10–12
34. Hebrews 11:1; Romans 4:21
35. Matthew 3:8; James 2:14–26
36. 2 Corinthians 13:5; 2 Peter 1:10

It is the great task of the Christian evangelist to both proclaim as a herald and expound as a scribe.[37] The Scriptures abound with such examples. Philip pointed the Ethiopian eunuch to Christ through his explanation of Isaiah's prophecies.[38] Priscilla and Aquila took Apollos aside and explained to him the way of God more accurately.[39] The apostle Paul met with the Jews of Thessalonica for three consecutive Sabbaths and reasoned with them from the Scriptures, "explaining and demonstrating that the Christ had to suffer and rise again from the dead."[40] Finally, there is the greatest Expositor of them all, our Lord Jesus Christ, who revealed God to man in His incarnation and expounded the gospel to His bewildered disciples on the road to Emmaus: "Then beginning with Moses and with all the prophets, He explained to them the things concerning Himself in all the Scriptures."[41]

---

37. In this discussion, "Christian evangelist" loosely refers to any Christian who preaches or shares the gospel.

38. Acts 8:26–35

39. Acts 18:26

40. Acts 17:3

41. John 1:18 NASB. The word *explained* is from the Greek word *exegéomai,* which means to draw out or unfold a teaching or truth. Luke 24:27 NASB: Here, the word *explained* is from the Greek word *diermeneúo,* which means to unfold the meaning of something, explain, or expound.

PART TWO

The Power of God for Salvation

‍⁌

For I am not ashamed of the gospel of Christ, for it is the power of God to salvation for everyone who believes, for the Jew first and also for the Greek.

—Romans 1:16

CHAPTER SIX

The Gospel

For I am not ashamed of the gospel.
—Romans 1:16

Before we consider Paul's boldness in preaching the gospel, we must understand something of the gospel that He preached. It is a sound principle of communication to define terms prior to any debate or proper discussion. This clears the playing field and allows those involved to know where the others stand or what they mean when they speak. Evangelicals today define theological terms so broadly that we can no longer suppose that we are all talking about the same thing even though we are using the same words. This is especially true regarding the gospel.

The first thing worth considering in our text is the definite article *the*. Paul did not have *a* gospel that was peculiar to him. His was not a Pauline gospel as opposed to a Petrine or Johannine gospel.[1] Though something of the personalities of these apostles shines through in their presentation, the gospel they shared was the same. They would know nothing of the frequent language of our day that speaks of different variations, versions, and flavors of the gospel as though there could be more than one.[2]

---

1. The words *Petrine* and *Johannine* refer to the gospel as preached by Peter and John respectively.

2. The differing opinions regarding the gospel are often categorized as different variations of the same truth, or coming at the same truth from different angles, or even emphasizing different aspects of the same truth. This fails to recognize that the different "variations" are often altogether different gospels. The Reformed gospel is completely different from the Roman Catholic gospel; a faith-based gospel is in direct contradiction to a works-based gospel; a truly evangelical gospel stands in contrast to an ultracharismatic gospel.

Secondly, Paul did not have *a* gospel that was peculiar to a certain culture. He did not preach one variation to the Jews and another to the Gentiles. Though he was aware of cultural differences and used the unique inroads provided by each culture, his gospel was not adapted to fit the culture or to be less offensive to it. In fact, the offensiveness of the gospel to both Jew and Gentile was the very thing that put his life in constant danger. It is doubtful that the apostle Paul would understand contemporary evangelicalism's overwhelming preoccupation with minutely understanding a specific culture and adapting its message and methodologies to it. Paul understood that, ultimately, all men of every culture suffer from the same malady, and only one message has the power to save them.

Finally, Paul did not have *a* gospel that was peculiar to a single epoch in world history. There undoubtedly were significant changes in the Roman Empire with each passing decade of Paul's life, yet he preached the same gospel at his death that he did at the start of his apostolic ministry several decades earlier. Without doubt, he would be surprised at the contemporary Christian conviction that each passing decade brings a new generation of people who require a new presentation or adaptation of the gospel.

PARALLELS BETWEEN THE TEACHINGS OF JESUS AND PAUL

It is clear from Scripture that there was an unbroken continuum between what Jesus did and communicated to His followers and what Paul believed and preached. This truth holds up under the greatest scrutiny. In the gospel of Jesus, God is love. He causes His sun to rise on the evil and the good, and He sends rain on the righteous and unrighteous alike.[3] At the fullness of time, He gave His greatest demonstration of love by sending His beloved Son so that men might not perish but have eternal life through Him.[4]

In the gospel of Paul, God is love. He has not left Himself without a witness of His mercy, but He does good to all men and gives them rain from heaven and fruitful seasons, satisfying their hearts with food and gladness.[5] In the fullness of time, His love reached its crescendo in the

---

3. Matthew 5:45
4. Mark 1:15; John 3:16
5. Acts 14:17

giving of His Son to die for our fallen race while we were yet helpless sinners and enemies of God.[6]

In the gospel of Jesus, men are evil and enslaved to sin.[7] They are bad trees bearing bad fruit.[8] They hate the light of God's revelation and do not come to it for fear that their evil deeds will be exposed.[9] Their hearts are full of evil thoughts, murders, adulteries, fornications, thefts, false witness, and slanders. Even the highest and most lofty moralists among men are nothing but whitewashed tombs full of dead men's bones.[10]

Paul serves the same indictment against our fallen race: "For all have sinned and fall short of the glory of God."[11] There is no one righteous, not even one. There is no one who understands or seeks after God. They have all turned away and become worthless. There is no one who does good, and there is no fear of God before their eyes.[12] For this reason, the law serves only to convict men of their sin, crush their self-righteous hopes, and leave them without excuse and totally dependent upon the mercies of God.[13]

In the gospel of Jesus, all unbelieving men stand condemned before God, and His wrath abides upon them.[14] The Galileans who died at the hands of Pilate and the eighteen upon whom the tower of Siloam fell did not suffer these things because they were greater sinners than other men, but rather all men deserve the same fate and it is only divine mercy that keeps them from it. All deserve death under the wrath of God and will die in due time if they do not repent.[15] In the gospel of Paul, the wrath of God is revealed from heaven against the ungodliness and unrighteousness of men who suppress the truth in their unrighteousness.[16] Those who continue with a stubborn and unrepentant heart are storing up wrath against themselves that will be revealed on the day of judgment.[17]

---

6. Galatians 4:4; Romans 5:6–10
7. Matthew 7:11; John 8:34
8. Matthew 7:17
9. John 3:20
10. Matthew 23:27; 15:19
11. Romans 3:23
12. Romans 3:10–18
13. Romans 3:19
14. John 3:18, 36
15. Luke 13:1–5
16. Romans 1:18
17. Romans 2:5

In the gospel of Jesus, the cross is the great essential and the culminating work of redemption. It was necessary for the Christ to suffer and to enter into His glory.[18] Thus, He taught His disciples that He must go to Jerusalem, suffer many things, be killed, and be raised on the third day.[19] At Gethsemane and Golgotha, He revealed that His sufferings were not confined to the mistreatment of men or devils.[20] On the cross, He drank the full cup of God's wrath and died a forsaken man.[21]

In the gospel of Paul, this same great theme occurs on every page. Paul preached to men as of first importance what he had also received: Christ died for our sins according to the Scriptures, He was buried, and He was raised on the third day according to the Scriptures.[22] Paul demonstrated with great and irrefutable proofs that Christ was the sin-bearer who became a curse and died under the wrath of God as a propitiation for His people.[23] He proclaimed Christ crucified even though it was a stumbling block to the Jews and foolishness to the Gentiles.[24] The cross was not a minor theme for Paul. It was everything. It held him captive and constantly constrained him.[25]

The gospel of Jesus calls men to repent of their sins and believe.[26] He promises those who obey the call will receive eternal life.[27] He warns the rest that they will perish under the wrath of God if they continue in their unrepentant and unbelieving state.[28] The gospel of Paul provides the very same promises and warnings. The apostle solemnly testified, to both Jews and Greeks, of the need for repentance toward God and faith in our Lord Jesus Christ. He proclaimed that God has commanded all people everywhere to repent, and he warned men not to be deceived by empty works, for the wrath of God is coming upon the disobedient.[29]

---

18. Luke 24:26
19. Matthew 16:21
20. Gethsemane being the garden where Jesus prayed and was captured the night before His crucifixion, and Golgotha being the location of the cross and His crucifixion.
21. Luke 22:42; Matthew 27:46
22. 1 Corinthians 15:3–4
23. 2 Corinthians 5:21; Galatians 3:10–13; Romans 3:23–26
24. 1 Corinthians 1:23
25. Romans 1:1; 2 Corinthians 5:14
26. Mark 1:15
27. John 5:24
28. Luke 13:1–5; John 3:18–36
29. Acts 20:21; Ephesians 5:6

In the gospel of Jesus, sincere and costly discipleship always accompanies genuine conversion. Jesus frequently culled the large crowds that followed Him by making radical demands upon them: "If anyone comes to Me and does not hate his father and mother, wife and children, brothers and sisters, yes, and his own life also, he cannot be My disciple."[30] He even warned His own disciples, "If anyone desires to come after Me, let him deny himself, and take up his cross, and follow Me. For whoever desires to save his life will lose it, but whoever loses his life for My sake will find it."[31]

The gospel of Paul contains the same radical demands of discipleship. With regard to holiness, Paul admonishes believers to come out from this world and be separate.[32] With regard to righteousness, he commands believers to consider themselves dead to sin and alive to God as instruments of righteousness.[33] With regard to faithfulness, they are encouraged to endure in spite of the many tribulations and persecutions that are certain to come against all who desire to live godly in Christ Jesus.[34]

The gospel of Jesus teaches men that a mere profession of faith alone is no sound evidence of salvation. Jesus warned that not everyone who says to Him, "Lord, Lord," will enter the kingdom of heaven, but only he who does the will of His Father in heaven.[35] He was adamant that the fruit of one's life is the proof of salvation, and that everyone who does not bear good fruit is cut down and thrown into the fire.[36]

The gospel of Paul contains the same solemn warnings. He admonished those who have professed faith in Christ to examine and test themselves to see if they are truly in the faith.[37] He warned men about having a form of godliness but negating its power, and professing to know God but denying Him with their deeds.[38]

Finally, the gospel of Jesus abounds with warnings about future judgment and the terrors of hell. In fact, Jesus spoke more about this dreadful

---

30. Luke 14:26
31. Matthew 16:24–25
32. 2 Corinthians 6:14–18
33. Romans 6:11–14
34. Acts 14:22; 2 Timothy 3:12
35. Matthew 7:21
36. Matthew 7:16, 19–20
37. 2 Corinthians 5:17
38. 2 Timothy 3:5; Titus 1:16

matter than all the other prophets and apostles combined. According to Jesus, a great day of judgment is coming when men will be separated as sheep from goats, and a great multitude will hear, "Depart from Me, you cursed, into the everlasting fire prepared for the devil and his angels."[39] The matter was so crucial to Jesus that He gave the following warning even to those whom He considered His friends: "And I say to you, My friends, do not be afraid of those who kill the body, and after that have no more that they can do. But I will show you whom you should fear: Fear Him who, after He has killed, has power to cast into hell; yes, I say to you, fear Him!"[40]

The gospel of the apostle Paul agrees with Christ in the matter of judgment and hell. He writes that the wicked are storing up wrath for themselves to be revealed in the day of God's righteous judgment and wrath.[41] He warns believers and unbelievers alike that they should not be deceived by the empty words of those who would deny the coming reality of divine retribution and wrath. God will not be mocked. Whatever the disobedient sows, he will also reap.[42] Like Christ, Paul is both explicit and unapologetic in his warnings: "The Lord Jesus is revealed from heaven with His mighty angels, in flaming fire taking vengeance on those who do not know God, and on those who do not obey the gospel of our Lord Jesus Christ. These shall be punished with everlasting destruction from the presence of the Lord and from the glory of His power."[43]

From the texts we have just considered, it is obvious that there is no contradiction or deviation between the gospel of Jesus Christ and that which the apostle Paul preached and defined in his epistles. In like manner, Moses and the prophets, the writers of the four Gospels, and the other contributors to the New Testament stand in perfect agreement with Christ regarding this "faith which was once for all delivered to the saints."[44] There is but one gospel, which stands above the editor and the censor, and which must not be changed, adapted, or repackaged. Any attempt to do so, regardless of the reason or motivation, will result in a

---

39. Matthew 25:41
40. Luke 12:4–5
41. Romans 2:5
42. Galatians 6:7; Ephesians 5:6
43. 2 Thessalonians 1:7–9
44. Jude v. 3

different gospel which is no gospel at all.[45] We must put aside every foolish and dangerous notion that we can improve upon the gospel for the
sake of the gospel, and stand with that great cloud of witnesses throughout the history of the church, who preached Christ crucified and raised
according to the Scriptures.

---

45. Galatians 1:6–7

CHAPTER SEVEN

A Scandalous Gospel

For I am not ashamed of the gospel.
—Romans 1:16

Now that we have a general understanding of the gospel of the apostle Paul, we can begin to comprehend something of why it generated such disdain and hostility among those who heard him. Although the gospel is the power of God for salvation to everyone who believes, it is nevertheless a scandalous and unbelievable message to a fallen world.

RADICALLY EXCLUSIVE

Paul's flesh had every reason to be ashamed of the gospel he preached because it contradicted absolutely everything that was held true and sacred among his contemporaries. To the Jew, the gospel was the worst sort of blasphemy because it claimed that the Nazarene who died accursed on Calvary was the Messiah. To the Greeks, it was the worst sort of absurdity because it claimed that this Jewish Messiah was God in the flesh. Thus Paul knew that whenever he opened his mouth to speak the gospel he would be utterly rejected and ridiculed to scorn unless the Holy Spirit intervened and moved upon the hearts and minds of his hearers. In our day, the primitive gospel is no less offensive, for it still contradicts every tenet, or "ism," of contemporary culture: relativism, pluralism, and humanism.[1]

We live in an age of relativism—a belief system based upon the absolute certainty that there are no absolutes. We hypocritically applaud men

---

1. The term *primitive gospel* refers to the gospel of the first century that was preached by Jesus and the apostles.

for seeking the truth but call for the public execution of anyone arrogant enough to believe he has found it. We live in a self-imposed Dark Age, the reason for which is clear. Natural man is a fallen creature, morally corrupt, and hell-bent on autonomy (i.e., self-government). He hates God because He is righteous and hates His laws because they censure and restrict his evil. He hates the truth because it exposes him for what he is and troubles what still remains of his conscience. Therefore, fallen man seeks to push truth, especially the truth about God, as far away as possible. He will go to any extent to suppress the truth, even to the point of pretending that no such thing exists, or that if it does exist, it cannot be known or have any bearing on our lives. It is never the case of a hiding God but a hiding man. The problem is not the intellect but the will. Like a man who hides his head in the sand to avoid a charging rhino, modern man denies the truth of a righteous God and moral absolutes in hopes of quieting his conscience and putting out of mind the judgment he knows to be inevitable. The Christian gospel is a scandal to man and his culture because it does the one thing he most wants to avoid: it awakens him from his self-imposed slumber to the reality of his fallen and rebellious state, and it calls for him to reject autonomy and submit to God through repentance and faith in Jesus Christ.

We live in an age of pluralism—a belief system that puts an end to truth by declaring everything to be true, especially with regard to religion. It may be difficult for the contemporary Christian to comprehend, but the Christians living in the first few centuries of the faith were actually marked and persecuted as atheists. The culture surrounding them was immersed in theism. Images of deities filled the world, and religion was a booming business.[2] Men not only tolerated one another's deities but also swapped and shared them. The entire religious world was going along just fine until the Christians showed up and declared, "They are not gods which are made with hands."[3] They denied the Caesars the homage they demanded, refused to bend the knee to all other so-called gods, and confessed Jesus alone as Lord of all.[4] The entire world looked on this as jaw-dropping arrogance and reacted with fury against the Christian's intolerable intolerance to tolerance.

---

2. Acts 19:27
3. Acts 19:26
4. Romans 10:9

This same scenario abounds in our world today. Against all logic, we hear that all views regarding religion and morality are true, no matter how radically different and contradictory they may be. The most overwhelming aspect of all this is that through the tireless efforts of the media and the academic world, this has quickly become the majority view. However, pluralism does not address the issue or cure the malady. It only anesthetizes the patient so that he no longer feels or thinks. The gospel is a scandal because it awakens man from his slumber and refuses to let him rest on such an illogical footing. It forces him to come to some conclusion—"How long will you falter between two opinions? If the LORD is God, follow Him; but if Baal, follow him."[5]

The true gospel is radically exclusive. Jesus is not *a* way; He is *the* way, and all other ways are no way at all. If Christianity would only move one small step toward a more tolerant ecumenicalism and exchange the definite article *the* for the indefinite article *a*, the scandal would be over, and the world and Christianity could become friends. However, whenever this occurs, Christianity ceases to be Christianity, Christ is denied, and the world is without a Savior.

We live in an age of humanism—over the last several decades, man has fought to purge God from his conscience and culture. He has torn down every visible altar to the one true God and has erected monuments to himself with the zeal of a religious fanatic. He has managed to make himself the center, measure, and end of all things. He praises his inherent worth, demands homage to his self-esteem, and promotes his own self-fulfillment or self-realization as the greatest good. He explains away his gnawing conscience as the remnant of an antiquated religion of guilt, and he excuses himself from any responsibility for the moral chaos surrounding him by blaming society, or at least that part of society that has not yet attained his enlightenment. Any suggestion that his conscience might be right in its testimony against him or that he might be responsible for the almost infinite variations of maladies in the world is unthinkable. For this reason, the gospel is a scandal to fallen man because it exposes his delusions about himself and convicts him of his fallen state and his guilt. This is the essential first work of the gospel, and this is why the world so loathes true gospel preaching. It ruins man's party, rains on his parade, exposes his make-believe, and points out that the emperor has no clothes.

---

5. 1 Kings 18:21

The Scriptures recognize that the gospel of Jesus Christ is a "stumbling block" and "foolishness" to all men of every age and culture.[6] However, to seek to remove the scandal from the message is to make void the cross of Christ and its saving power.[7] We must understand that the gospel is not only scandalous—it is supposed to be scandalous! Through the foolishness of the gospel, God has ordained to destroy the wisdom of the wise, frustrate the intelligence of the greatest minds, and humble the pride of all men to the end that no flesh may boast in His presence.[8] As it is written, "He who glories, let him glory in the LORD."[9]

Paul's gospel not only contradicted the religion, philosophy, and culture of the day, it also declared war on them. It refused truce or treaty with the world and would settle for nothing less than culture's absolute surrender to the lordship of Jesus Christ. We would do well to follow Paul's example. We must be careful to shun every temptation to conform our gospel to the trends of the day or the desires of carnal men. We have no right to water down its offense or civilize its radical demands in order to make it more appealing to a fallen world or carnal church members.

Our churches have plenty of strategies to become more seeker friendly by repackaging the gospel, removing the stumbling block, and taking the edge off the blade so that it might be more acceptable to carnal men. We ought to be seeker friendly, but we ought to realize this: there is only one Seeker, and He is God. If we are striving to make our church and message accommodating, let us make them accommodating to Him. If we are striving to build a church or ministry, let us build it upon a passion to glorify God and a desire not to offend His majesty. To the wind with what the world thinks about us. We are not to seek the honors of earth, but the honor of heaven should be our desire.

AN UNBELIEVABLE GOSPEL

As we have argued, Paul's flesh had every reason to be ashamed of the gospel that he preached because it contradicted absolutely everything that was held true and sacred among his contemporaries. Yet there is still

---

6. 1 Corinthians 1:23
7. 1 Corinthians 1:17, 23
8. 1 Corinthians 1:19–20, 29
9. 1 Corinthians 1:31

another reason for fleshly shame: the gospel is an absolutely unbelievable message, a seemingly ludicrous word to the wise of the world.

As Christians, we sometimes fail to realize how utterly astounding it is when anyone truly believes our message. In a sense, the gospel is so far-fetched that its spread throughout the Roman Empire is proof of its supernatural nature. What could ever bring a Gentile, completely unaware of Old Testament Scriptures and rooted in either Greek philosophy or pagan superstitions, to believe such a message about a man named Jesus?

- He was born under questionable circumstances to a poor family in one of the most despised regions of the Roman Empire, *and yet* the gospel claims that He was the eternal Son of God, conceived by the Holy Spirit in the womb of a Jewish virgin.

- He was a carpenter by trade and an itinerant religious teacher with no official training, *and yet* the gospel claims that He surpassed the combined wisdom of every Greek philosopher and Roman sage of antiquity.

- He was poor and had no place to lay His head, *and yet* the gospel claims that for three years He fed thousands by a word, healed every manner of illness among men, and even raised the dead.

- He was crucified outside of Jerusalem as a blasphemer and an enemy of the state, *and yet* the gospel claims that His death was the pivotal event in all of human history and the only means of salvation from sin and reconciliation with God.

- He was placed in a borrowed tomb, *and yet* the gospel claims that on the third day He rose from the dead and presented Himself to many of His followers. Forty days later, He ascended into heaven and sat down at the right hand of God.

- Thus, the gospel claims that a poor Jewish carpenter, who was rejected as a lunatic and a blasphemer by His own people and crucified by the state, is now the Savior of the world, the King of Kings and Lord of Lords. At His name, every knee, including Caesar's, will bow.

Who could have ever believed such a message except by the power of God? There is no other explanation. The gospel would have never made its way out of Jerusalem, let alone beyond the Roman Empire and into every nation of the world, except that God had ordained to work through it. The message would have died at its birth had it depended upon the organizational abilities, eloquence, or apologetic powers of its preachers. All the missionary strategies in the world and all the clever marketing schemes borrowed from Wall Street could never have advanced this foolish stumbling block of a message.

This truth brings both encouragement and warning to those of us who endeavor to advance the faith in which we have believed. First, it is an encouragement to know that the simple and faithful proclamation of the gospel will ensure its continued advance in the world. Secondly, it is a warning to us that we not succumb to the lie that we can advance the gospel through our brilliance, eloquence, or clever strategies. Such things have no power to bring about the "impossible" conversion of men.[10] We must cast ourselves with hopeful urgency upon the only biblical means of advancing the gospel—the bold and clear proclamation of a message about which we are not ashamed because "it is the power of God to salvation for everyone who believes."[11]

We live in an unbelieving and skeptical age. The culture ridicules our faith as a hopeless myth, viewing us as either narrow-minded bigots or weak-minded victims of a religious ruse. Such an attack often puts us on the defensive, and we attempt to fight back and prove our position and relevancy with apologetics. Although some forms of this discipline are quite helpful and necessary, we must realize that the power still lies in the proclamation of the gospel. We cannot convince a man to believe any more than we can raise the dead. Such things are the work of God's Spirit. Men are brought to faith only through the supernatural working of God, and He has promised to work—not through human wisdom or intellectual expertise, but through the preaching of Christ crucified and resurrected from the dead![12]

We must come to grips with the fact that our gospel is an unbelievable message. We should not expect anyone to give us a hearing, let alone believe, apart from a gracious and powerful working of God's Spirit. How very hopeless is all our preaching apart from God's power! How very dependent is the preacher upon God! All our evangelism is nothing more than a fool's errand unless God moves upon the hearts of men. However, He has promised to do just that if we will be faithful to preach that one singular message that has the power to save: the gospel!

---

10. 1 Corinthians 1:17–25
11. Romans 1:16
12. 1 Corinthians 1:22–24

CHAPTER EIGHT

A Powerful Gospel

For it is the power of God to salvation.
—Romans 1:16

The absolute inability of man to save himself from his sin and its condemnation is a constant theme throughout the Scriptures. Job declared, "If I wash myself with snow water, and cleanse my hands with soap, yet You will plunge me into the pit, and my own clothes will abhor me."[1] The psalmist lamented that his sin was always before him, and the apostle Paul cried out in desperation, "O wretched man that I am! Who will deliver me from this body of death?"[2]

Man's total helplessness and inability to save himself is one of the darkest truths in Scripture. However, it serves the very high purpose of humbling man and magnifying the power of the gospel to save. In his letter to the church in Rome, Paul declared that it was because of man's impotence or utter inability to save himself that Christ died for the ungodly.[3] Left to himself, man cannot be saved. However, God has not left man to himself but has provided a means of salvation through the gospel of His Son! That which is impossible for men is possible with God.[4] He is mighty to save, and He can save to the uttermost.[5]

---

1. Job 9:30–31
2. Psalm 51:3; Romans 7:24
3. Romans 5:6. The word *powerless* (NIV), or *helpless* (NASB), is from the Greek word *asthenés*, which means impotent, weak, feeble, without strength, infirm.
4. Mark 10:24–27
5. Isaiah 63:1: "Who is this who comes from Edom, with dyed garments from Bozrah, this One who is glorious in His apparel, traveling in the greatness of His strength?—'I who speak in righteousness, mighty to save.'" Hebrews 7:25: "Wherefore he is able also to save them to the uttermost that come unto God by him, seeing he ever liveth to make intercession for them" (KJV).

THE POWER OF GOD IN THE GOSPEL

The Scriptures abound with demonstrations of God's power. He creates the world with a word.[6] He leads forth the starry host by number. He calls them all by name, and because of the greatness of His might and the strength of His power, not one of them is missing.[7] He separates the sea with a blast from His nostrils.[8] The mountains melt under Him like wax before the fire and water poured down a steep place.[9] He plays with Leviathan as with a bird.[10] He does according to His will in the host of heaven and among the inhabitants of earth. No one can ward off His hand or say to Him, "What have You done?"[11] Such is the power of our God, and yet none of these demonstrations of divine strength can compare with that power revealed through the gospel of Jesus Christ.

In our text, Paul refers to the gospel as the *power* of God. The word is translated from the Greek word *dúnamis*. Although the word itself is not exceptional, it takes on extraordinary meaning within the context of Scripture. Here, Paul is undoubtedly drawing upon the countless references in the Old Testament to the power of God manifested in the saving of His people. God brought Israel out from the land of Egypt with great power and with a mighty hand.[12] He raised up Pharaoh in order to show him His power and to proclaim His name throughout all the earth.[13] He saved His people for the sake of His name, that He might make His power known.[14] Finally, He reminded Israel time and time again that their salvation had nothing to do with their own power, but everything to do with His.[15]

Here in the first chapter of Romans, the word *dúnamis* occurs in two places other than verse 16. At the beginning of the chapter, it refers to the power that raised Jesus from the dead and vindicated His sonship.[16] Following our text, it also refers to power as an attribute of God that is manifest

6. Genesis 1:3; Hebrews 11:3
7. Isaiah 40:26
8. Exodus 15:8
9. Micah 1:4
10. Job 41:5
11. Daniel 4:35
12. Exodus 32:11; Deuteronomy 9:29; 2 Kings 17:36; Nehemiah 1:10; Psalm 77:14–15
13. Exodus 9:16
14. Psalm 106:8
15. Deuteronomy 8:16–17
16. Romans 1:4

in the creation and sustaining of the universe.[17] Both of these are two of the greatest demonstrations of God's omnipotence in the Scriptures. However, the gospel stands on an equal footing with them, for it is the power of God for the salvation of men, a salvation which includes not only their deliverance from the condemnation of sin but also their spiritual resurrection as new creations and their ongoing preservation, or sanctification.

With regard to the power of the gospel, it is helpful to ask ourselves two questions. The first is, "Do we recognize the great power required to save sinful men?" Salvation is not a light work; it is an impossibility for all but God.[18] This is due to man's fallen state and moral corruption. The Scriptures teach that the image of God in man has been seriously disfigured and moral corruption has polluted his entire being.[19] As such, man has declared war on God and does everything in his power to restrain or stifle His truth.[20] The Scriptures teach that man *cannot* come to God because He *will not* come to God, and he will not come to God because his heart is evil. Jesus taught this truth in John 3:19–20: "And this is the condemnation, that the light has come into the world, and men loved darkness rather than light, because their deeds were evil. For everyone practicing evil hates the light and does not come to the light, lest his deeds should be exposed."

The walls of depravity around the heart of a man are much stronger and made of harder stuff than those that surrounded Jericho. If men could not bring down the walls of that great city by their own power, they cannot conquer the depravity of their own hearts. It must be the power of God. For this reason, we often hear that the power of God manifested in the salvation of one man far exceeds the power of God manifested in the very creation of the universe. God created the world *ex nihilo*, out of nothing. However, when God saves a man, He does an exceedingly more difficult thing. It is far easier to create good out of nothing than it is to recreate good out of a fallen and corrupt humanity.

At the risk of redundancy, we must reiterate that we cannot truly appreciate the power of the gospel in the salvation of man until we comprehend

---

17. Romans 1:20

18. Matthew 19:26

19. Moral corruption pervades the body (Romans 6:6, 12; 7:24; 8:10, 13), reason (Romans 1:21; 2 Corinthians 3:14–15; 4:4; Ephesians 4:17–19), emotions (Romans 1:26–27; Galatians 5:24; 2 Timothy 3:2–4), and will (Romans 6:17; 7:14–15).

20. Romans 1:18, 30; 5:10

something of the fallen state and moral corruption of man. The more we sound the depths of man's depravity, the more we will soar in our understanding and appreciation of the power of the gospel. We will also become acutely aware that the methodologies and marketing strategies and the props and gimmicks on display in much of contemporary evangelicalism are useless vanity. If men are going to be saved, they will be saved by the supernatural power of God manifested in the preaching of the gospel!

The second question we must ask ourselves is, "Do we recognize that the power to save is found uniquely in the gospel?" The gospel of Jesus Christ *is* the power of God for salvation. It is not just the core, or part of what is needed, but the whole. For it to have great effect upon men, it only needs to be proclaimed. It does not require a revision to make it relevant, an adaptation to make it understood, or a defense to validate it. If we stand up and proclaim it, it will do the work itself. A single preacher who has stripped himself of all his carnal weaponry and fights with only the proclamation of the gospel, the work of intercession, and the labor of sacrificial love will do more for the world than all the schemes of strategists and innovators combined.

Although Scripture and the history of the church both confirm this truth, a study of contemporary evangelicalism shows that evangelicals no longer believe this bold thought. It sounds good in the old hymns, but to actually believe it and apply it would seem naive to say the least. Thus, many of the "model churches" of the day look more like a Six Flags over Jesus than a ship of Zion. Not only do they offer a reduced or modified gospel but also they promote so many other attractions that a biblical gospel becomes difficult, if not impossible, to find. Power no longer resides in a simple message but in bold leadership, cutting-edge strategies, cultural sensitivity, and the ability to morph the church into whatever the culture dictates.

As our world becomes increasingly irreligious and anti-Christian, evangelicalism runs around aimlessly, looking for a remedy. We carefully study the fads and fashions of the culture and then make the necessary changes in the gospel in order to keep it relevant. When our culture no longer desires what we have, then we give them what they want. When a certain model of ministry draws a crowd of carnal men, we write a how-to book that lays out a strategy for the rest to follow. However, in all of this we fail to see that we are not making the gospel relevant. We are only catering to a godless culture in order to keep it within our walls. In the end, the gospel is gone, God is not honored, and the culture goes to hell.

The church needs men who will stand before the opposing masses with nothing to help them or defend them except the gospel and the God who has promised to work through it. How cumbersome was Saul's armor to David, and how ridiculous did David appear when he wore it? The sheer weight of it sapped his agility and strength. Yet he made the crucial decision to put it off and face the giant with nothing more than the name of the Lord. Likewise, we must refuse Saul's armor and weaponry and go to battle with nothing more than the smooth stones of the gospel. We must make that crucial decision to throw off the props, strategies, and clever techniques of modern-day evangelism, facing the twin giants of unbelief and skepticism with open Bibles and the clear, uncompromising message of Christ crucified and resurrected from the dead. Then we will see the power of God manifested in the genuine conversion of even the greatest sinners. Is there anything too difficult for the Lord?[21]

Now that we recognize the depravity of man and the impossibility of his salvation through any means even remotely associated with the arm of the flesh, we can begin to appreciate Paul's exultation in the power of the gospel. It was for this reason that he was able to walk into the Areopagus and declare a crucified Jew to be the God of the universe and the Savior of the world![22] He needed no persuasive argument or eloquence of speech. He knew that men would be converted if he endured in preaching this singular message boldly and clearly.[23] This is the same confidence that sustained William Carey and countless other missionaries through the long years of drought before the harvest. The gospel is the power of God for salvation. Men will be converted if it is preached!

A SAVING GOSPEL

In the Scriptures, we read that salvation is the end, or goal, of faith.[24] The same is true of the gospel. In Paul's estimation, the greatest gift that the gospel affords a man is the salvation of his soul. God sent His Son into

---

21. Genesis 18:14
22. Acts 17:22
23. Acts 17:34
24. 1 Peter 1:9

the world that the world might be saved through Him.[25] Throughout the ages, salvation has been the glorious theme of the church and the subject of her greatest hymns. Saints of old viewed salvation as not just one of the many gospel benefits to be considered, but as the one great benefit that when received, it so consumed the believer's life that he wanted nothing more. Salvation from self and sin, deliverance from judgment and wrath, reconciliation with God and the knowledge of Christ was enough!

Lamentably, in recent decades, it seems that salvation has lost something of its value. In the opinion of many, the promise of salvation is no longer a strong enough motivation to move the sinner to repentance or the saint to true devotion, so we must add many other promises to make the gospel call appealing. Health and wealth, purpose and power, and getting the most out of this present life are the real drawing cards of contemporary Christianity. In fact, the very things that the pulpit now promises and people in the pews seek the most are often the very things that Jesus warned could be lost in the course of true discipleship.[26] According to Him, a man may have to lose the whole world in order to be saved, and yet in His estimation, it was a bargain to get salvation at such a small cost.[27]

In light of the high value that Scripture places upon salvation, why is it that the lone promise of salvation no longer thrills the modern soul? Why must other more earthly promises be added to the gospel in order to make it appealing to contemporary man? First, it is because men do not comprehend their deplorable condition. As a rich man sees no reason for rejoicing in a meager gift of bread until a turn of events leaves him impoverished, so the sinner finds no joy in salvation until the horrid nature of his sin is revealed and he sees himself as wretched, miserable, poor, blind, and naked.[28] Secondly, it is because men do not understand the great danger they are in. A man will esteem salvation only to the degree that he understands something of the terrors from which he is being saved. A clearer view of hell and the wrath of God will give man a more appropriate appreciation of the salvation offered through the gospel. Thirdly, it is because men do not understand the infinite cost that was paid to secure their salvation. The redemption of a soul is costly

---

25. John 3:17
26. Matthew 16:24–26
27. Mark 8:36–37
28. Revelation 3:17

and beyond the wages of men.[29] Only God possessed the payment price, and He paid it in full with the precious blood of His own Son.[30] Sinners who remain uninformed regarding the worth of Christ have little hope of appreciating what He has done for them in the gospel. Fourthly, it is because unregenerate men are always this way. Blind men find no beauty in a sunset, deaf men are not moved by even the most beautiful sonata, and brute beasts have no appreciation for art. In a similar fashion, unregenerate, unconverted, carnal men are spiritually blind, deaf to God's Word, and in bondage to a brutish heart that would sooner feed its animal lusts than taste and see that the Lord is good.[31] For this reason, Jesus exclaims that unless a man is born again he cannot even "see" the kingdom of heaven, let alone esteem its worth.[32] For this reason, carnal people fill our church rosters—people who come for all sorts of reasons other than Christ and a hunger for righteousness.[33] The more practical and present-day promises that have been added to the gospel make it appealing to them, and they remain in church as long as they continue to get what they want. This feeds their flesh in a religious fashion, but their souls remain dead to God and the hope of true salvation.

SALVATION DEFINED

The apostle Paul writes that the gospel is the power of God for salvation. It seems simple enough, but once again, there is a great need to define our terms. What does Paul mean by *salvation*? There is an overabundance of conflicting ideas regarding the matter, and it would be wrong to assume that we are all of the same opinion. The salvation afforded by the gospel is multifaceted, but we will concern ourselves with its three primary themes: salvation from the condemnation of sin, from the power of sin, and, ultimately, from the presence of sin. These same themes may also be arranged in a temporal or chronological order—past, present, and future. The one who believes in the gospel has been saved from the condemnation of sin, is being saved from the power of sin, and will ultimately be saved from the presence of sin.

---

29. Psalm 49:8
30. 1 Peter 1:18–19
31. Psalm 34:8
32. John 3:3
33. Matthew 5:6

In the past tense, the Christian has been saved from the condemnation of sin. The Scriptures teach that all men stand condemned in Adam and by merit of their own sinful deeds.[34] This condemnation ultimately takes place before the judgment throne of God, where the sinner is exposed, weighed, and exiled to hell.[35] Yet for the Christian, the scenario is quite different. The moment a Christian repented and believed the gospel, his standing before God completely changed forever.[36] He was justified by faith and obtained peace with God.[37] As the Scriptures declare, "There is therefore now no condemnation to those who are in Christ Jesus."[38]

In the present tense, the Christian is being saved from the power of sin. The God who began a good work in him has promised to perfect that work until that final day, and to cleanse him from all his filthiness and idols.[39] In the Scriptures, God is the God who not only justifies but also sanctifies.[40] Every Christian, without exception, is God's workmanship.[41] He works powerfully and effectually in the life of all true believers, directing their will and empowering them to act according to what most pleases Him.[42] This work of sanctification is an essential element of salvation, and every true Christian has entered into this inescapable process that is designed, directed, and empowered by God. It is a long-standing gospel truth that the greatest evidence of having been justified is that we presently are being sanctified. We have assurance that God has saved us from the condemnation of sin because He is currently saving us from its power. Because of our human frailties, this process is a real struggle, and our advancement in holiness may be marked by three steps forward and one step back. Nevertheless, over the course of every Christian life, there will be a marked advance. Only a weak and perverted gospel puts forth the possibility of salvation without sanctification. As the Scriptures declare, "Pursue…holiness, without which no one will see the Lord,"

---

34. Romans 5:12–19; 3:23
35. Revelation 20:11–15
36. Mark 1:15
37. Romans 5:1. The word *justified* is a forensic or legal term. To be justified means that one has been legally declared right with God, not by his own virtue and merit, but by the virtue and merit of Jesus Christ and His death on Calvary.
38. Romans 8:1
39. Philippians 1:6; Ezekiel 36:25
40. 1 Thessalonians 5:23
41. Ephesians 2:10
42. Philippians 2:13

and "if you are without chastening, of which all have become partakers, then you are illegitimate and not sons."[43]

In the future tense, the Christian will one day be saved from the presence of sin and its corrupting influence. In this work, two things are required. First, the Christian must be changed, his corrupt flesh put away and his body redeemed.[44] This will happen in the twinkling of an eye, at the trumpet sound, when the body is raised imperishable and the mortal is dressed in immortality.[45] Secondly, a new heaven and earth must be prepared—a creation set free from the curse and corruption under which it has groaned into the freedom of the glory of the children of God.[46] Though still in the future, this final stage of salvation is as certain as the other two. The Scriptures state it in this way: "Moreover whom He predestined, these He also called; whom He called, these He also justified; and whom He justified, these He also glorified."[47]

The immeasurable power of God manifests itself in the gospel. Nothing less than the gospel can bring a man to repentance and faith. Nothing less than the gospel can transform a man from sinner to saint. Nothing less than the gospel can bring many sons home to glory![48]

---

43. Hebrews 12:14, 8. The word *discipline* refers to God's intervention in the life of the believer to train them in holiness.
44. 1 Corinthians 15:50; Romans 8:23
45. 1 Corinthians 15:52–53
46. Revelation 22:3; Romans 8:21–22
47. Romans 8:30
48. Hebrews 2:10

CHAPTER NINE

A Gospel for All Who Believe

For everyone who believes, for the Jew first and also for the Greek.
—Romans 1:16

The gospel call is universal. The redemptive work of Christ did not take place in some remote corner of the planet, but in the very center of the religious world.[1] News of His death and resurrection spread quickly throughout the entire known world.[2] Furthermore, Christ did not come to save only a certain people group, but He shed His blood to redeem a people from every tribe and tongue and people and nation.[3] The Old Testament prophecies declared that the Messiah would receive the nations as an inheritance, and the Great Commission is the working out of that promise.[4] Christ has commanded His church to go into all the world and preach the gospel to all creation. Those who believe and show their faith by their public identification with Christ through baptism will be saved, but those who do not believe will be condemned.[5]

SALVATION TO ALL WHO BELIEVE

Both the Old and New Testament Scriptures give the comprehensive testimony that men can only receive the gospel benefits by faith. Habakkuk's creed is the foundation of all true religion: "The just shall live by faith."[6] These words are the key to salvation and the spark of every true

---

1. Acts 26:26
2. Colossians 1:5–6
3. Revelation 5:9
4. Psalm 2:8
5. Mark 16:15; Matthew 28:18–20
6. Habakkuk 2:4; Romans 1:17

revival of religion. Without these words, the door of salvation is sealed shut. The only password into glory is "I believe." Paul drives home this truth in a passage that is remarkable for its redundancy: "Knowing that a man is not justified by the works of the law but by faith in Jesus Christ, even we have believed in Christ Jesus, that we might be justified by faith in Christ and not by the works of the law; for by the works of the law no flesh shall be justified."[7]

Salvation is not of works for two fundamental reasons. First, man has no works of which to speak. There is nothing in his life that merits salvation, but everything that would evoke the condemnation of a holy God. It is the testimony of Scripture that there is no one righteous, not even one. There is none who does good.[8] In fact, the very best of man's labors and his greatest acts of altruism are nothing more than filthy rags before God.[9] These truths devastate the pride of man, but they must be pressed upon his conscience in order to extinguish any hope of self-promotion before God and to crush every thought of gaining favor with the Deity by the strength of his own arm. A man comes to God by faith only after he has realized his destitute condition and cries out with the old hymn writer, "In my hand no price I bring, simply to Thy cross I cling."[10]

Secondly, salvation is not of works because that would not glorify God; it would make Him a debtor bound to reward the supposed virtue of the creature. Salvation by works is nothing more than humanism clothed in religion. It is the mythological man raising himself from the dust by his own strength of will to overcome all odds and earn the prize. On the other hand, faith is true religion. It is man as he is, "lost and ruined by the fall," emptied of all confidence in self, and trusting in the faithful promises of a saving God.[11] In the epic drama of salvation by faith, God is the hero, and upon Him alone do we lavish praise. Just as it is written, "Not unto us, O LORD, not unto us, but to Your name give glory," and "He who glories, let him glory in the LORD."[12]

Given that salvation is by faith alone, it is imperative that we understand something of what faith is. After all, the demons believe and even

---

7. Galatians 2:16

8. Romans 3:10–12

9. Isaiah 64:6

10. Augustus M. Toplady, "Rock of Ages," 1775.

11. Joseph Hart, "I Will Arise and Go to Jesus," 1759.

12. Psalm 115:1; 1 Corinthians 1:31; Romans 3:27

tremble, and in their trembling, they show more piety than some men who make a claim to saving faith.[13] According to the Scriptures, faith is being fully assured that what God has promised, He is also able to perform.[14] Regarding the gospel, it means that the repentant sinner has turned from every vain hope in the flesh and has thrown himself upon Christ alone. In doing so, he becomes fully assured that Christ's death made atonement for his sin and reconciled him to God. This is what faith is, but how can we know that this is the faith we have? What are the evidences of true saving faith? How is it validated? Fortunately, the Scriptures have not left us to ourselves in this matter. The apostle James answers our questions with marked simplicity and clarity: "But someone will say, 'You have faith, and I have works.' Show me your faith without your works, and I will show you my faith by my works."[15] It is a gross misinterpretation of the text even to suggest that James might be promoting salvation through works. His argument is not that works result in salvation, but rather that all true salvation results in works. In other words, the work or fruit of one's life is the evidence of truly being saved by faith.

This teaching is not exclusive to James alone. John the Baptist exhorted men to "bear fruits worthy of repentance." Jesus warned, "You will know them by their fruits.... Not everyone who says to Me, 'Lord, Lord,' shall enter the kingdom of heaven, but he who does the will of My Father in heaven."[16] Paul commanded those who professed faith in Christ to "examine" and "test" their lives to find evidence or proof of their faith.[17] Furthermore, he warned about men who professed to know God but denied Him by their deeds.[18] Finally, Peter admonished his readers to be diligent to make their "calling and election sure" by examining their lives for evidence of growth in Christian virtue or Christlike character.[19] From these texts and others, we can rightly conclude that salvation comes to everyone who believes. However, a man's life proves the validity of his confession of faith.

13. James 2:19
14. Romans 4:21
15. James 2:18
16. Matthew 3:8; 7:16, 21
17. 2 Corinthians 13:5
18. Titus 1:16
19. 2 Peter 1:5–10

Before we leave behind this brief discussion regarding the gospel of Christ and salvation by faith alone, we must address a very important matter. The Scriptures not only teach that the gospel is *for* everyone who believes, but they also warn that the gospel is *against* everyone who does not believe. Jesus explains it this way: "He who believes in Him is not condemned; but he who does not believe is condemned already, because he has not believed in the name of the only begotten Son of God.... He who believes in the Son has everlasting life; and he who does not believe the Son shall not see life, but the wrath of God abides on him."[20] How important it is to see the whole picture! The gospel is a two-sided coin with forgiveness and life on the one side, and condemnation and death on the other. It is not "salvation to everyone"; it is only to "everyone who believes." To the rest, the gospel is a death sentence, a constant reminder that they stand condemned before God and that the wrath of God abides upon them. For this reason, the unbelieving world hates the gospel and does everything in its power to suppress or restrain its truths.[21] For this reason, the unbeliever loathes the messengers of the gospel and seeks to silence them. Gospel messengers are like barbs in his eyes and thorns in his sides.[22] They are the "troubler[s] of Israel" and the ones who "turned the world upside down."[23] Though they may be a fragrance of life to the believer, they are the smell of death to everyone else.[24]

A GOSPEL FOR ALL

Throughout the history of the Old Testament, two distinct groups made up the world—the descendants of Abraham and everyone else. The former were Israelites, who received the adoption as sons, the covenants, the law, the temple, and the promises.[25] The latter consisted of the Gentiles, who experienced futility of mind, hardness of heart, and exclusion from the life of God.[26] They were polar opposites, with almost nothing in common except their humanity. However, one dreadful Friday afternoon,

---

20. John 3:18, 36
21. Romans 1:18
22. Numbers 33:55
23. 1 Kings 18:17; Acts 17:6
24. 2 Corinthians 2:15–16
25. Romans 9:4–5
26. Ephesians 4:17–19

everything changed as the Savior of both peoples bowed His head and gave up His life. Through Him, a multitude from the Jews and Gentiles would be united together as one man and reconciled to God.[27] As it is written: "And He came and preached peace to you who were afar off [Gentiles], and to those who were near [Jews]."[28]

In the death of Christ, the door of salvation opened to all peoples. The fact that God was not constrained in any way to provide salvation for anyone just magnifies this amazing demonstration of grace. If He had turned away from man's plight and let every son of Adam run headlong into hell, He would have been just, and His reputation would have remained untarnished. If He had sent a Savior to Israel alone and left the Gentiles to continue in their self-imposed exile, no accusation could have been made against His throne. The angels were made of greater stuff than men, but God passed them over and left them to their own destruction.[29] He could have done the same with us! He did not owe the world a Savior!

One may question the usefulness of discussing such a dark and disturbing theme. Yet it is only in light of such truths that we are able to appreciate the grace given to us in the gospel. We were a fallen and sinful race. We had made our decision, declared our independence, and charted our own course for destruction. There was no virtue in us that He should seek us out, nor was there any worth in us that He should redeem us. His glory would not have diminished and creation would have suffered no loss if He had simply let us run our course straight into hell without the slightest intervention. Yet He has opened the door of salvation to every tribe, tongue, people, and nation through a most costly payment—the precious blood of His only Son![30]

Although the gospel is for all, it is noteworthy that it is first for the Jew and then the Gentile. This is one of the many demonstrations of the sovereignty of God that runs throughout the full length of biblical history. It demonstrates that God deals with men according to His character and choice, not the merits of the recipient.[31] God chose Israel and placed it first, above all the nations of the earth—not because of some merit found in them, but according to His good pleasure and sovereign love:

---

27. Ephesians 2:13–16
28. Ephesians 2:17
29. Hebrews 2:7
30. Revelation 5:9; 1 Peter 1:18–19
31. Romans 9:15–16

The LORD your God has chosen you to be a people for Himself, a special treasure above all the peoples on the face of the earth. The LORD did not set His love on you nor choose you because you were more in number than any other people, for you were the least of all peoples but because the LORD loves you.[32]

The only explanation for God's special love for Israel must rest in God Himself: He loved them because He loved them.[33] Merit did not prompt His love. He did not find something in the Jew that was lacking in the Gentile. One was not better than the other. The apostle Paul proves this when he asks, "Are we better than they? Not at all. For we have previously charged both Jews and Greeks that they are all under sin."[34] God chose to manifest His salvation to Israel for the same reason that He has now opened a door of salvation to the Gentiles—because it was pleasing in His sight. He loved us because He loved us—not because of human merit or worth, but in spite of our utter lack of both. He could have left us to ourselves. He could have given us over to the lusts of our own hearts and to the practice of every kind of impurity.[35] He could have extended the prohibition, "Do not go into the way of the Gentiles."[36] Yet, according to His good pleasure and to demonstrate His great mercy, the gospel call extends to the far reaches of the earth. The Scriptures give abundant testimony to this great and glorious truth: "The people who sat in darkness have seen a great light, and upon those who sat in the region and shadow of death light has dawned."[37] "Behold! My Servant whom I have chosen,…He will declare justice to the Gentiles…. And in His name Gentiles will trust."[38] "I have set you as a light to the Gentiles, that you should be for salvation to the ends of the earth."[39] And again he says: "Rejoice, O Gentiles, with His people!"[40]

The universal call of the gospel is a great part of its beauty. God has concerned Himself with taking a people from among the Jews and

---

32. Deuteronomy 7:6–8
33. Deuteronomy 7:8
34. Romans 3:9
35. Acts 14:16; Romans 1:24, 26; Ephesians 4:17–19
36. Matthew 10:5
37. Matthew 4:16
38. Matthew 12:18, 21
39. Acts 13:47
40. Romans 15:10

Gentiles, opening a wide door of faith for whosoever will—Greek and Jew, circumcised and uncircumcised, barbarian, Scythian, slave and freeman.[41] Through the gospel, the Gentile hope has now advanced far beyond that of the Syrophoenician mother who begged to feed on the crumbs that fell from Israel's table.[42] By faith, the greatest sinner from the most backward and vile people may now take his chair at the Lord's Table and dine as a son.

God offers the gospel freely to the Jew and the Gentile alike, and this brings to mind one more truth that ought to be expounded before we leave this theme behind: the gospel that saves the Jew is the same that saves the Gentile. Although we should be aware of the differences in cultures, we must not allow culture to shape our gospel or to dictate how to communicate it. Our point of origin must always be the Scriptures. The Bible alone tells us what the gospel is and how to teach it to men. Consequently, it should be the exegete (one who is dedicated to the interpretation of Scripture) and the theologian among us who shape our message, not the anthropologist, sociologist, missiologist, or church growth expert.

Recent years show a growing preoccupation with cultural sensitivity and the need to adapt the gospel message to specific cultural circumstances. The great majority of evangelicals seem convinced that the raw or primitive gospel will not work, and that man has somehow become too complex or too simple a being to be saved and transformed by such a message. There is now more emphasis on understanding and catering to the culture than to understanding and proclaiming the only message that has the power to save it.

We must regain our foothold in the Scriptures until once again they birth in us the conviction that the gospel alone is the power of God for salvation. While it is true that it is a scandalous and incomprehensible message, it is also true that it is the only message through which God has promised to save fallen man. To revise or repackage the gospel in hopes of making a greater impact upon each specific culture is to pervert the truth of the gospel, diminish its power, and leave the world without the only message that has the power to save it!

---

41. Acts 15:14; 14:27; Colossians 3:11
42. Mark 7:28

PART THREE
The Acropolis of the Christian Faith

*For all have sinned and fall short of the glory of God, being
justified freely by His grace through the redemption that is in
Christ Jesus, whom God set forth as a propitiation by His blood,
through faith, to demonstrate His righteousness, because in His
forbearance God had passed over the sins that were previously
committed, to demonstrate at the present time His righteousness, that He might be just and the justifier of the one who has
faith in Jesus. Where is boasting then? It is excluded. By what
law? Of works? No, but by the law of faith.*

—Romans 3:23–27

CHAPTER TEN

Making Much of Sin

For all have sinned.
—Romans 3:23

The center of the gospel is the death of Christ, and Christ died for sin. Therefore, there can be no gospel proclamation apart from a biblical treatment of sin. This includes explaining the heinous nature of sin and exposing men as sinners. Although the subject of sin is somewhat out of vogue, even in some evangelical circles, any honest consideration of Scripture as it relates to contemporary culture will demonstrate that there is still a need to make much of sin.

The need for clear communication about sin is acute since we live in a generation born in and cultivated by sin.[1] We are a people that drinks down iniquity like water, and cannot discern our fallen condition any more than a fish can know that it is wet.[2] Because of this, we must endeavor to rediscover a biblical view of sin and the sinfulness of man. Our understanding of God and the gospel depends on it.

As stewards of the gospel of Jesus Christ, we do no service to men by making light of sin, skirting around the issue, or avoiding it altogether. Men have only one problem: they are under the wrath of God because of their sin.[3] To deny this is to deny one of the most foundational doctrines of Christianity. It is not unloving to tell men that they are sinners, but it is the grossest form of immorality *not* to tell them! In fact, God declares that their blood will be on our hands if we do not warn them of their sin

1. Psalms 51:5; 58:3
2. Job 15:16
3. John 3:36

and the coming judgment.[4] To seek to preach the gospel without making sin an issue is like trying to heal the brokenness of people superficially, saying, "Peace, peace," when there is no peace.[5]

The book of Romans is the closest thing we have to a systematic theology in the Scriptures. In this letter, the apostle Paul set forth his theology before the church in Rome. He sought to prepare them for his upcoming visit and hoped that they would join with him in his missionary endeavors in Spain.[6] It is extremely important to note that the first three chapters of this letter, with the exception of a brief introduction, are dedicated to hamartiology, or the doctrine of sin.[7] For three chapters, the apostle labors with all his intellect and under the inspiration of the Holy Spirit to achieve one great purpose: to prove the sinfulness of man and to condemn the entire world!

It is popular for Christians to insist that God has not given us a ministry of condemnation and death, but of righteousness, reconciliation, and life.[8] This is very true, but this does not mean that we are not to speak much about sin or use the Scriptures to bring men under the conviction of the Holy Spirit regarding their sin. It is true that there is now no condemnation "in Christ Jesus," but also there is nothing but condemnation apart from Him.[9]

The Scriptures tell us that the law was not given as a means of salvation, but as an instrument for exposing both the vileness of sin (i.e., that sin through the commandment might become exceedingly sinful) and the sinfulness of man (i.e., all the world may become guilty before God).[10] Although we rarely use the law for such a purpose today, there is no evidence in the New Testament that this ministry of the law should not continue to be an essential part of our gospel proclamation. The old preachers called it the breaking up of fallow ground, turning over rocks, and pulling back curtains.[11] They saw the need to hold men up to the mirror of God's law so that they might see their destitute condition and

---

4. Ezekiel 33:8

5. Jeremiah 6:14

6. Romans 15:23–24

7. *Hamartiology* is derived from the Greek words *hamartía*, meaning "sin," and *lógos*, meaning "word" or "discourse." Hamartiology is literally a discourse on sin.

8. This statement is based upon 2 Corinthians 3:7–9 and 2 Corinthians 5:17–18.

9. Romans 8:1; 5:18

10. Romans 7:13; 3:19

11. Jeremiah 4:3; Hosea 10:12

cry out for mercy. Of course, this is not to be done with a spirit of pride or arrogance, and we are not to handle people roughly. God has not called us to be a belligerent or offensive people, even though the truth we preach with all humility may be a great offense to many.

The ministry of the apostle Paul did not have condemnation as it goal, but there is a very real sense in which he labored for condemned men in the hope that they might recognize their utter moral ruin and turn to Christ in repentance and faith. In the book of Romans, Paul first sets out to prove the moral corruption of the entire world, its hostility toward God, and its absolute refusal to submit to the truth it knows.[12] Then he turns his attention to the Jew, and proves that although uniquely blessed through the gift of special revelation, he is just as guilty before God as the Gentile.[13] Finally, he concludes his argument by presenting some of the most direct and offensive accusations against man found in Scripture.[14] What is his purpose? He tells us in his closing arguments: "That every mouth may be stopped, and all the world may become guilty before God."[15]

Like Jeremiah before him, Paul was called not only to "build and to plant" but also to "root out and to pull down, to destroy and to throw down."[16] He was, in his own words, "casting down arguments and every high thing that exalts itself against the knowledge of God."[17] Under the ministry of the Holy Spirit and through the Scriptures, Paul endeavored to end the hope of the pagan moralist, the religious Jew, and everyone in between. He wrote and preached to close the mouths of men so that they would never again boast in self-righteousness or make excuses for sin. He cut them off from every other hope so that they might turn to Christ.

Was the apostle Paul merely an angry and bitter man with an ax to grind against humanity? No! He loved humanity to such an extent that he poured out his life like a drink offering on behalf of the Gentiles, and he even wished himself accursed, separated from Christ for the sake of his fellow Jew.[18] Paul preached against sin for the same reason that the physician works to diagnose his patient's illness and is willing to tell

---

12. Romans 1:18–32
13. Romans 2:1–29
14. Romans 3:1–18
15. Romans 3:19
16. Jeremiah 1:10
17. 2 Corinthians 10:5
18. Philippians 2:17; Romans 9:3

him even the worst of news. It is a labor of love for the salvation of the hearer. Any other response by a doctor or preacher would be loveless and immoral.

It may be appropriate at this time to ask ourselves if our gospel preaching has such a purpose. Do we love enough to teach truth, expose sin, and confront our hearers? Do we possess a biblical compassion that tells men the truth in hope that their hearts will be broken under the weight of their sin and they must look to Christ alone? Are we willing to risk being misunderstood and maligned in order that truth might be told and men might be saved? There seems to be a growing conviction even among evangelicals that contemporary Western man already carries so many psychological fractures and burdens of guilt that we dare not press him further lest we crush him. Such a view fails to realize that there is a tremendous difference between a psychological fracture and biblical repentance leading to life. Modern man has become the feeble character that he is because he is self-absorbed and living in rebellion against God. He is loaded down with guilt because he *is* guilty. He needs God's Word to expose his sin and bring him to repentance. Only then will there be a biblical brokenness that leads to life.

God's dealings with the nation of Israel provide a wonderful example of this truth. Through the prophet Isaiah, God describes Israel's condition: "Why should you be stricken again? You will revolt more and more. The whole head is sick, and the whole heart faints. From the sole of the foot even to the head, there is no soundness in it, but wounds and bruises and putrefying sores; they have not been closed or bound up, or soothed with ointment."[19] The nation of Israel was as fractured and frail as one could ever imagine, yet God dealt with them for their own good by pointing out their rebellion and calling them to repentance. He used many hard words against them, but each was necessary to expose their sin and turn them from it. "Alas, sinful nation, a people laden with iniquity, a brood of evildoers, children who are corrupters! They have forsaken the LORD, they have provoked to anger the Holy One of Israel, they have turned away backward."[20] Also, "'Come now, and let us reason together,' says the LORD, 'though your sins are like scarlet, they shall be

---

19. Isaiah 1:5–6
20. Isaiah 1:4

as white as snow; though they are red like crimson, they shall be as wool. If you are willing and obedient, you shall eat the good of the land.'"[21]

Identifying a malady and explaining its seriousness are always the first steps to finding a cure. A man who has no knowledge of his cancer will not seek the aid of medicine, and a man will not flee from a burning house unless he knows of a fire. To the same degree, a man will not seek salvation until he knows that he is thoroughly lost, and he will not flee to Christ until he knows that there is no other means of salvation. Men must be told of their sin before they will acknowledge it; they must be informed of the danger of it before they will flee from it; and they must be convinced that salvation is found in Christ alone before they will leave behind all their self-righteous hopes and run to Him.

In light of the previous truths, it is a travesty that many within the evangelical community do not even consider making much of sin. There even seems to be a conscious effort to discourage such preaching as negative and destructive even though this is one of the primary ministries of the Holy Spirit: "And when He has come, He will convict the world of sin, and of righteousness, and of judgment: of sin, because they do not believe in Me; of righteousness, because I go to My Father and you see Me no more; of judgment, because the ruler of this world is judged."[22]

According to the Lord Jesus Christ, God sent the Holy Spirit into the world to convict men of sin, righteousness, and judgment. Bringing sin to light and pressing the sinner to repentance is one of His primary ministries. Should not we as ministers of the gospel have the same goal? Should not our preaching reflect the same work? Is it possible to evangelize in the power of the Holy Spirit while refusing to work with the Spirit in this essential ministry? Although the Holy Spirit is not dependent upon human instruments, God has ordained that men come to conviction of sin, repentance, and saving faith through preaching.[23] Yet how can the Spirit use our preaching if we are not willing to expose sin or call men to repentance? The Scriptures teach us that the sword of the Spirit is the Word of God, but if God's ministers only reluctantly use the sword in convicting men of sin, will it not quench both the ministry and the

---

21. Isaiah 1:18–19
22. John 16:8–11
23. 1 Corinthians 1:21

person of the Holy Spirit?[24] We must not be afraid to follow the Spirit's example in dealing with sinners. If He deems it necessary to convict men of sin, we must join Him in this work. Those preachers and churches that have found a "better" way have no grounds for hoping that the Spirit of God is working among them to bring men to Christ.

Before we conclude this chapter, it is important to make one final note. The greatest reason for making much of sin is that it exalts the gospel. You cannot see the beauty of the stars in the midday sky because the light of the sun eclipses them. However, after the sun sets and the sky becomes black as pitch, you can see the stars in the full force of their splendor. So it is with the gospel of Jesus Christ. We can only see its true beauty against the backdrop of our sin. The darker man appears, the brighter the gospel shines.

It seems that men never even notice the beauty of Christ or consider His worth until they see the heinous nature of their sin and see themselves as absolutely destitute, lacking any merit. There are countless testimonies of Christians through the ages who never once esteemed Christ until the day the Holy Spirit came and convicted them of sin and righteousness and judgment. After the unrelenting darkness of their own sin engulfed them, Christ appeared like the morning star and became precious to them.[25]

It is striking that when true believers in Jesus Christ hear a sermon regarding man's depravity, they walk out of church bursting with joy and filled with a new zeal to follow Christ. It is not because they take sin lightly or find some satisfaction in their former sinful state. Rather, the truth fills them with joy unspeakable, because in the greater darkness they saw more of Christ! We rob men of a greater vision of God because we will not give them a lower vision of themselves.

---

24. Ephesians 6:17
25. 2 Peter 1:19; Revelation 22:16

CHAPTER ELEVEN

Making Much of God

For all have sinned.
—Romans 3:23

Against You, You only, have I sinned.
—Psalm 51:4

The divine verdict levied against man in the above texts will have little meaning to a culture that laughs at sin and embraces it as though it were a virtue. Our culture calls evil good and good evil; we substitute darkness for light and light for darkness![1] To stem the tide, we must preach in a way that demonstrates to men the gravity of their sin. The best method to accomplish this is by teaching not only the biblical view of man but also the biblical view of God. To understand the heinous nature of the sin they are committing, men must come to understand Scripture's exalted view of the One against whom they are sinning. If the bravest and most hardened infidel understood even the smallest portion of who God is, he would immediately collapse under the weight of his sin.

If sin receives mention at all in our contemporary context, it is sin against man, sin against society, or even sin against nature, but rarely does our culture ever consider sin against God. In contrast, the Scriptures view all sin as ultimately and most importantly sin against God. King David betrayed the trust of his people, committed adultery, and even orchestrated the murder of an innocent man, yet when the rebuke of Nathan the prophet finally brought him to repentance, he cried out in confession to God: "Against You, You only, have I sinned, and done this evil in Your sight."[2]

---

1. Isaiah 5:20
2. Psalm 51:4

From this text, we learn two important truths. First, although sin may be committed against our fellow creatures and even against creation itself, all sin is first and foremost against God. Secondly, sin is heinous not merely because of the devastation it might bring upon other men or creation as a whole, but primarily and especially because it is an offense committed against an infinitely glorious God who is worthy of the most perfect love, devotion, and obedience from His creation. Therefore, the more a man comprehends something of the glory and supremacy of the God against whom he has sinned, the more he will comprehend the atrocious nature of his sin. A true knowledge of God will lead men to treat even the smallest infraction of God's law as an unspeakable crime, yet an ignorance of God will lead them to treat sin as a small matter of little consequence.

It is a foundational tenant of the Christian faith that a true knowledge of God is essential if one is to have a right view of reality. A wrong view of God will ultimately lead to a wrong view of everything else. This is particularly true with regard to sin. In Psalm 50, God scorns the people of Israel for having forgotten or rejected the most essential truths of His character. They had come to believe that He was just like them—apathetic and unaffected by unrighteousness.[3] Their wrong view of God led to a wrong view of sin. They threw off every moral restraint and perverted their way without fear or shame. Their rebellion led to destruction. They perished for a lack of knowledge.[4] It is for this reason that the prophet Jeremiah declared that a true knowledge of God was of greater value than all other merits, virtues, or blessings: "Thus says the LORD: 'Let not the wise man glory in his wisdom, let not the mighty man glory in his might, nor let the rich man glory in his riches; but let him who glories glory in this, that he understands and knows Me' says the LORD."[5]

It is no exaggeration to say that ignorance of God's attributes abounds in the streets and in the pew. Men may have some near-biblical opinions about God in certain matters, but the great majority of individuals have been utterly deceived about sin and God's disposition toward it. Men may say great things about God's love, compassion, and mercy, but they are suspiciously silent about His holiness, righteousness, and sovereignty.

3. Psalm 50:21
4. Hosea 4:6
5. Jeremiah 9:23–24

Because of this, most hold to a very low view of God and are blind to the true nature of their sin.

In the preaching of the gospel, we must expose the sinfulness of sin by spreading abroad the true knowledge of God. We must proclaim the full counsel of Scripture concerning all His attributes, especially those that are less popular and less palatable to the carnal man: His supremacy, sovereignty, holiness, righteousness, and love.

THE SUPREMACY OF GOD

We must come to grips with the twisted age we live in, in which man has made himself the measure of all things. The secular humanist looks below and sees that he is the highest on the evolutionary scale. He looks above and finds nothing. Thus, he is king by default, the definer of his own destiny, the rule maker, and the caretaker of the planet. Since he has no one greater with whom to compare himself, he lives a delusion, unaware that at his best he is a nose full of breath and vanity, a blade of grass that vanishes with the wind, and a vapor that appears for a moment.[6]

The religious humanist is not much better off than his secular counterpart, even though he dresses in evangelical garb.[7] His heightened sense of self-importance coupled with the influences of the present-day psychology of self-realization and self-fulfillment have been devastating. To make matters worse, the very preachers called to expose such error in the church are now in the business of promoting it. Although much of the teaching about God is orthodox, His glory has been made subservient to man's felt needs so that God now exists for man rather than the reverse. Furthermore, God's purposes and eternal good pleasure are now viewed as so completely dependent upon and intertwined with man's good that He cannot be fulfilled or complete without us. Although these statements may seem to be an exaggeration, an honest consideration of what the evangelical community is actually communicating to the world will demonstrate that they are not.

This humanistic trend in contemporary Christianity has had a ruinous effect upon the gospel that we preach to the world. Our low view of God that cannot but manifest itself in our preaching has allowed our

---

6. Isaiah 2:22; Psalm 103:15; James 4:14

7. *Garb* refers to clothing or dress and metaphorically describes an external appearance that betrays the inward reality.

hearers to continue in their heretical high view of self, insulating them from ever fearing the Lord, desiring His person, or finding their ultimate good and fulfillment in the exaltation of His glory. We have fallen so far in our thinking and proclamation that the answer to the first and greatest question in our most orthodox and respected catechisms is all but unknown to the vast majority of evangelicals: "What is the chief and highest end of man? To glorify God and fully to enjoy Him forever."[8]

In light of all the noise and confusion, what can be done? The course we must take is as simple as it will be difficult. We must commit ourselves to proclaiming the attributes of God as they are found in Scripture—raw, uncut, unedited, and unfiltered by the humanistic philosophies of our age. God has no need for us to make a defense on His behalf. If we proclaim Him as He reveals Himself to be in the Scriptures, He will defend Himself![9] We must stand in the midst of self-absorbed men, challenge their beliefs, and point their eyes upward through the proclamation of truth. We must tell them that the Lord is the only God, eternal, immortal, and invisible, the "most high above all the earth."[10] We must warn them that the nations are like a drop from a bucket before Him, and He regards them as a speck of dust on the scales.[11] We must lead them to the conclusion that to Him belong greatness and power and glory and majesty, indeed everything that is in the heavens above and on the earth beneath.[12] For of Him and through Him and to Him are all things.[13] We must proclaim with the greatest clarity and precision that this is the God against whom we have sinned, and it is because He is so great that our sin is so evil.

THE SOVEREIGNTY OF GOD

Without doubt, carnal man views God's sovereignty as His least palatable attribute. This is especially true in the modern West where individualism, self-autonomy, and democracy are sacred themes, inherent rights, and

---

8. Westminster Larger Catechism, Q. 1.

9. The author borrowed this thought from Spurgeon, who makes a similar claim regarding the Scriptures: "Scripture is like a lion. Who ever heard of defending a lion? Just turn it loose; it will defend itself."

10. Psalm 97:9; Isaiah 57:15; 1 Timothy 1:17

11. Isaiah 40:15–18

12. 1 Chronicles 29:11

13. Romans 11:36

self-evident truths. Although these are noble themes that should define and limit man's government of man, we must constantly be on guard against presuming that God is so limited in the exercise of His government. The Scriptures unapologetically declare that the Lord has established His throne in the heavens, and His sovereignty rules over all.[14] There are no limitations to His government, nor is there any creature or activity beyond the boundaries of His scepter. Every living being, every created thing, and all events of history are His. He does whatever He pleases in every realm of creation.[15] He works all things after the counsel of His will and none can turn Him.[16] He kills and makes alive.[17] He causes well-being and creates calamity.[18] There is no one who can ward off His hand or say to Him, "What have You done?"[19] His counsel stands forever, and the plans of His heart are from generation to generation.[20] There is no wisdom, understanding, or counsel that can prevail against Him.[21] His dominion is an everlasting dominion, and His kingdom endures without end.[22] There will never be a changing of the guard, and His office will never be taken by another. He will always be the Lord with whom we must deal.

Men must understand that when they sin, they have not rebelled against some minor deity or the superintendent of some small province, but against the great King above all gods, the Lord of heaven and earth, the blessed and only Sovereign, the King of Kings and the Lord of Lords![23] They must see every sin as a declaration of war against the very One who created the universe with a word and governs the same freely and effortlessly. He commanded the stars to set their watch in the midnight sky, and they took their place. He gave word to the planets to find their orbits, and they followed His decree. He ordered the valleys to be cast down and the mountains to be lifted up, and they obeyed in fear. He drew a line in the sand and told the brave sea to come no further, and it bowed in reverence. Yet in spite of the unaltered obedience of creation's greatest powers, man

---

14. Psalm 103:19
15. Psalms 115:3; 135:6
16. Ephesians 1:11; Job 23:13
17. 1 Samuel 2:6
18. Isaiah 45:7
19. Daniel 4:34–35
20. Psalm 33:11
21. Proverbs 21:30
22. Daniel 4:34–35
23. Psalm 95:3; Acts 17:24; 1 Timothy 6:15

continues to lift his puny fist in the face of God. He is as pathetic as a mite beating its head against a world of granite, and as self-destructive as a man on life support who seeks to rip the power cord from the wall.

As preachers of the gospel, we must make much of the sovereignty of God and thus prove to men that their sin is an atrocious crime that reveals the insanity and self-destructive nature of the fallen heart. However, if we refuse to make known the fullness of God and speak these hard truths to our hearers, then we do them a great injustice and condemn them to a life of ignorance and idolatry. The Scriptures tell us that God revealed Himself to Israel so that they might fear Him.[24] In turn, we must preach the full counsel of God's revelation concerning Him so that all nations might fear and be saved. To the degree that they know Him, they will comprehend something of the heinous nature of their sinning and possibly seek a remedy for it in the gospel of Jesus Christ.

THE HOLINESS OF GOD

Both testaments of Scripture describe God as holy, holy, holy.[25] This tripart formula is often referred to as the *trisagion* and is the strongest form of superlative in the Hebrew language.[26] The writers of Scripture exalt no other attribute of God so highly. His holiness is not merely one attribute among many but is the very context in which all other divine attributes must be defined and understood. Therefore, above all things, men must know that God is holy! What they understand about this one attribute will determine what they understand about God, self, sin, salvation, and the whole of reality. The sage of Proverbs teaches us that the knowledge of the Holy One is understanding.[27] To be ignorant of this one attribute of singular importance is to be ignorant of God and to open oneself to the misinterpretation of all other divine attributes and works. Not only this, but a lack of the knowledge of the Holy One will lead men to a skewed or distorted view of self. Thus, if men are ever to understand the horrid nature of their sin, they must first comprehend something of the holy nature of God!

---

24. Exodus 20:20

25. Isaiah 6:3; Revelation 4:8

26. From the Greek, *tris*: three; *agion*: holy. John N. Oswalt, *The Book of Isaiah: Chapters 1–39*, The New International Commentary of the Old Testament (Grand Rapids: Eerdmans, 1986), 181.

27. Proverbs 9:10

The word *holy* comes from the Hebrew word *qadosh*, which means separated, marked off, placed apart, or withdrawn from common use. With regard to God, the word denotes two important truths. First, the holiness of God refers to His transcendence.[28] As Creator, He is above all of His creation and is totally distinct from everything that He has made and sustains. This distinction or separation between God and everything else is not merely quantitative (i.e., God is greater) but qualitative (i.e., God is a completely different being). Regardless of personal splendor, all other beings on earth and in heaven are mere creatures. God alone is God, separate, transcendent, and unapproachable.[29] The most splendid angel that stands in the presence of God is no more like God than the smallest worm that crawls upon the earth. No one is holy like the Lord.[30] He is incomparable!

It is this otherness of God that causes men to stand in awe and fear Him. The most awesome and terrible creatures in heaven and on earth are still creatures like us. Though they dwarf us in size, overpower us with strength, and shame us with their wisdom and beauty, they are still just creatures, and their difference is merely quantitative. But God is holy, unique, and separate—not just greater, but wholly and completely other. For this reason, Moses and the people of Israel sang: "Who is like You, O LORD, among the gods? Who is like You, glorious in holiness?"[31]

Secondly, the holiness of God refers to His transcendence over the moral corruption of His creation. He is separate from all that is profane and sinful. He is impeccable and pure![32] He is light, and in Him there is no darkness at all.[33] He is the Father of lights, with whom there is no variation or shifting shadow.[34] He cannot be tempted by evil, and He does not tempt with evil.[35] His eyes are too pure to approve it, and He cannot look on it with favor.[36] All sin is an abomination to Him—a loathsome thing that evokes hatred and disgust. Everyone who acts unjustly is

---

28. The word *transcendence* comes from the Latin verb *transcendere* (*trans*: over; *scandere*: to climb), meaning to go beyond, rise above, or exceed.

29. Deuteronomy 4:35; 1 Timothy 6:16

30. 1 Samuel 2:2

31. Exodus 15:11

32. The word *impeccable* comes from the Latin word *impeccabilis* (*im*: not; *peccare*: to sin; *abilis*: able), meaning not capable of sinning or free from fault or blame.

33. 1 John 1:5

34. James 1:17

35. James 1:13

36. Habakkuk 1:13

an abomination before His throne, and His face is set against all who do iniquity.[37] For this reason, the holiest and most devout men of Scripture who were granted a closer look at God's person fell before Him as dead men and cried out, "Woe is me, for I am undone! Because I am a man of unclean lips, and I dwell in the midst of a people of unclean lips; for my eyes have seen the King, the LORD of hosts."[38]

There is something of a logical progression in the salvation of men. They must know that they are lost before they can be saved. However, they must know that they are sinners before they can realize that they are truly lost. And finally, they must understand that God is holy before they can fully comprehend the grievous nature of their sin! In light of these truths, it should be clear to us that we do no good for men when we withhold from them the truth of their sin, and we grant them no favors when we neglect to instruct them in the knowledge of the Holy One. The Lord Jesus Christ was adamant that the gospel and the kingdom advance only to the degree that men learn to "hallow" God's name, or to esteem Him as holy.[39] Therefore, the preaching of the gospel has not been performed with any degree of faithfulness unless much has been made of the holiness of God.

THE RIGHTEOUSNESS OF GOD

The word *righteous* is translated from the Hebrew word *tsaddik* and the corresponding Greek term *dikaíos*. Both terms denote the rightness, correctness, or moral excellence of God. According to the Scriptures, God's righteousness is not merely something that He decides to be or do, but it is essential to His very nature. He *is* a righteous God; His righteousness is everlasting, and He does not change.[40] He is a God of faithfulness who will not pervert what is right.[41] He will always act in a way that is consistent with who He is. Thus, all His works are perfect, and His ways are just.[42]

God's just dealings with His creation especially reveal His righteous character. His Word assures us that righteousness and justice are the foundation of His throne, and He rules over all without caprice, partiality, or

---

37. Deuteronomy 25:16; Psalm 5:4
38. Isaiah 6:5
39. Matthew 6:9
40. Psalms 7:9; 119:142
41. Deuteronomy 32:4; Job 8:3
42. Deuteronomy 32:4

injustice.[43] Being a righteous God, He loves righteousness with all His being and hates the contrary with a perfect hatred.[44] Thus, He cannot be morally neutral or apathetic towards the character and works of men or angels, but He will judge them with uncompromised justice and equity without mixture. As the psalmist declares, "But the LORD shall endure forever; He has prepared His throne for judgment. He shall judge the world in righteousness, and He shall administer judgment for the peoples in uprightness."[45]

Based on such truths, we have the guarantee that on the day when God judges the deeds of all men, even the condemned will bow their heads and declare that He is right! For the Lord of hosts will be exalted in judgment and will show Himself holy in righteousness.[46] There will never be an accusation of wrongdoing that stands against Him, for He is a righteous God whose works, decrees, and judgments are nothing short of perfect.[47]

This news regarding the righteousness or justice of God is both good and bad. It is good news in that we would want an infinitely powerful and all-sovereign God to be righteous and just. It would be difficult to imagine anything more terrifying than a being who is both omnipotent and evil. An immoral deity of unbridled power would make the Hitlers of this world look like petty criminals, guilty of a mere misdemeanor. If there is a God, we do want Him to be righteous!

On the other hand, a righteous God does present great problems for man. In fact, it may be said that man's greatest problem is the righteousness of God. Simple logic leads to this conclusion:

First Premise: The Creator and Sovereign of the universe is both righteous and good.

Second Premise: A righteous and good God will oppose and bring to judgment all that is unrighteous or evil.

Third Premise: All men are evil and guilty of unrighteousness.

Conclusion: Therefore, God will oppose and bring to judgment all men.

The righteousness of God is good news to righteous creatures, but it is a terrifying broadcast to the unrighteous. The writer of Proverbs confirms

43. Psalm 89:14
44. Psalms 11:7; 5:5
45. Psalm 9:7–8
46. Isaiah 5:16
47. Job 36:23

this truth: "It is a joy for the just to do justice, but destruction will come to the workers of iniquity."[48]

If we were righteous as God is righteous then news of certain judgment would be a cause for celebration. However, we are not righteous; in fact, there is none righteous, no not one.[49] Therefore, the expectation of God's righteous judgment should produce a great terror in every man and drive him to seek an advocate. The fact that most men are unmoved by the news of coming judgment can only lead us to one of the following conclusions. First, their conscience is seared, and they believe the whole thing to be myth. Second, they think themselves more righteous than they are. Third, they think God to be less righteous than He is. Fourth, they are simply ignorant of such themes because the evangelical pulpit rarely proclaims them with clarity.

In many cultures throughout the world, justice is often portrayed as a lady with a scale in her hands and a veil covering her eyes. The image intends to show that justice is blind to partiality and bribery, yet for fallen man the image demonstrates something far less noble: we are blind to justice, righteousness, and equity. We are a people of false balances and unjust weights.[50] We point to the speck in our neighbor's eye and yet are seemingly unaware of the log protruding from our own.[51] We rail against corrupt political despots who pillage their own people and protest the unchecked greed of corporate giants, but we fail to see that there are striking similarities between them and us. The difference is only in degrees. We too eat stolen bread, wipe our mouths, and say we have done nothing wrong. We fail to understand that when we call for divine judgment against the great sinners of this world, we bring judgment down upon our own heads. We seem oblivious to the universal accusation of Scripture against all of us: "There is none righteous, no, not one."[52]

As preachers of the gospel, we must proclaim the righteousness of God and thus expose the unrighteousness of men. We must show the strictness of God's righteousness and prove that the smallest deviation from His perfect standard both disqualifies and condemns. Men must know that it required only one act of unrighteousness on the part of our

---

48. Proverbs 21:15
49. Romans 3:10
50. Proverbs 11:1
51. Matthew 7:3–4
52. Romans 3:10

first parents to bring condemnation to all men and to cast the world into seemingly irretrievable chaos.[53] Only then will they realize that their countless acts of unrighteousness disqualify them from any favorable relationship with God based upon their own virtue and merit. When asked by the unbelieving world what men must do to dwell in the presence of God, our answer should be strict and pointed. If a man seeks a relationship with God, then God demands only one thing of him: that he live a life of absolute moral perfection without flaw or failure every moment of every day of his life.[54] When our hearers admit the impossibility of such a thing, we then point them to Christ.

THE LOVE OF GOD

Nothing so exposes the depravity and sin of man more than clear and consistent preaching on the love of God. When a preacher contrasts this exalted attribute of the Most High with the apathy and hostility of His creatures toward Him, it exposes man's vileness and shows sin to be utterly sinful.[55]

The gospel preacher must inundate men with the love of God. Men must know that it is not their merit or virtue but God's love that moves Him to give Himself freely and selflessly to others for their benefit or good.[56] They must know that His love is much more than an attitude, emotion, or work. It is an *attribute*, a part of His very being or nature. God not only loves—He *is* love.[57] He is the God of love.[58] He is the very essence of what true love is, and all true love flows from Him as its ultimate source. Men must know that it would be easier to count all the stars in the heavens or each grain of sand on the earth than to measure or even seek to describe the love of God. Its height, depth, and width are beyond the comprehension of even the greatest and most discerning creatures.

The gospel preacher must display the love of God toward sinful men by setting forth His benevolence—His disposition to seek the good of

53. Romans 5:12–19
54. I owe this thought to Pastor Michael Durham of Oak Grove Baptist Church in Paducah, Kentucky.
55. Romans 7:13
56. Deuteronomy 7:7–8
57. 1 John 4:8, 16
58. 2 Corinthians 13:11

others, to bless them, and promote their welfare. It is the testimony of Scripture that He is a loving Creator who seeks the blessing and benefit of angels, men, and lower animals.[59] He is the very opposite of any opinion that would portray Him as a capricious or vindictive deity who seeks the downfall and misery of His creation. He is good to all, and His mercies are over all His works.[60] He causes His sun to rise on the evil and the good and sends rain on the righteous and the unrighteous alike.[61] He is kind to ungrateful and evil men.[62] Every good thing and every perfect gift come from Him.[63]

The gospel preacher must display the love of God toward sinful men by defining and illustrating His mercy and grace. Men must know the mercy of God as a reference to His loving-kindness, tenderheartedness, and compassion towards even the most miserable and pitiful of His creatures. The Scriptures call Him the Lord of mercy and describe Him as both "full of" and "rich in" mercy.[64] Men must know the grace of God as a reference to His willingness to treat His creatures not according to their own merit or worth but according to His own kindness and generosity. He is the God of all grace.[65] He longs to be gracious to men and waits on high to have compassion on them.[66] By grace, He saves men when they are helpless to save themselves, so that in the ages to come He might show the surpassing riches of His grace in kindness toward the undeserving.[67]

The gospel preacher must display the excellencies of God's love by making much of His patience, or long-suffering. Men must know that God has always demonstrated a willingness to "suffer long" and "bear with" the weaknesses and wrongdoings of His creatures. He restrains His anger and does not arouse all His wrath, because He remembers that men are but flesh, a wind that passes and does not return.[68] He is slow to anger, not wishing for any to perish but for all to come to repentance.[69] He

---

59. Jonah 4:11; Proverbs 12:10
60. Psalm 145:9
61. Matthew 5:45
62. Luke 6:35
63. James 1:17
64. Psalm 145:8; 2 Corinthians 1:3; Ephesians 2:4
65. 1 Peter 5:10
66. Isaiah 30:18
67. Ephesians 2:7–8
68. Psalm 78:38–39
69. Exodus 34:6; 2 Peter 3:9

desires all men to be saved and to come to the knowledge of the truth.[70] He has no pleasure in the death of the wicked, but rather that they should turn from their ways and live.[71]

Finally, and most importantly, the gospel preacher must constantly labor to exalt the love of God through the proclamation of the Father's gracious giving of His Son. God's love is beyond comprehension, manifested to all of His creatures in an almost infinite number of ways. Nevertheless, the Scriptures teach us that there is one manifestation of the love of God that rises above them all—the giving of His only Son for the salvation of His people. The Scriptures testify that God is love, and He has manifested His love to us in that He sent His only begotten Son to die that men might live through Him. Our disposition and deeds do not define or measure love; real love is God's love for us shown by the sending of His Son to be the propitiation for our sins.[72] It is common knowledge that one will hardly die for a righteous man, though perhaps for a good man someone would dare to die. Nevertheless, God demonstrated His own love toward us in that while we were yet sinners, Christ died for ungodly and utterly helpless men.[73] It is in paying this great redemptive price that God's love proves most lovely and our sin most heinous.

These are only a few of the truths that we must lay before men if they are to have a biblical view of God and comprehend the true nature of the sin they have committed against Him. All sin is ultimately and primarily evil because it is committed against an infinitely good God who is worthy of all love, devotion, and obedience. The more we make of this God in our preaching, the more men will see the extent of their sin and their great need of salvation.

---

70. 1 Timothy 2:4
71. Ezekiel 18:23, 32
72. 1 John 4:8–10
73. Romans 5:6–8

CHAPTER TWELVE

Sinners One and All

For all have sinned and fall short of the glory of God.
—Romans 3:23

Apart from a biblical view of God, man's greatest need is a biblical view of self. Here we discover a great contrast between secular thought and biblical truth. The contemporary view is that man is basically good, and his greatest problems stem from unhealthy external influences—social, political, economic, and educational factors, to name a few. In contrast, the Scriptures teach that man is a fallen creature and that the moral corruption of his heart is the source of all his maladies.

In preaching the gospel of Jesus Christ, we must strive to communicate to our hearers a biblical view of sin and the sinner. The exposition of the Scriptures in the power of the Holy Spirit is the only way to accomplish such an endeavor. The work is difficult and oftentimes misunderstood, but it is as necessary as plowing before the sowing of seeds. It is our task to speak about the one subject that most men would rather forget. Ours is an unusual work because the degree of conviction, brokenness, and repentance created in the hearts of our hearers is our measure for success. It is a hard way, but it is the only road to salvation.

In Romans 3:23, the phrase *have sinned* is translated from the most common Greek word for sin, *hamartáno*, which means to miss the mark, err, or wander from the path. The most common Hebrew word for sin is *chata*, and it carries the same meaning. The writer of Judges communicates the idea behind both these words when he tells us that the men of Benjamin could "sling a stone at a hair's breadth and *not miss*."[1] The sage of Proverbs also warns that "he *sins* [or, *misses his way*] who hastens with

---

1. Judges 20:16, emphasis added

his feet."[2] From a biblical viewpoint the mark toward which a man is to aim and the path in which he is to walk are the will of God. Any thought, word, or deed that does not perfectly conform to this standard is sin. Even the slightest deviation brings guilt. For this reason, the Westminster Larger Catechism defines sin as "any want of conformity unto any law of God" (Q. 24). It is important to note that Scripture never presents "missing the mark" as an innocent mistake or honest error. It is always an act of willful disobedience resulting from man's moral corruption and enmity toward God.

In our text, the accusation of sin has been laid at the feet of every man without exception, "for all have sinned." This same sentiment echoes throughout all of Scripture. In the Old Testament, we read, "There is no one who does not sin," and, "No one living is righteous."[3] The wise and somber King Solomon saw through man's thin veneer of morality and declared, "For there is not a just man on earth who does good and does not sin."[4] Finally, the prophet Isaiah scoured the whole of humanity and cried out, "All we like sheep have gone astray; we have turned, every one, to his own way."[5]

The Old Testament writers were unrelenting in their condemnation of man, but we should not think that the New Testament writers were of any different opinion or that their censure was less pronounced. In Romans 3, the apostle Paul strings together a collection of Old Testament quotes to demonstrate the universality of sin and the depths of man's depravity. It is one of the most lengthy and straightforward denunciations of humanity in all of Scripture: "What then? Are we better than they? Not at all. For we have previously charged both Jews and Greeks that they are all under sin. As it is written: 'There is none righteous, no, not one; there is none who understands; there is none who seeks after God. They have all turned aside; they have together become unprofitable; there is none who does good, no, not one.'"[6]

From the Scriptures, we see that sin is not a rare or unusual phenomenon confined to a small minority of humanity, but it is universal in its scope. Every member of Adam's race has joined him in the rebellion he

---

2. Proverbs 19:2, emphasis added
3. 1 Kings 8:46; Psalm 143:2
4. Ecclesiastes 7:20
5. Isaiah 53:6
6. Romans 3:9–12

began. Those who would deny such a truth must deny the testimony of Scripture, of human history, and of their own sinful thoughts, words, and deeds. The apostle John even goes so far as to tell us that those who would deny the reality of their sin are making God a liar and proving that they are void of any relationship with Him: "If we say that we have no sin, we deceive ourselves, and the truth is not in us.... If we say that we have not sinned, we make Him a liar, and His word is not in us."[7]

The slightest glance at Scripture will show that sin is man's greatest malady, yet it cannot be denied by any stretch of the imagination that sin is treated as a light matter in our contemporary culture and in the so-called Christianity it has produced. For this reason, we must be all the more careful to follow the example of the writers of Scripture, who labored with intense effort to expose sin and make it utterly sinful. We must not speak of sin in harmless generalities that tend to leave the soul undisturbed and unconverted, but we must employ a precise language which defines its true character and exposes its every manifestation. Our goal is to paint a picture of sin in the hearts and minds of our hearers so horrid that it cannot be removed except by the blood of the Lamb. To achieve this goal, we must examine some of the most common and frequent characteristics of sin.

SIN IS TRANSGRESSION

"Cry aloud, spare not; lift up your voice like a trumpet; tell My people their transgression."[8]

In this text, God commands His spokesperson Isaiah to clearly and passionately expose the transgressions of His people. God directs the prophet to cry aloud, to raise his voice like a trumpet, to declare, publish, and expound on the sins that would soon result in Israel's destruction. God also mixes the command with a divine warning to the prophet: spare not. He must not hold back in his preaching against sin because of some false sense of compassion. He must lay aside his fear of wounding. Israel had to be cut with the sword of the Spirit. A deep and painful surgery was required if she was to be saved. This is both a rebuke and an exhortation for the contemporary evangelist who is often neglectful in this necessary element of true gospel preaching.

7. 1 John 1:8, 10
8. Isaiah 58:1

In the Old Testament, the word *transgression* is translated from the Hebrew word *abar*, which means to cross, pass over, or pass by. In the New Testament, the term is translated from the Greek word *parabaíno*, which means to go by the side of, to pass over, or step over. To sin is to step over or go around God's law with a total disregard for His person and authority. It is to go beyond what His commands permit and to ignore the restrictions His law imposes on us. It is to run beyond the fence and trespass into places that do not belong to us, like sheep that have gone astray and turned to their own way.[9] Unlike the great oceans that obey the voice of God and stay within the lines He has drawn, men are constantly seeking to break through and trespass the boundaries He has marked out for them.

To preach sin as transgression has many benefits. First, it reveals the arrogance that dwells in the heart of man. Who is this puny creature who runs boldly beyond the limits God has placed for Him? He is a scandal and a disgrace to the rest of creation! The ox and donkey have greater understanding.[10] Secondly, it exposes our foolishness. We were born yesterday, and what we know can be poured into a thimble with room to spare.[11] Yet we would choose to rebel against the counsel of the eternal God whose knowledge has no limits and whose wisdom has no match. Thirdly, it tells us the real reason for all our maladies—we have despised the Holy One and turned away from Him.[12] Because of our transgressions, our heads are sick and our hearts are faint. From the soles of our feet to the tops of our heads, there is nothing sound in us. We are covered in bruises, welts, and raw wounds, all of them self-imposed.[13]

SIN IS REBELLION AND INSUBORDINATION

"For rebellion is as the sin of witchcraft, and stubbornness is as iniquity and idolatry."[14] We live in a culture that redefines and ranks sin for its own convenience. Although most would admit to some moral failure in their lives, they would not consider themselves to be evil or their sin to

---

9. Isaiah 53:6
10. Isaiah 1:3
11. Job 8:9
12. Isaiah 1:4
13. Isaiah 1:5–6
14. 1 Samuel 15:23

be as bad as that of others. The great benefit of 1 Samuel 15:23 is that it demonstrates that there are no small sins. In God's view, the slightest rebellion is as evil as partaking in some demonic ritual, and even a hint of insubordination is equal to the grossest iniquity or the worshiping of false gods. Although certain sinful acts have more devastating consequences than others do, at the core of every sin is the same rebellion and insubordination. The child who ruins the carpet by purposely throwing his plate on the floor and the child who merely refuses to pick up his toys are both united in the same rebellion against the authority of their parents. Though the consequences of their sinful acts may differ in degree, the rebellion that birthed them is the same.

First Samuel 15:23 describes sin in terms of rebellion and insubordination. The word *rebellion* refers to a revolt, uprising, insurgence, or mutiny. The word *insubordination* is translated from the Hebrew word *patsar*, which literally means "to press or push." It denotes one who is stubborn, pushy, insolent, presumptuous, and arrogant. These definitions help us to see the horrid nature of man's disobedience. The sinner is a mutinous traitor against God. He stands in opposition to the kingdom of heaven and calls for the advancement of his own kingdom. He is doing the work of his father, the devil, who would storm the throne of God and slaughter Him in His own temple.[15] The sinner is a stubborn and insolent beast who not only refuses the will of his Maker but also seeks to impose his own upon Him.

In light of what the Scriptures teach us about the supremacy, sovereignty, and power of God, our sin must be seen as the grossest form of arrogance and the height of insanity. Should men who are a vapor and less than nothing revolt against the eternal God?[16] Should broken shards of pottery stubbornly refuse the Master's hand? Yet men deny God's sovereignty and seek their own autonomy. They not only refuse His will but also seek to bend Him to theirs. Modern man rarely sees himself in this light and would hardly categorize his sin as rebellion and insubordination. Therefore, it is the labor of the gospel preacher to help him see what may be difficult for him to accept and yet is necessary for him to be saved.

---

15. John 8:44
16. James 4:14

SIN IS LAWLESSNESS

"Whoever commits sin also commits lawlessness, and sin is lawlessness."[17] There is no doubt that this text proves the gravity of every kind or type of sin. Every sinful deed, from the greatest to the smallest according to human estimation, is lawlessness, and to practice any kind of sin is to practice lawlessness. The word *lawlessness* is translated from the Greek word *anomia*, meaning literally "no law" or "without law." To practice lawlessness is to live as though God were morally neutral or apathetic, or to live as though God had never revealed His will to mankind. Both of these opinions directly contradict Scripture. According to the Scriptures, God is a righteous being. He has revealed His law, or will, to all men through the work of the law written on the heart, and to some men through the greater revelation of Scripture.[18] In either case, the Scriptures testify that all men have been given enough light regarding the will of God so that all will be without excuse on the day of judgment.[19] What the prophet Micah said to the Jews can be said in varying degrees to every man: "He has shown you, O man, what is good; and what does the LORD require of you but to do justly, to love mercy, and to walk humbly with your God?"[20]

It is important to understand that a man may practice lawlessness by openly defying God's law, or by simply being unconcerned and willingly ignorant of it. In either case, he shows contempt for God and His authority. It is also imperative that we understand that the severity of one's rebellion is not dependent upon the supposed greatness or smallness of the law being broken. All sin is lawlessness, and "whoever shall keep the whole law, and yet stumble in one point, he is guilty of all."[21] Furthermore, the fact that the Antichrist is referred to as the "son of perdition" shows the abominable nature of lawlessness, and Jesus commands those who practice lawlessness to depart from Him on the day of judgment.[22] All sin is lawlessness, birthed in hell and deserving of all condemnation.[23]

---

17. 1 John 3:4
18. Romans 2:14–16; 2 Timothy 3:15–17
19. Romans 1:20
20. Micah 6:8
21. 1 John 3:4; James 2:10
22. 2 Thessalonians 2:3; Matthew 7:23
23. All sin is of the devil (John 8:44). See James 3:6, which contains a similar phrase regarding the tongue: "It is set on fire by hell."

As preachers of the gospel, God calls us to expose such lawlessness and stem the tide of its advance among men. We can accomplish this only through the proclamation of the full counsel of God. The writer of Proverbs warns us: "Where there is no revelation, the people cast off restraint; but happy is he who keeps the law."[24] Men and their societies run headlong into unrestrained lawlessness when there is no vision or revelation of the will of God. However, God restrains lawlessness when He confronts men with His law, and the Holy Spirit convicts them and brings them to a saving knowledge of Jesus Christ. Gospel preaching is not a dainty work for men with faint hearts. God calls us to stand in the middle of the tide and against the flow, to expose sin as lawlessness and men as lawbreakers, and to point them to Christ, the only mediator between God and men.[25]

SIN IS HOSTILITY

"Because the carnal mind is enmity against God; for it is not subject to the law of God, nor indeed can be."[26] One of the most disturbing truths about man's sin is that it is an expression or manifestation of his hostility, enmity, and even hatred toward God. To understand this truth, we must first explore the reason behind it. Why would man, as a dependent creature, harbor such antagonism against an infinitely good God? According to the Scriptures, it is because fallen man is a morally corrupt being who loves unrighteousness and demands the autonomy (a state of being free and self-directing) to do what is right in his own eyes.[27] Consequently, he also hates God, who is righteous, and hates His law, which is an expression of that righteousness.[28] Thus, as our text teaches us, man *cannot* obey or subject himself to the law of God because he *will not*, and he *will not* because he *hates* God. The problem is not free will, but ill will. Fallen man so hates God that he will not submit to Him even if it leads to eternal destruction.

The Lord Jesus Christ taught, "If you love Me, keep My commandments."[29] This is further evidence that a direct relationship exists between

---

24. Proverbs 29:18
25. 1 Timothy 2:5
26. Romans 8:7
27. Romans 3:12; Isaiah 64:6; Job 15:16; Judges 17:6; Proverbs 14:12
28. Romans 1:30
29. John 14:15

our disposition toward God and our relationship to His will. Genuine obedience to the will of God reveals a genuine love toward Him. Sin demonstrates the very opposite—an aversion or enmity. This despicable and inexcusable disposition toward God stands at the very core of every kind of sin committed. Thus, all sin, whether large or small in the eyes of society, is an immeasurable evil because it proceeds from a heart that is at war with the very God who is infinitely worthy of all love, gratitude, and adoration.

The gospel preacher must press these truths upon men. Sin is only a symptom of a much darker inward malady—a depraved heart that loves evil and is hostile toward the sovereign dictates of a righteous God. All the rules and religious reforms of every ecclesiastical institution combined cannot change a man inwardly or remove the hostility from his heart. Man's case is hopeless apart from a genuine work of the gospel, faithfully preached and accompanied by the regenerating power of the Holy Spirit.

SIN IS TREACHERY

"But like men they transgressed the covenant; there they dealt treacherously with Me."[30] All sin of whatever kind is a form of treachery. The word *treacherously* is translated from two Hebrew terms: *maal* and *bagad*, both of which mean "to act treacherously, deceitfully, or unfaithfully." *Webster's Dictionary* defines the term as a violation of allegiance, a betrayal of trust, or an act of treason. Hosea 6:7 describes the first sin of our father Adam as "treachery" against the Lord, and throughout the Scriptures, treachery is a common element in all sin.[31] We find sin in the act of rebellion, in forsaking the true God for idols, and in any form of apostasy or turning away from God.[32]

When we consider the nature and works of the God against whom man commits his treachery, we see the treachery of sin more clearly. He is the faithful God, whose faithfulness reaches to the skies and extends to all generations.[33] He accomplishes all His plans and works with perfect faithfulness.[34] He keeps faith forever and does not change.[35] He

---

30. Hosea 6:7
31. Ezekiel 18:24
32. Isaiah 48:8; 1 Chronicles 5:25; Psalm 78:57
33. Deuteronomy 7:9; Psalms 36:5; 100:5
34. Psalm 33:4; Isaiah 25:1; 1 Thessalonians 5:24
35. Psalm 146:6; Malachi 3:6

guards His covenant and His loving-kindness to a thousand generations, and not one of His words or promises have ever failed.[36] Therefore,
when man sins against God, he betrays the one who is worthy of his
greatest allegiance, loyalty, commitment, and duty. For this reason, sin
is the worst of treacheries—the highest form of treason—and evokes
the penalty of death.[37] Every sin that man commits proves his kinship
or brotherhood with Judas, the guide for those who arrested Jesus.[38]
As preachers of the gospel, we must proclaim these hard words about
man's treachery lest we betray the God whom we are called to serve, the
gospel we have been called to preach, and the men who so desperately
need to hear the truth.

SIN IS AN ABOMINATION

"These six things the LORD hates, yes, seven are an abomination to
Him."[39] "For all who do such things, all who behave unrighteously, are
an abomination to the LORD your God."[40] Out of all the words employed
to describe the heinous nature of sin, the word *abomination* may be the
most appropriate. This word is from the Hebrew word *tow'ebah* and the
Greek word *bdélugma*. In both languages, it is one of the strongest words
available to denote something that is foul, vile, or disgusting. *Webster's
Dictionary* defines an abomination as something worthy of loathing or
hatred, something abhorrent, revolting, or causing extreme disgust. To
put it simply, any and all forms of sin are an abomination before the Lord,
resulting in His extreme disgust, loathing, and hatred. These are hard
words, but we should not expect anything less from a holy and righteous
God whose eyes are too pure to approve evil, and who cannot look on
wickedness with favor.[41]

According to the Scriptures, everyone who acts unjustly is an abomination to the Lord,[42] and to sin is to act abominably.[43] In fact, the wicked
so displease God that even their religious rituals are an abomination to

36. Deuteronomy 7:9; Joshua 23:14; 1 Kings 8:56
37. Ezekiel 18:24
38. Acts 1:16
39. Proverbs 6:16
40. Deuteronomy 25:16
41. Habakkuk 1:13
42. Deuteronomy 25:16
43. Ezekiel 16:52

Him.[44] The writer of Proverbs informs us that sin is not only an abomination to God but also an object of His righteous indignation or hatred.[45] He also warns us that those who have made themselves an abomination through their disobedience will certainly not go unpunished.[46] The book of Revelation concludes with the warning that the abominable and those who practice abominations will suffer eternal punishment cut off from the favorable presence of God.[47]

How can we who know and believe these things about sin not make them known to others? Should we withhold such information from men in the name of politeness and etiquette? Is it wrong to use the very words used by God to expose the sins of our fellow men who languish in ignorance and die without Christ? Sin is an abomination and leads to the destruction of countless lives. As preachers of the gospel, we must put away self-preservation and the desire to be esteemed by men. Boldly and lovingly, we must employ the harsh words that best expose the vileness of sin so that men might turn from it like the plague and run to salvation in Christ.

CONCLUSION AND WARNING

Having reached the end of this chapter, the reader may be thinking, "This is a hard saying; who can understand it?"[48] The truth about sin is disturbing and the language is harsh. Nevertheless, we must understand that forthright teaching on sin is an essential part of the gospel of Jesus Christ. Men must understand what they are and what they have done. Although such truths are scandalous and even painful, they are biblical and necessary.

We rarely use the word *sin* in our contemporary culture. It is not because it has been replaced by one that is more appropriate but because the idea itself has been lost. We live among people that are either unable or unwilling to practice moral discernment or pronounce judgment upon anything. Sin is no longer utterly sinful, and men are no longer totally depraved. Even to suggest that something might be wrong is intolerable,

---

44. Proverbs 15:8
45. Proverbs 6:16
46. Proverbs 16:5
47. Revelation 21:27
48. John 6:60

to proclaim that something is sin is unthinkable, and to teach that men are sinners is criminal. Nevertheless, our culture must know that a holy, righteous, and unchanging God will one day judge them. That which was sin in earlier times is still sin today, and that which has led to the eternal ruin of a countless multitude will continue to engulf countless more.

As preachers of the gospel, we must impress these truths upon men. Although men may consider our language scandalous and question our motives, we must not shrink back from using God's language and calling things what they are, so that men might see things as they are.

CHAPTER THIRTEEN

Sinners Falling Short

For all have sinned and fall short of the glory of God.
—Romans 3:23

The phrase *fall short* is from the Greek word *hustereó*, which means to fail to reach the goal or to fall short of the end. According to the above text, the goal or end which man has fallen short of is the glory of God. Throughout the history of the church, there have been many opinions regarding the exact meaning of this phrase; however, the most common and most approved interpretation is this: man's falling short of the glory of God means that he has failed to glorify God as he ought, and he has forfeited his unique privilege to bear or reflect God's glory.

GLORIFYING GOD

The Scriptures teach that God made man for His own honor, praise, and good pleasure. We draw breath only so it might be returned to Him in praise and adoration. Our hearts beat with a rhythm so they might beat for Him and be completely satisfied. Our minds have their great complexity in order to think great thoughts about Him and stand in awe. Our physical strength makes us able to serve Him and carry out His will. In short, we are from Him, through Him, and to Him.[1] We find our *summum bonum* in loving Him with all our heart, soul, mind, and strength, and in doing all that we do for His glory.[2]

Man is to be besotted—utterly fascinated—with God. Any satisfaction that does not find its origin in Him is an idol, and even the most menial

---

1. Romans 11:36
2. *Summum bonum* is a Latin phrase meaning "greatest good." Man finds his greatest purpose or end in God. Matthew 22:37; 1 Corinthians 10:31.

tasks of eating and drinking should be done for His glory or not at all.[3]
The Westminster Shorter Catechism is right to declare, "Man's chief end
is to glorify God and to enjoy Him forever" (Q. 1). It is man's privilege and
duty to esteem God above all things, to be completely satisfied in Him,
and to live before Him with reverence, gratitude, obedience, and worship. This was how man was in his original state before the fall, and he
will never be whole until he returns to what he was and to the purpose
for which he was made.

It is the clear testimony of Scripture that God made man for His own
glory, but man has willfully fallen short of this purpose. Paul's letter to the
church in Rome best illustrates this terrible reality: "Because, although
they knew God, they did not glorify Him as God, nor were thankful, but
became futile in their thoughts, and their foolish hearts were darkened.
Professing to be wise, they became fools, and changed the glory of the
incorruptible God into an image made like corruptible man—and birds
and four-footed animals and creeping things."[4] According to this text, all
men know enough about the one true God to be without excuse before
Him in judgment. Yet man suppresses what he knows to be true and
rebels against the very purpose for which he was made—the glory and
honor of God. In turning away from the truth, he becomes engulfed in
darkness and vanity. Rather than repent, he fights against what he knows
to be true and continues his downward spiral into greater and greater
moral darkness, degradation, and futility.

The sin that marks the life of all men is the very antithesis of glori-
fying God, and it demonstrates how disjointed and dislocated man has
become.[5] He has wrenched himself from the very purpose for which God
made him and cut himself off from the only reason for his existence. He
has cast aside the glory of the incorruptible God and made himself an
object of worship.[6] He has refused the will of God and subjected himself
to himself. Is it any wonder that he gropes for meaning to no avail, and
that his greatest attempts at significance are utterly ridiculous?

It is important to note that man's failure to glorify God not only leads
to a meaningless existence but it is the birth mother of all other sins. The

---

3. 1 Corinthians 10:31
4. Romans 1:21–23
5. Sin is the antithesis or direct opposite of glorifing God.
6. Romans 1:23

long list of debauchery and vice listed in Paul's opening address to the Romans is merely the result of the one great sin above them all—man's refusal to acknowledge God and honor Him as such.[7] It is the Pandora's box of Scripture and fills the entire world with chaos and destruction.[8]

This brief discussion of the glory of God is particularly important whenever we address the mythological "good" atheist. People often attempt to dispel the claims of Christianity by referring to the atheist who does not believe in God, nor render praise unto God, but is a moral man who seeks the good of his fellow human beings. The argument is that it is unjust to bring such a man into judgment and condemn him simply because he does not see enough evidence to support belief in the existence of God.

This argument, although popular, does not stand the test of Scripture. First, the Scriptures argue that there are no real atheists. All men have a knowledge of the one true God, because that which is known about God is evident within them; for God made it evident to them through what has been made so that they are without excuse.[9]

Secondly, the Scriptures argue that the atheist's problem is not intellectual but moral. According to the psalmist, it is the fool who says in his heart that there is no God, and he does so not for intellectual reasons, but because of his own corruption and desire to do evil. He does not want God or His morality, so he denies them both.[10] It is not the intellectual refinement of the atheist that prohibits him from believing in God, but it is his ungodliness and unrighteousness that move him to suppress the truth.[11]

Thirdly, the Scriptures argue against the possibility of a moral atheist, because apart from the grace of God, "There is none righteous, no, not one."[12] The fact that a man boasts of morality does not make him moral. It is not the hearers or the proponents of morality who are truly righteous, but those who actually do what they advocate.[13]

---

7. Romans 1:21–32

8. In mythology, Pandora's box contained all the ills of mankind. Zeus gave it to Pandora, who opened it against his command.

9. Romans 1:19–20

10. Psalms 14:1–3; 53:1–3. The word *fool* is translated from the Hebrew word *nabal*, which denotes a foolish or senseless person. It should be noted that *nabal* is a moral term and does not refer to a victim of ignorance who desires wisdom, but to one who disdains wisdom and is willingly ignorant.

11. Romans 1:18

12. Romans 3:10–12

13. Romans 2:13; James 1:22

Fourthly, the argument that it is unjust to condemn the moral atheist represents a distinctly humanistic and man-centered view of reality. In a man-centered universe, man is responsible to man, but in a God-centered universe, he is responsible primarily to God and only secondarily to man. Even if the atheist's boast of righteousness towards his fellow man were true, he has failed in his primary relationship and responsibility to the God who gives to him life and breath and all things.[14] This sin against God is infinitely greater than any immorality he could ever commit against his fellow man.

Finally, the seemingly moral atheist is guilty not only of refusing to give glory to God but also of seeking to pilfer glory from Him. All men are born morally corrupt and radically depraved. The only thing that restrains the evil of men and causes them to have any semblance of goodness is the common grace of God. If God were to withdraw this grace, and men were left to be governed by the depravity of their own hearts, the human race would quickly annihilate itself; it would be a literal hell on earth—at least while it lasted. Divine grace holds society together in order that God might accomplish a work of redemption in the midst of humanity's depravity and hopelessness. It is not the atheist's humanism or some highly evolved morality that prevents him from being a serial killer and enables him to do the semblance of good that he does, but the gracious providence of God who works all thing according to the counsel of His will.[15] So then, the crime of the atheist is that he adamantly denies the God who restrains him in his evil and grants a semblance of good by His grace. The atheist then claims the work as his own and receives the glory that ought to be given to God. He is a thief of the worst sort, a despicable charlatan. His condemnation is just.[16]

BEARING THE GLORY OF GOD

God created man to bear something of His glorious image.[17] We do not understand the fullness of this terminology, but we know that by divine decree, God made man to be more than clay—a recipient and reflector of glory. He received the incomprehensible and unspeakable privilege of

14. Acts 17:25
15. Ephesians 1:11
16. Romans 3:8
17. Genesis 1:26

walking in communion with God and being transformed "from glory to glory" as he beheld Him with an "unveiled face."[18] However, man forfeited all on that day when Adam exalted self over deity and chose the autonomy of a finite creature over the lordship of an infinitely wise and benevolent God. In return, Adam became destitute and naked of the glory that once had been his in abundance. Sin defaced the image of God and *Ichabod* was written on man's forehead, for the glory of the Lord had departed.[19] Thus, Adam became the very opposite of what he was created to be, a marred and fractured mirror of no use.[20] His heart became hollow and empty on the inside and encased in a vault as hard as granite. His outward man became the image of his inward condition. He became a deformed and dislocated creature that had lost his place, and he perverted the very reason for his existence.

This is the inheritance that Adam has left his sons and daughters. Although several millennia have passed, man has been unable to recoup the family fortune. All are born in the image of the one who fell from the image in which he was made.[21] Mankind now ekes out its existence under the curse, yet there is enough of the image of God left in man so that he cannot be satisfied by anyone or anything except the One from whom he runs.[22] He can dress himself in the fame and fortune of this world, and yet he will still be naked. He can wash himself in self-esteem and surround himself with support groups to affirm his every thought and deed, but he will not escape the relentless accusations of his conscience. He can gain the world and thousands more, but his real poverty will continue to gnaw at his insides. God made man's heart to be His dwelling place that can be filled with nothing less than Him. As Augustine wrote: "Thou movest us to delight in praising Thee; for Thou hast formed us for Thyself, and our hearts are restless till they find rest in Thee."[23]

Though man's reality is extremely dark, this man-made debacle has a bright side. It provides the church with an excellent opportunity for the

---

18. 2 Corinthians 3:18

19. 1 Samuel 4:21

20. Romans 3:12. One of the characteristics of fallen man is his utter uselessness: "They have together become unprofitable."

21. Genesis 5:3

22. Genesis 3:16–24; James 3:9

23. Augustine, *The Confessions of St. Augustine, Bishop of Hippo* (London: J. M. Dent, 1950), 1.1.

preaching of the gospel, but only if the church and her message are truly Christian. First, we must find freedom from the trappings of this present age and its futile attempts to find a substitute for God. To be a witness to an empty world, God must fill us and satisfy us in the doing of His will. It is a mark against us that even though the Christians of the West are the wealthiest and most protected in the history of the church, they are also the emptiest. Our Christian bookstores are a witness against us. How many volumes are written to heal our emptiness, correct our lack of purpose, and shore up our self-esteem? Yet we are empty for all the reasons that Jesus never was. He was often tired, hungry, misunderstood, persecuted, and abandoned, but He was never empty. The reason Jesus gave for His fullness is also the explanation for our lack: "But He said to them, 'I have food to eat of which you do not know.... My food is to do the will of Him who sent Me, and to finish His work.'"[24] The Western Christian is empty because he is full of the world, absorbed in self, and given to the doing of his own will. To move from emptiness to true fullness will require a drastic shift from self to God and from self-will to His will.

Secondly, the church must seek to be biblical rather than relevant. We are not going to leave a mark upon our culture because we have studied its ways and adapted ourselves to it. We will leave a mark and be a light only to the degree that we have studied God's ways and remained faithful to them in the midst of the raging and ever-changing river of culture. We are not relevant to the world because we are like it. We are relevant when we reject the world outright and are its polar opposite!

This present darkness provides a great opportunity for the church to be the salt of the earth, but if we mix with the very impurities we are supposed to expose, we are no longer good for anything but to be thrown out and trampled underfoot by the very men we are called to influence.[25] We have the greatest opportunity to be a city set upon a hill, but if the light we put forth is nothing more than a Christianized reflection of our culture's ideas and desires, we are as useless as our culture already believes us to be.[26] We must confront the emptiness of our age with the unrelenting and uncompromising truths of the biblical gospel. We must be satisfied in God alone, devoted to His will alone, and conformed to His

---

24. John 4:32, 34
25. Matthew 5:13
26. Matthew 5:14–16

image alone. Then we will be blameless and innocent children of God. We will be above reproach in the midst of this crooked and perverse generation. We will stand in the midst of its darkness as lights in the world as we hold fast the word of life until the day of Christ.[27]

This way of life will require great courage. We must be willing to stand up and tell men that they are fundamentally and radically wrong in their search for significance, self-esteem, and self-realization. We must unmask the false hopes of humanism and materialism, and we must expose any form of so-called Christianity that seeks to heal men by leading them to a baptized version of the same. We must defy all attempts at getting the most out of Jesus, finding purpose in purpose, or attaining our best life now. We must not adopt the world's view and then tweak it to make it Christian. We must draw a line in the sand and stand firm in the radical teachings of Christ and His gospel. We must preach the truth and be the examples of the truth we preach. We must count all things as loss in view of the surpassing value of knowing Christ Jesus our Lord, and count them but rubbish so that we may gain Christ and be found in Him.[28]

---

27. Philippians 2:15–16
28. Philippians 3:7–9

CHAPTER FOURTEEN

Sinners Through and Through

For all have sinned and fall short of the glory of God.
—Romans 3:23

In this chapter, we will confront a crucial truth: men sin because they are born morally corrupt.[1] One of the most important terms theologians use to describe the depth of man's inherited moral corruption is the word *depravity*. The word is derived from the prefix *de-*, which communicates intensity, and the Latin word *pravus*, which means twisted or crooked. To call something depraved means that its original state or form has been thoroughly perverted. To say that the human race is depraved means that it has fallen from its original state of righteousness and that all men are born as morally corrupt sinners by nature. To describe the extent of this moral corruption, theologians will often employ various terms to communicate the same truth. The most common are: *total depravity, spiritual death,* and *moral inability.*

TOTAL DEPRAVITY

The phrase *total depravity* has long been employed by Reformed theologians and others to describe the fallen state of man. Although the language is adequate when properly defined, the phrases *pervasive depravity* and *radical depravity* may be more appropriate.[2] To say that every man is totally depraved does not mean that he is as bad as he could be or that his every deed is entirely or perfectly evil. Rather it means that depravity,

---

1. Psalms 51:5; 58:3; Genesis 8:21
2. The verb *pervade* means to move along through; to become diffused thoughout every part (*Webster's Dictionary*). Thus, depravity relates to the root of who we are by nature; depravity proceeds directly from the root of our soul.

or moral corruption, has affected his entire being—body, intellect, and will. In the following, we will consider what total depravity does mean and does not mean.

First, total depravity does not mean that the image of God in man was totally lost in the fall. In several texts, Scripture still refers to man as being made "in the image of God."[3] Total depravity does mean that the image of God in man has been seriously defaced or disfigured, and that moral corruption has polluted the entire person—body, reason, emotions, and will.[4]

Secondly, total depravity does not mean that man has no knowledge of the person or will of God. The Scriptures teach us that all men know enough about the true God and His will to be without excuse before Him on the day of judgment.[5] What it does mean is that apart from a special work of grace, all men reject God's truth in favor of their own futile speculations. They are hostile towards God's truth and seek to suppress it so that it will not disturb what is left of their conscience.[6] Men know enough about God to hate Him and enough about His will to reject it and fight against it.

Thirdly, total depravity does not mean that man has no conscience or that he is totally insensible to good and evil. The Scriptures teach that all men possess a conscience, which, if not seared, is able to lead them to admire virtuous character and actions.[7] What it does mean is that men are not wholeheartedly obedient to the directives of their conscience. A man is not righteous because he knows what is good or denounces what is evil, but because he does the good he knows.[8]

Fourthly, total depravity does not mean that man is incapable of demonstrating virtue. There are men who love their families, sacrifice their own lives to save others, complete their civic duties, and perform good deeds in the name of religion. It does mean that such virtue is not motivated by genuine love for God or any true desire to obey His commands. The Scriptures testify that no man loves God in a worthy manner or as the law commands, neither is there a man who glorifies God in every

---

3. Genesis 9:6; 1 Corinthians 11:7; James 3:9

4. Body (Romans 6:6, 12; 7:24; 8:10, 13), reason (Romans 1:21; 2 Corinthians 3:14–15; 4:4; Ephesians 4:17–19), emotions (Romans 1:26–27; Galatians 5:24; 2 Timothy 3:2–4), and will (Romans 6:17; 7:14–15).

5. Romans 1:20

6. Romans 1:21–23; 1:18

7. Romans 2:15; 1 Timothy 4:2

8. Romans 3:10–12; 2:13, 17–23; James 4:17

thought, word, and deed.[9] All men prefer self to God, and it is the love of self or the love of others—not the love of God—that moves men to acts of altruism, heroics, civic duty, and external religious good.[10]

Fifthly, total depravity does not mean that all men are as immoral as they could be, that all men are equally immoral, or that all men indulge in every form of evil that exists. Not all men are delinquents, fornicators, or murderers. It does mean that all men are born with a great propensity or inclination towards evil, and that all men are capable of the most unspeakable crimes and the most shameful perversions. As a whole, all of humanity is inclined to greater and greater moral corruption, and this moral deterioration would be incalculably more rapid than it is were it not for the common grace of God which restrains it.[11] Man, by his own doing, cannot free or recuperate himself from this downward spiral.[12]

Finally, total depravity does not mean that men do not possess the necessary faculties to obey God. Man is not a victim who desires to obey but is unable to because of factors beyond his control. God has endowed man with an intellect, a will, and a freedom to choose. Man is therefore responsible before God as a moral agent. Total depravity does mean that man *cannot* submit himself to God because he *will not*, and he will not because of his own hostility toward God.[13]

SPIRITUAL DEATH

Another important phrase theologians use to describe the depth of man's moral corruption is *spiritual death*. In the garden, God warned Adam that he would surely die the very day he ate of the forbidden tree.[14] Although Adam did not die physically until many years later, there is a very real sense in which he died spiritually at the very moment he chose self-determination over submission and sinned against God.[15] Through his fateful choice, Adam became alienated from God, and death passed over that part of his being that had enabled him to know and commune with

---

9. Deuteronomy 6:4–5; Matthew 22:37; 1 Corinthians 10:31; Romans 1:21
10. 2 Timothy 3:2–4
11. A. A. Hodge, *Outlines of Theology* (Edinburgh: Banner of Truth), 329.
12. Jeremiah 13:23; Romans 7:23–24
13. Romans 8:7–8
14. Genesis 2:17
15. Genesis 5:5

his Creator. In short, he became a spiritual corpse. He was physically alive but spiritually dead. He became responsive to every sort of wicked stimulus, both human and demonic, but he was unresponsive to the person and will of God.

The Scriptures teach us that this devastating consequence of Adam's disobedience was not limited to him alone, but that all members of Adam's race are born spiritually dead. This is the meaning of Paul's foundational statement to the Ephesians: "And you He made alive, who were dead in trespasses and sins, in which you once walked according to the course of this world, according to the prince of the power of the air, the spirit who now works in the sons of disobedience, among whom also we all once conducted ourselves in the lusts of our flesh, fulfilling the desires of the flesh and of the mind, and were by nature children of wrath, just as the others."[16] In this text, we find that all men enter this world as spiritual stillborns, void of true spiritual life and unresponsive to the person and will of God. They are "alienated from the life of God" and live as though they were dead to Him, and He to them.[17] It is for this reason that the psalmist tells us that fallen men do not seek God, and in all their thoughts, there is no room for Him.[18] Fallen man does not take into account the reality of God or the need to walk according to His commands. He lives as a practical atheist. Although he may acknowledge the existence of God or some sort of deity, it has no practical or real effect on his life. He is dead even while he lives and boasts of life.[19] He has a heart of stone toward God, and he is like an autumn tree without fruit, doubly dead and uprooted.[20] He is a living corpse whose righteousness is like filthy rags and whose most religious deeds are dead works.[21]

MORAL INABILITY

Another phrase that is closely related to the doctrine of spiritual death is *moral inability*. This phrase is commonly employed to describe the extent

---

16. Ephesians 2:1–3
17. Ephesians 4:18
18. Psalm 10:4 NASB: "The wicked, in the haughtiness of his countenance, does not seek Him. All his thoughts are, 'There is no God.'" NIV: "In his pride the wicked man does not seek him; in all his thoughts there is no room for God."
19. 1 Timothy 5:6; Revelation 3:1
20. Ezekiel 11:19; Jude v. 12
21. Isaiah 64:6; Hebrews 6:1; 9:14

of man's moral corruption, and this doctrine teaches us that fallen man is unable to love, obey, or please God.

Upon hearing of such a doctrine, one may ask, "How is man responsible before God when he is unable to do anything that God commands?" The answer is very important. If man did not love or obey God because he lacked the mental faculties to do so or was somehow physically restrained, then it would be unfair for God to hold him accountable—he would be a victim. However, this is not the case with man. His inability is moral and stems from his hostility toward God.[22] Man is unable to love God because he hates God.[23] He is unable to obey God because He disdains his commands. He is unable to please God because he does not hold the glory and good pleasure of God to be a worthy goal.[24] Man is not a victim but a culprit. He *cannot* because he *will not*. His corruption and enmity toward God are so great that he would rather suffer eternal punishment than acknowledge God to be God and submit to His sovereignty.

For this reason, moral inability may also be called willing hostility. The relationship between Joseph and his brothers best illustrates this truth: "But when his [Joseph's] brothers saw that their father loved him more than all his brothers, they hated him and could not speak peaceably to him."[25] The text states that Joseph's brothers could not speak to him on friendly terms. It was not because they lacked the physical ability to speak but because their hatred toward him was so great that they were unwilling to be friendly to him. In the same way, fallen man's hostility toward God is so great he cannot bring himself to love God or to submit to His commands.

Imagine a political prisoner justly locked away in a dungeon for his betrayal of king and country. One day the just and merciful king visits the cell and throws open the door. He then promises to give full pardon to the prisoner and restore his freedom on the singular condition that he renounce his rebellion, honor the king, and submit to the king's law. Upon hearing the word of the king, the prisoner races to the door and slams it closed, confining himself once again to the horrid dungeon. Then, in a fit of rage, he spits at the king and exclaims, "I would rather rot

---

22. Romans 5:10; 8:7–8
23. Romans 1:30
24. Romans 1:21
25. Genesis 37:4

in this cell than bow my knee to you!" This is the case of the unregenerate heart. Man's enmity toward God is so great that he would rather waste in hell than render unto Him the esteem, glory, and obedience He deserves!

It is a biblical truth that man's will is subject to his nature. If man possessed a morally pure nature, then his will would be inclined toward morally pure acts: he would love a holy and righteous God, and he would esteem and obey His commands. However, fallen man possesses a morally corrupt nature, and so his will is inclined toward morally corrupt acts. Thus, he hates a holy and righteous God, turns away from His truth, and rebels against His commands.

It is in this inseparable relationship between the nature and will of fallen man that we find the answer to the frequently debated question, "Does man possess free will?" The scriptural answer is that man is free to choose as he pleases, but because he is depraved, it pleases him to choose evil. In other words, fallen man does have free will, but he does not have a good will. His will is in bondage to his own depraved nature, and therefore he will always freely choose in opposition to the person and will of God. Jesus' scathing rebuke of the Pharisees clearly reveals this: "Brood of vipers! How can you, being evil, speak good things?"[26]

The biblical truth of moral inability prompted Martin Luther to write his famous treatise *The Bondage of the Will*. The title conveys that man cannot escape what he is. He is evil by nature, and he does works of evil willfully and freely. Fallen man bears bad fruit because he is a "bad tree."[27] His will is subject, or in bondage, to his corrupt nature. In the following pages, we will consider a few of the dire consequences of this truth.

FALLEN MAN CANNOT KNOW GOD

Through God's gracious providence, the human race has gained great intellectual achievements in areas such as science, technology, and medicine. Nevertheless, fallen man's knowledge of God is nothing more than a twisted maze of heresy and futile thinking.[28] This ignorance is not the result of a hidden God but of a hiding man. God has clearly revealed Himself to men through creation, His sovereign works in history, the

---

26. Matthew 12:34
27. Matthew 7:18
28. Romans 1:21–23; Ephesians 4:17–19

Scriptures, and finally, through His incarnate Son.[29] Nevertheless, man has responded to this revelation by closing his eyes and covering his ears. He cannot know the truth because He hates the truth and seeks to repress it.[30] He is against the truth because it is God's truth. It speaks against him, and therefore he cannot bear it.

FALLEN MAN CANNOT LOVE GOD

Most men, even the irreligious, claim some degree of love or affection toward God. Nevertheless, the Scriptures testify that fallen man cannot love God. In fact, the Scriptures teach that, prior to conversion, all of Adam's race hates God and lives at war against Him.[31] This hostility exists because a morally corrupt creature simply cannot tolerate a holy and righteous God or bear to submit to His will.

It is important to note that most who claim a genuine love for God know very little about His attributes and works as Scripture describes them. Therefore, the god they love is nothing more than a figment of their own imagination. They have made a god in their own image, and they love what they have made. As God declares through the psalmist, "You thought that I was altogether like you; but I will rebuke you."[32]

If most men, even those who consider themselves religious, were to investigate the Scriptures, they would most certainly find a God much different from the god they claim as the object of their affections. If they took at face value the Scripture's teaching on such divine attributes as holiness, justice, sovereignty, and wrath, they would most likely respond in disgust and declare, "My God's not like that!" or, "I could never love a God like that!" Thus, we would quickly see that when fallen man meets the God of the Scriptures, his only reaction is repulsion and rejection. What is the reason for this adverse reaction? Again, it has to do with who man is at the very core of his nature. If man were holy and righteous by nature, then he could easily love a holy and righteous God. However, man is by nature depraved, and therefore he cannot.

---

29. Romans 1:19–20; 2 Timothy 3:16; John 1:18
30. Romans 1:18; Job 21:14–15
31. Romans 1:30; 5:10
32. Psalm 50:21

FALLEN MAN CANNOT SEEK GOD

We live in a world full of self-proclaimed seekers after God, and yet the Scriptures destroy all such boasting with one simple declaration: "There is none who seeks after God."[33] Often, we hear young converts to Christianity begin their testimonies with the words, "For years I was seeking after God," but the Scriptures again reply, "There is none who seeks after God."[34] Man is a fallen creature. He hates God because He is holy, and he opposes the truth of God because it exposes his depravity and rebellion.[35] Therefore, he will not come to God, but he will do everything in his power to avoid Him and to remove every fragment of His law from his conscience. The old preachers often summarized this truth with this declaration: "Man is no more inclined to seek God than a criminal at large is inclined to seek after an officer of the law."[36] Jesus agrees: "And this is the condemnation, that the light has come into the world, and men loved darkness rather than light, because their deeds were evil. For everyone practicing evil hates the light and does not come to the light, lest his deeds should be exposed."[37]

FALLEN MAN CANNOT OBEY OR PLEASE GOD

There is one great common denominator that binds together all other religions outside of Christianity: the belief that a right standing before God is based upon obedience, personal merit, or some ability to please God. Christianity stands alone in declaring that apart from a special work of God's grace, man cannot obey God or please Him.[38] Since man is truly unclean, he is destitute of merit. Even his most exemplary deeds are nothing but filthy rags before a holy and righteous God.[39] This is one of the most humbling truths of the Scriptures—and one of the most detested and opposed by Adam's race. Nevertheless, it is an essential part of the gospel and must be pressed upon a man until he bears the weight of its truth. He is hopelessly and helplessly lost. If he will be saved, he must be saved by God alone.

---

33. Romans 3:11
34. Romans 3:11
35. John 3:19–20
36. The futile "hiding" of Adam and Eve in Genesis 3:8 clearly illustrates this.
37. John 3:19–20
38. Romans 7:14–24; Ephesians 2:4–5
39. Isaiah 64:6

FALLEN MAN CANNOT REFORM HIMSELF

The twentieth century began with great optimism about man's ability to evolve into a greater and nobler creature. It was supposed to be the age of reform, but it ended in a stupor of despair and confusion. The Scriptures clearly teach that man is born spiritually dead and morally depraved. Every attempt at self-reformation is hopeless and will end in utter failure.[40] The patriarch Job cried out, "If I am condemned, why then do I labor in vain? If I wash myself with snow water, and cleanse my hands with soap, yet You will plunge me into the pit, and my own clothes will abhor me."[41] Through the prophet Jeremiah, God declared, "For though you wash yourself with lye, and use much soap, yet your iniquity is marked before Me."[42] And again, "Can the Ethiopian change his skin or the leopard its spots? Then may you also do good who are accustomed to do evil."[43] Man has only one hope, but before he can see it, he must be convinced of his utter inability and brought to the very end of himself. This is one of the essential works of gospel preaching.

FALLEN MAN IS A SLAVE TO SATAN

In the beginning, Adam was free to obey God and exercise dominion over all the earth.[44] Because of his rebellion against God, both he and his race fell into corruption and slavery. Since the fall, every man is born in bondage to his corrupt nature and in slavery to Satan. Although few men would ever consider themselves followers of the devil, the Scripture testifies that all men live "according to the prince of the power of the air" (the devil), and that he works powerfully through all who live in disobedience to God.[45] Furthermore, the Scriptures testify that the whole world lies in the power of the evil one, that all men are born under his dominion, and that he holds all men captive to do his will.[46]

Although it is proper to use the term *enslavement* to describe man's relationship with the devil, we must understand that man is not a victim

---

40. Job 9:29–31
41. Job 9:29–31
42. Jeremiah 2:22
43. Jeremiah 13:23
44. Genesis 1:27–28
45. Ephesians 2:2
46. 1 John 5:19; Acts 26:18; 2 Timothy 2:26

held against his will. Man has rejected the rule of God and has been "given over" to the rule of Satan. Both the captive and the capturer are fallen creatures, and there is great affinity between them.[47] They are alike in their moral corruption and in their enmity toward God. Although it is repulsive to most, it is nevertheless true: there is such a moral likeness between fallen man and Satan that prior to conversion, all men may rightly be called children of the devil.[48]

ARE WE REALLY THAT BAD?

We live in a decidedly optimistic but delusional age that places man at the very center of the universe and hails him as the measure of all things. Against the testimony of his own blighted history, his afflicted conscience, and the teaching of Scripture, he makes great claims to virtue and merit and boasts of a brighter future. He covers his countless immoralities and continual degeneracy by simply changing the rules of morality and christening what once was considered evil and calling it good.[49] Because of this powerful delusion, it is not surprising that we would respond to the indictment of Scripture with this question: Are we really that bad? The biblical answer is, "Yes! We really are that bad!"

Scripture clearly testifies that God brought a great flood upon the entire world during the days of Noah.[50] The reason for this divine act of judgment was the godlessness and gross immorality of man. The Scriptures provide us with the following explanation: "Then the LORD saw that the wickedness of man was great in the earth, and that every intent of the thoughts of his heart was only evil continually. And the LORD was sorry that He had made man on the earth, and He was grieved in His heart."[51] The thought that stands out in this text is not just the wickedness of man but also the extent of it—"Every intent of the thoughts of his heart was only evil continually." This is one of the most powerful statements in the Scriptures regarding what we have referred to as the total,

---

47. Because of this affinity, in John 8:44 Jesus calls the devil the "father" of the unbeliever.

48. 1 John 3:8; John 8:44

49. Isaiah 5:20–21: "Woe to those who call evil good, and good evil; who put darkness for light, and light for darkness; who put bitter for sweet, and sweet for bitter! Woe to those who are wise in their own eyes, and prudent in their own sight!"

50. Genesis 7–9

51. Genesis 6:5–6

radical, or pervasive depravity of man. At first, the indictment may seem extreme and applicable to only a few infamous persons in history whose consciences were completely seared. However, after closer investigation, it becomes apparent that it applies to each and every one of us.

Imagine if we possessed a device that was able to transform every thought that has ever entered into our minds into a visual image and then place all those images on a film for everyone to see. Imagine that all of our family, friends, and peers were going to see this film. Wouldn't we do everything within our power to keep them from seeing the film? If they did see the film, wouldn't we find it difficult, if not impossible, to look them in the eyes ever again? If, however, against all reason, we maintained a bold countenance and claimed that we would be ashamed of nothing, would it not be evidence that we are either lying, delusional, or already seared in our conscience? The truth is that the best of us have thought things so vile that we would not share them with our closest friends! All this demonstrates that there is something in us that is simply not right. We have a propensity for evil and are inclined toward the very things that our consciences oppose and censure. This has been the great predicament of the most enlightened philosophers, moralists, and theologians throughout the history of thought. The apostle Paul summarized man's dilemma when he lamented, "For what I am doing, I do not understand. For what I will to do, that I do not practice; but what I hate, that I do."[52]

It is important to understand that the wickedness we have described is not confined to the antediluvian period.[53] In other words, the flood did not wash away man's tendency toward evil, nor was Noah able to leave behind a better legacy than Adam. Immediately after the flood subsided and God commanded Noah to leave the ark, God exposed the ongoing depravity that remained in the heart of man and would be the mark of his unregenerate character until the end of the world: "And the LORD smelled a soothing aroma. Then the LORD said in His heart, 'I will never again curse the ground for man's sake, although the imagination of man's heart is evil from his youth; nor will I again destroy every living thing as I have done.'"[54]

---

52. Romans 7:15
53. The period in history prior to the flood of Noah.
54. Genesis 8:21

Before the flood, God declared that every intent of the thoughts of a man's heart was only evil continually.[55] After the flood, little changed. The intent of a man's heart is not only evil, but the origin of that evil is also exposed. It resides within the heart of man from birth. It is his inheritance from Adam.[56] Although Scripture does not explain the mystery to us, it does confirm it as true. Man is conceived in sin and brought forth in iniquity; he is estranged from the womb and goes astray from birth.[57] For this reason, there is no need to teach children to be selfish or deceitful. Instead, parents and others must labor diligently to teach them to restrain their selfishness, speak the truth, and be concerned for the welfare of others. Anyone who would hope that children might one day govern the world has never witnessed the brutal and merciless pecking order that is often established among the youngest children, or what can happen when one child covets the toy of another. Anyone who would say otherwise has history and the daily news against him!

The Scriptures teach that man does evil because he has evil residing within him. This indwelling depravity permeates and affects his every thought, word, and deed. This lament of the prophet Isaiah powerfully illustrates this truth: "But we are all like an unclean thing, and all our righteousnesses are like filthy rags; we all fade as a leaf, and our iniquities, like the wind, have taken us away."[58] There are many opinions regarding what Isaiah meant by the words *filthy garment*. However, most think that he is referring to a garment that has become ceremonially unclean by contact with the dead, a flow of blood, or leprosy. We will concern ourselves with the last of the three.

Throughout history, leprosy has been considered one of the most terrifying of all diseases; therefore, it provides a powerful and graphic illustration of sin. Leprosy ravages the body until it is little more than a mass of rot and stench. It is unbearable to him who suffers from the malady, and it is equally unbearable for those who must witness it. In light of this information, imagine that the local Optimist Club decides to take in a poor leper and make him presentable. They wash him ever so carefully and mask his smell in the most expensive perfumes. Finally,

55. Genesis 6:5–6
56. Genesis 5:3; Romans 5:12
57. Psalms 51:5; 58:3
58. Isaiah 64:6

they dress him in a pure white garment made of the finest silk and present him for all the world to see. Although their labors may produce a momentary benefit for the leper and evoke applause for themselves, it will not take long for the veneer to fall away. The rot of the man's body will quickly bleed through the cloth and his stench will soon overpower the fragrances. Within moments, the man, the garment, and everything he touches becomes corrupted and leprous.

The same may be said of a man. Regardless of the religious or moral reforms that he might impose upon himself, he remains the same inside. Jesus describes him as a cup that is clean on the outside but is full of filth within; a whitewashed tomb filled with dead bones.[59] Like the leper whose corruption bleeds through the cloth and makes it as vile as his person, so the corruption of the man's heart or nature bleeds through his every thought, word, and deed and makes it unclean. For this reason, the unregenerate man is unable to gain a right standing before God by means of his works or merit. The best of all he does is like a filthy and loathsome garment before God!

Our understanding of the nature of man is foundational to our understanding of the gospel and evangelism. If man is basically good, or if there is a remnant or spark of goodness residing in man, then the preacher has the power to convince and men have the power to respond. However, if man is radically depraved, then only the supernatural power of God can open hearts and minds, grant repentance, and give faith leading to salvation.[60]

As Christians and ministers of the gospel, God calls us not only to proclaim the greatness of God and the riches of His grace but also to expose the true condition of man's heart by the light of God's Word and the power of the Holy Spirit. It is this later work of exposing man's moral corruption that leads men to put no confidence in the flesh and to glory in Christ Jesus.[61] The moral darkness of man serves as a background of pitch-black night upon which the twin stars of God's grace and mercy shine forth.

---

59. Matthew 23:25–28
60. Acts 16:14; Luke 24:45; 2 Timothy 2:25; Ephesians 2:8; Romans 12:3
61. Philippians 3:3

CHAPTER FIFTEEN

Righteous Indignation

God is a just judge, and God is angry with the wicked every day.
—Psalm 7:11

The boastful shall not stand in Your sight;
You hate all workers of iniquity.
—Psalm 5:5

Most of the evangelical community has forgotten the above verses to the point that they are no longer even controversial. How often do preachers proclaim to sinners the righteous indignation of God against the sinner? How often does the pulpit even address themes such as divine anger or holy hatred? Is it because we no longer study the Scriptures? Or have we concluded that certain parts are now uninspired or obsolete? Could it be that we have cowered under the shadow of political correctness and the whims of culture? Or are we convinced that preaching the truth is no way to grow a church?

Regardless of whether it is palatable to our present age, the righteous indignation of God is a reality in the Scriptures and an essential part of all true gospel proclamation. Therefore, we must understand this doctrine and the truths that surround it. We must also bear in mind that once understood, they are also to be proclaimed. The end of our study is not that we merely obtain a balanced theology for ourselves but that we proclaim the truths we discover for the benefit of God's people. There is little risk in learning, but there is often great risk in proclaiming what we have learned. The truths we know will cause us little harm and bring little benefit to the church if we confine them to our libraries.

DO WE WANT A RIGHTEOUS GOD?

The first question we must ask both our fellow man and ourselves is, "Do we really want a righteous God?" This may seem like an unusual question, even an unnecessary one, but in reality, it reveals much about our human condition and our problem before God.

On the one hand, we want a righteous God. It would be terrifying even to think of living in a universe under the absolute sovereignty of an unrighteous and omnipotent being. The Hitlers of this world appear for only a moment on the theater of history, and their own evil quickly sweeps them away. Yet the wake of their destruction seems to reach far beyond their own generation. What then would it be like to live under the unrighteous rule of an immoral and eternal deity? The thought of it is the stuff of nightmares. His unrighteousness would make him inconsistent and even capricious. His power would make him terrifying. Even if he were good to us for the longest time, there would still be no certainty that his goodness would continue. We would be like sailors on a calm sea who go mad anticipating a possible fatal storm. There would be no certainty and no reasonable grounds for faith. There would be no hope of a future rectification of wrongs for a present world that staggers under the weight of unpunished injustice and unchallenged immorality. For these reasons, if it were left up to a vote, the sane among men would cast their ballots for a perfectly righteous God who "will have no part in unrighteousness."[1] A God who is absolutely trustworthy will judge the world in righteousness and execute judgment among all men with a perfect and impartial justice.[2]

A just God is the kind of God that most men want and even demand. When great injustices run wild in our world without any apparent divine intervention or judgment, unlearned men stand like brute beasts and demand justice from heaven, but the thinking man sits silently in the corner with his head hidden in his hands. He knows that he is caught between a rock and a hard place. By the indicting finger of his own conscience, he realizes that if God gives men the justice they demand, then all men, including those making the greatest demands, will be condemned. As it is written, "There is none righteous, no, not one."[3] Those who demand

1. 2 Chronicles 19:7 NASB
2. Deuteronomy 7:9; Psalm 9:8
3. Romans 3:10

that others be brought to the bar of justice must realize that they are making petition for their own judgment at the same bar. Though all have not committed the same atrocities, all have sinned, and all are under the condemnation of death and eternal separation from a holy and righteous God. Any who would seek to segregate themselves from the greatest of sinners is blind to his own depravity and the wickedness of his deeds.

This is the dilemma that gives birth to the question, "Do we really want a righteous God?" Would we really want Him to survey every aspect of our lives—thoughts, words, and deeds—and then grant us the exact sentence due us? Only the man or culture whose conscience has already been seared would offer to stand before such scrutiny and take what may come from the judgment seat of a perfectly righteous God.

The truth that God is a righteous God is a double-edged sword. It brings comfort to know that an immoral, omnipotent being does not rule the world. However, to those who still have a conscience with which to contemplate, the truth is absolutely terrifying. If God is truly righteous, loving all that is right with a perfect love and hating unrighteousness with a perfect hatred, what must be His response to our own personal evil?

IS GOD ANGRY?

It is not uncommon for contemporary preachers and evangelists to assure their hearers that God is not an angry God, but this statement is misleading at best and heretical at worst.[4] It cannot offer any real comfort to men. According to the Scriptures, God is an angry God, and it is a good thing for us that He is. The Scriptures declare the following: "God is jealous, and the LORD avenges; the LORD avenges and is furious. The LORD will take vengeance on His adversaries, and He reserves wrath for His enemies"; "God is a just judge, and God is angry with the wicked every day"; "You, Yourself, are to be feared; and who may stand in Your presence when once You are angry?"[5]

When the holiness, justice, and love of God meet the depravity, injustice, and lovelessness of man, the inevitable result is divine anger or indignation, a wrath so great that the psalmist cries out: "Who knows

---

4. Many preachers have unknowingly retitled Jonathan Edward's sermon "Sinners in the Hands of an Angry God" as "Slightly Dysfunctional Individuals in the Hands of a Mildly Disgruntled Deity."

5. Nahum 1:2; Psalms 7:11; 76:7

the power of Your anger? For as the fear of You, so is Your wrath."[6] The word translated *wrath* in the Old Testament comes from three Hebrew words. The first is *qetsep,* which refers to wrath, anger, or indignation. The second is *hema,* which denotes wrath, anger, disgust, fury, heat, and even poison. The third is *'aph,* which is literally translated "nostril" or "nose." It represents the anger of God in the same way that the flaring of the nostrils represents the anger of an enraged animal. The representation is not at all refined, but it is powerful.

In the New Testament, the word *wrath* is translated from two Greek words. The first is *orge,* which refers to wrath or anger. The second is *thumos,* which denotes anger, indignation, passion, and rage. In the broad spectrum of the Scriptures, divine wrath refers to God's holy displeasure and righteous indignation directed towards the sinner and his sin.

In considering the wrath of God, it is important to understand that it is not an uncontrollable, irrational, or selfish emotion, but His wrath is the result of His holiness, righteousness, and love. It is also a necessary element of His government. Because of who God is, He must react adversely to sin. *God is holy.* Therefore, evil repulses Him, and He breaks fellowship with the wicked. *God is love* and zealously loves all that is good. Such intense love for righteousness manifests itself in an equally intense hatred of all that is evil. Thus, the love of God does not negate the wrath of God; rather, it confirms or guarantees it. *God is righteous.* Therefore, He must judge wickedness and condemn it. If man is an object of God's anger, it is because he has chosen to challenge God's sovereignty, violate His holy will, and expose himself to judgment.

In His holiness, righteousness and love, God hates sin and comes with a terrible and often violent anger against it. Before His wrath, the earth quakes and the rocks break up. The nations cannot endure His anger, and no one can stand before His indignation.[7] The strongest among men and angels alike will melt before Him like a tiny wax figurine before a blast furnace.[8]

Today, many reject the doctrine of divine wrath or any similar teaching that would even suggest that a loving and merciful God could be

---

6. Psalm 90:11

7. Jeremiah 10:10; Nahum 1:6

8. I owe this thought to Pastor Charles Leiter of Lake Road Chapel in Kirksville, Missouri.

wrathful or that He would manifest such anger in the judgment and con-demnation of the sinner. They argue that such ideas are nothing more than the erroneous conclusions of primitive men who saw God as hostile, vengeful, and even cruel. As Christians, we should reject any doctrine that would portray God as cruel or ignore His compassion. Neverthe-less, we must not forsake the Scripture's clear teaching on the doctrine of divine wrath and punishment. There are enough references in the Scrip-tures with regard to the anger and wrath of God to make it at least as prominent a theme as His love, kindness, and compassion.

God is compassionate and gracious, slow to anger and abounding in loving-kindness, and yet He will punish the unrepentant sinner with a view to administering justice among His creatures and vindicating His holy name.[9] In the greatness of His excellence, He will overthrow those who rise up against Him and send forth His burning anger to consume them as chaff.[10] Even in the New Testament, He is described as a consum-ing fire and as a God who "inflicts wrath" to such an extent that the great among the wicked will cry out for the mountains and rocks to fall upon them to hide from the wrath of His Lamb.[11] For this reason, the apostle Paul pleads with men not to be deceived but to live in the light of the truth that the wrath of God will come upon the sons of disobedience.[12]

The oft-repeated statement that God is not an angry God is untrue and it cannot offer any real comfort to man! What comfort could be found in a God who is neutral toward evil and demonstrates no indignation against it? How could God be good, loving, or even moral if He did not burn with indignation over the slave trade, Auschwitz, or the slaughter of millions of unborn children in the name of convenience? When we hear of such atrocities, we feel an overwhelming sense of moral indignation or anger. Furthermore, we would consider any man who was unmoved by such immoral horrors to be as much a monster as those who commit-ted them. What then are we communicating when we declare that God is not an angry God? Can we justify our own indignation towards unrigh-teousness and all the while deny such a right to God?

---

9. Exodus 34:6–7
10. Exodus 15:7
11. Hebrews 12:29; Romans 3:5; Revelation 6:16
12. Ephesians 5:6

In contrast to the poetic musings of preachers who desire to make God palatable to this carnal world, the Scriptures teach us that the infinitely holy, righteous, and loving God is a God of wrath. He is never apathetic toward evil; He burns with an unquenchable fire against it. He directs His righteous indignation toward the almost infinite number of sins committed against Him at every tick of the clock. "Behold, the name of the LORD comes from afar, burning with His anger, and His burden is heavy; His lips are full of indignation, and His tongue like a devouring fire."[13] "The sinners in Zion are afraid; fearfulness has seized the hypocrites: 'Who among us shall dwell with the devouring fire? Who among us shall dwell with everlasting burnings?'"[14] "Behold, the whirlwind of the LORD goes forth with fury, a continuing whirlwind; it will fall violently on the head of the wicked."[15]

We must not be deceived into thinking that God's unquenchable and consuming fire is only kindled for the most heinous crimes or that it comes only for the most despicable among us. In the mind of God, there are not two separate categories for sin: one category that makes Him angry and another that evokes no such response. The Scriptures teach us that all sin is lawlessness, every form of rebellion is as witchcraft, and every act of insubordination is as the most wicked immorality and idolatry.[16] For all and every sin, the wrath of God comes upon the son of disobedience, and the wages of any sin is death.[17]

The sin of our first parents and the anger it evoked from God clearly demonstrate the heinous nature of every form or category of sin. The eating of a forbidden fruit seems rather harmless when compared to the atrocities of human history and those that make the headlines of the nightly news, yet this one act of rebellion resulted in the wrath of God and the condemnation of the world. If nothing else, it teaches us that all sin is heinous before a holy and righteous God, and all who commit such sin are objects of His wrath.[18]

---

13. Isaiah 30:27
14. Isaiah 33:14
15. Jeremiah 30:23
16. 1 John 3:4; 1 Samuel 15:23
17. Epheisans 5:6; Romans 6:23
18. Ephesians 2:3; 5:6; Colossians 3:6

DOES GOD HATE?

Does God hate? Is that hatred ever directed toward men? Most have never heard a sermon on this subject matter or even entertained such an idea. The question alone is enough to cause a controversy and put the mildly religious in a fighting stance. Even to suggest the possibility of such a thing contradicts much of what evangelical preachers teach today. However, in the Scriptures, the hatred of God is just as much a reality as His love. According to the Scriptures, there are things that a holy and loving God hates, abhors, detests, and even loathes. Furthermore, that hatred is oftentimes directed toward fallen men.

Many object to any such teaching about the hatred of God on the false assumption that God is love and therefore cannot hate. While the love of God is a reality that goes beyond comprehension, it is important to see that the love of God is the very reason for His hatred. We should not say that God is love and therefore He *cannot* hate, but rather, God is love and therefore He *must* hate. If a person truly loves life, acknowledges its sanctity, and cherishes all children as a gift from God, then they must hate abortion. It is impossible to passionately and purely love children and yet be neutral toward that which destroys them in the womb. In the same way, if God loves with the greatest intensity all that is upright and good, then He must with equal intensity hate all that is perverse and evil.

The Scriptures teach us that God not only hates sin but also that He directs that hatred toward those who practice it. We have all been taught the popular cliché, "God loves the sinner and hates the sin," but this teaching is a denial of the Scriptures that clearly declare otherwise. The psalmist, under the inspiration of the Holy Spirit, wrote that God not only hates iniquity, but He also hates "all workers of iniquity."[19]

We must understand that it is impossible to separate the sin from the sinner. God does not punish sin, but He punishes the one who commits it. It is not sin that is condemned to hell but the man who practices it. For this reason, the psalmist declared: "The boastful shall not stand in Your sight; You hate all workers of iniquity."[20] And also, "The LORD is in His holy temple, the LORD's throne is in heaven; His eyes behold, His eyelids test the sons of men. The LORD tests the righteous, but the wicked and

---

19. Psalm 5:5: "You hate all who do iniquity" (NASB); "Thou hatest all workers of iniquity" (KJV); "You hate all who do wrong" (NIV); "You hate all evildoers" (ESV).
20. Psalm 5:5

the one who loves violence His soul hates. Upon the wicked He will rain coals; fire and brimstone and a burning wind shall be the portion of their cup. For the LORD is righteous, He loves righteousness."[21]

It is important to understand that the above texts are not alone in Scripture but are accompanied by other passages that strengthen the case for such a response from a holy God. In the book of Leviticus, the Lord warned the people of Israel that they must not follow the customs of the nations He would drive out before them, and then He added, "For they commit all these things, and therefore I abhor them."[22] Again, in the book of Deuteronomy, He warned His people that the Canaanites would be driven out because they were "an abomination to the LORD," and that anyone who participated in the same unjust acts would likewise be an "abomination" to Him.[23] In the book of Psalms, God described His disposition toward the unbelieving Israelites who refused to enter the Promised Land, saying, "For forty years I was grieved with that generation."[24] Finally, in the book of Titus, Paul describes those who made empty or superficial confession of faith in God as "abominable" before Him, and John on the Isle of Patmos describes the lake of fire as the eternal dwelling of all those who are "abominable."[25]

DIVINE HATRED EXPLAINED

What does it mean when the Scriptures declare that God hates sinners? First, *Webster's Dictionary* defines hate as a feeling of extreme enmity toward someone, to regard another with active hostility, or to have a strong aversion toward another: to detest, loathe, abhor, or abominate. Although these are hard words, Scripture uses most, if not all of these to describe God's relationship to sin and the sinner. Secondly, we must understand that God's hatred exists in perfect harmony with His other attributes. Unlike man, God's hatred is holy, just, and a result of His love. Thirdly, we must understand that God's hatred is not a denial of His love. Psalm 5:5 is not a denial of John 3:16 or Matthew 5:44–45. Although God's wrath abides upon the sinner, although He is angry with the wicked

---

21. Psalm 11:4–7
22. Leviticus 20:23
23. Deuteronomy 18:12; 25:16
24. Psalm 95:10
25. Titus 1:16; Revelation 21:8

every day, and although He hates all who do iniquity, His love is of such a nature that He is able to love those who are the very objects of His hatred and work on their behalf for their salvation.[26] Fourthly, although God is long-suffering toward the objects of His hatred and holds salvation out to them, there will come a time when He will withdraw His offer and reconciliation will no longer be possible.[27]

---

26. John 3:36; Psalms 7:11; 5:5
27. Romans 10:21

CHAPTER SIXTEEN

Holy War

But they rebelled and grieved His Holy Spirit; so He turned Himself against them as an enemy, and He fought against them.
—Isaiah 63:10

God is jealous, and the LORD avenges; the LORD avenges and is furious. The LORD will take vengeance on His adversaries, and He reserves wrath for His enemies.
—Nahum 1:2

Having considered the righteous indignation of God manifested in His anger and wrath, we will now turn our attention to a related theme—the hostility that exists between God and the unrepentant sinner. It is the obligation of the gospel preacher to warn men of the holy war that God has declared against His enemies and to plead with sinners to be reconciled to Him before it is too late. God's promise of amnesty to the rebel is genuine, but it is not to be presumed upon. A day is coming when the olive leaf will be withdrawn and the offer of peace will be rescinded. At that time, all that will remain for the sinner is "but a certain fearful expectation of judgment, and fiery indignation which will devour the adversaries.... It is a fearful thing to fall into the hands of the living God."[1]

WHO IS AT WAR WITH WHOM?

The popular announcement that "God loves the sinner and hates the sin" often accompanies a similar cliché: "Man is at war with God, but God is never at war with man." Consequently, much is made of the sinner's

---

1. Hebrews 10:27, 31

enmity and unceasing war against God, but little or nothing is said of God's unceasing war against the sinner.

Regardless of this current trend in evangelical thought, it is extremely important to understand that the hostility between God and the sinner is not one-sided—it is mutual. When men declare war on God, God turns Himself to become their enemy and fights against them.[2] Although it is an unsettling truth, the Scriptures clearly teach that God considers the unrepentant sinner to be His enemy and has written out a declaration of war against him. The sinner's only hope is to drop his weapons and lift the white flag of surrender before it is too late forever.[3]

The book of Nahum tells us, "The LORD will take vengeance on His adversaries, and He reserves wrath for His enemies."[4] The first truth this text teaches is that God is the one who considers the wicked to be His adversary. He is not lamenting that man has made Him an enemy, but He declares His own position against man. God is the one who draws the battle line and musters the troops. The second truth to be learned is that God is on the offensive. He does not merely stand against the attacks of wicked men, but He Himself gives the battle cry and runs to engage them with the full force of His wrath. As the psalmist warns, God has sharpened His sword for battle, bent His bow in readiness, and prepared deadly weapons against His enemies. If the wicked do not repent, they will certainly perish under His wrath.[5]

It is imperative that we understand and accept that this truth of "holy war" is not a relic from the old covenant or some primitive view of God nullified by the progressive revelation of the New Testament. Rather, it is a biblical and enduring truth found throughout the Scriptures. In the book of Romans, the apostle Paul writes: "When we were enemies we were reconciled to God through the death of His Son."[6] Although this text communicates the idea of mutual hostility between God and man, the greater emphasis is not the sinner's hostility toward God but God's opposition to the sinner. Realizing that this concept is foreign to the great majority of contemporary evangelicals, the following scholars offer further confirmation: Charles Hodge stated, "There is not only a wicked

---

2. Isaiah 63:10
3. Pastor Charles Leiter first brought this idea to my attention.
4. Nahum 1:2
5. Psalm 7:12–13
6. Romans 5:10

opposition of the sinner to God, but a holy opposition of God to the sinner."[7] Louis Berkhof said, "Not that men are hostile towards God, but that they are objects of God's holy displeasure."[8] And Robert L. Reymond explained, "The word 'enemies' most probably should be construed in the passive ('hated by God') rather than the active sense ('hating God'). In other words, the word 'enemies' does not highlight our unholy hatred of God, but rather God's holy hatred of us."[9]

According to our text, man had sinned, and God was the offended party. For reconciliation to occur, man's offense had to be removed, the justice of God had to be satisfied, and the wrath of God against man had to be appeased. We know that Christ's death did not make all men favorably disposed to God, because most men continue in their hateful opposition to His person and will. However, the death of Christ did satisfy the righteous demands of a holy God in order that He might be favorably disposed to His enemies and extend an olive leaf of peace toward them through the gospel. Those who repent and believe in Christ will be saved, but those who refuse are storing up wrath for themselves for the day of God's wrath when His righteous judgment will finally be revealed.[10]

We must never forget that the Christ who gave His life for the nations is the same who will strike them down and rule them with a rod of iron.[11] The Suffering Servant who trod the path to Calvary will one day tread the winepress of the fierceness and wrath of Almighty God.[12] The Savior who shed His blood for His enemies will appear a second time with His robe dipped in the blood of His enemies.[13] The Lamb who bore the wrath of God on the tree is the same who will pour out the wrath of God upon those gathered against Him to such an extent that they will cry out for the mountains to fall upon them to hide them from His presence.[14] The Prince of Peace who proclaimed the favorable year of the Lord will one

---

7. Charles Hodge, *A Commentary on the Epistle to the Romans* (London: Banner of Truth, 1989), 138.

8. Louis Berkhof, *Systematic Theology* (Edinburgh: Banner of Truth, 1993), 374.

9. Robert L. Reymond, *A New Systematic Theology of the Christian Faith* (Nashville: Thomas Nelson, 1998), 646.

10. Romans 2:5

11. Revelation 19:15

12. Revelation 19:15

13. Revelation 19:13

14. Revelation 6:16–17

day announce the day of His vengeance.[15] He is the same who will judge, wage war, and lead the armies of heaven against the enemies of God.[16] It is for this reason that the psalmist admonishes the nations to pay homage to the Son, that He not become angry and they perish in the way, for His wrath may soon be kindled.[17]

As preachers of the gospel, we must proclaim the love of God toward men and His willingness to save, but we must not set aside the warnings that are so obvious and frequent in the Scriptures. Men must be ready to meet their God.[18] They must "agree with [their] adversary quickly" while they are with Him on the way.[19] For if they do not repent, He will sharpen His sword, and He has already bent His bow of wrath.[20] To those who believe, the preacher must proclaim the promise of full amnesty and the certainty of peace. However, to those who refuse to obey the gospel, the faithful messenger must tell them that the wrath of God abides upon them still.[21]

What a wonderful and terrible calling has been bestowed upon the minister of the gospel. To some he is a fragrance of life, but to others he is the smell of death. Who is sufficient for these things?[22]

IS VENGEANCE BENEATH GOD?

God's vengeance closely relates to His wrath. The psalmist calls Him "God, to whom vengeance belongs," and the prophet Nahum introduces Him as the avenging and wrathful Lord who "will take vengeance on His adversaries, and He reserves wrath for His enemies."[23] The song of Moses even exalts the vengeance of God. It is one of the most terrifying depictions of God in all of the Scriptures: "Now see that I, even I, am He, and there is no God besides Me; I kill and I make alive; I wound and I heal; nor is there any who can deliver from My hand. For I raise My hand to heaven, and say, 'As I live forever, if I whet My glittering sword, and

---

15. Isaiah 9:6; 61:2; Luke 4:19
16. Revelation 19:11, 14
17. Psalm 2:12
18. Amos 4:12
19. Matthew 5:25
20. Psalm 7:12–13
21. John 3:36
22. 2 Corinthians 2:16
23. Psalm 94:1; Nahum 1:2

My hand takes hold on judgment, I will render vengeance to My enemies, and repay those who hate Me. I will make My arrows drunk with blood, and My sword shall devour flesh.'"[24]

How can we read such a text and not tremble? How can we believe such a truth and not proclaim it? The prophet Amos declared, "A lion has roared! Who will not fear? The Lord GOD has spoken! Who can but prophesy?[25] The apostle Paul wrote, "We also believe and therefore speak."[26] In like manner, if we believe that the Scriptures are infallible and God is immutable, how can we not declare such things? Is Nahum's warning nothing more than meaningless poetry with no practical application? Is it allegory with no concrete interpretation? Was it written for a heartier culture than our own, too strong for the fragile soul of modern man? If in Nahum's time, it was a true word about God and a necessary word for man, then it is the same today. It is the truth—and an essential element in our proclamation of the gospel!

According to the Scriptures, men should be warned that God is a God of vengeance. Yet how do we reconcile such a truth with other texts of Scripture that clearly depict vengeance as a vice of wicked men?[27] How can a holy and loving God also be a God of vengeance? First, we must understand that divine vengeance is a constant theme of Scripture and is therefore undeniable. Secondly, we must understand that God's vengeance differs from the vengeance of fallen man; His zeal for holiness, righteousness, and justice motivate His vengeance. God is compassionate and gracious, slow to anger, and abounding in loving-kindness, but He is also just. He will punish the sinner with the purpose of vindicating His name and administering justice among His creatures.[28] In light of the horrid nature of man's sin, God is right to avenge Himself. Three times in the book of Jeremiah, God asks, "Shall I not punish them for these things?... Shall I not avenge Myself on such a nation as this?"[29] Elsewhere in the Law and the Prophets we find the answer to this question: Moses affirms that God will not delay in repaying those who hate Him to their

---

24. Deuteronomy 32:39–42
25. Amos 3:8
26. 2 Corinthians 4:13
27. Leviticus 19:18; 1 Samuel 25:25, 30–33
28. Exodus 34:6
29. Jeremiah 5:9, 29; 9:9

faces, and Isaiah declares that He will be relieved of His adversaries and avenge Himself on His foes.[30]

Today, many reject the doctrine of divine vengeance or any other teaching that would even suggest that a loving and merciful God could be vengeful. Even those ministers who accept the doctrine as the plain teaching of Scripture will rarely proclaim it from the pulpit. As a result, the unbelieving world, as well as the sincere Christian, is unaware of God's true character and His radical response to the sinful deeds of men.

The Scriptures warn us that the wrath of God is coming upon the sons of men and admonishes us to prepare to meet our God.[31] Sinful men should consider these truths with fear and trembling, but first, preachers must make these truths known. With a clarion call, it is our responsibility to warn men of the certainty of the wrath to come.[32] If we refuse to fulfill this ominous facet of our ministry, we will be held responsible, and the blood of our listeners will be required from our hands. As God warned the prophet Ezekiel: "When I say to the wicked, 'O wicked man, you shall surely die!' and you do not speak to warn the wicked from his way, that wicked man shall die in his iniquity; but his blood I will require at your hand."[33]

In light of the few texts we have considered regarding the vengeance of God, one can only weep to think of how awkward and imbalanced our preaching has become! Our own sermons betray us and reveal how partial we are to some truths and how prejudiced we are against others! We are called to proclaim the full counsel of God, and we must not shrink from it![34] We are not given authority to pick and choose what should and should not be preached in light of what we think we know about the needs of modern man. Those of us who have been granted the privilege of instructing others should ask ourselves how often we proclaim what men most need to understand and yet least desire to hear: the judgment of God. We should understand that the lack of such preaching exposes the inconsistencies in our pulpits and explains the reason for the ignorance in our pews regarding some of the most fundamental truths about God's character and His dealings with men.

---

30. Deuteronomy 7:10; Isaiah 1:24
31. Amos 4:12
32. Ephesians 5:6
33. Ezekiel 33:8
34. Acts 20:27

We live in a time of great theological imbalance. Much is said of the love of God, and rightly so, but almost nothing is said of His wrath. If a preacher preached an entire sermon on the love of God without once mentioning His wrath, He most likely would not be called into account. However, if he preached only a portion of a sermon on the wrath of God, he most likely would be censured for being unbalanced, mean-spirited, and unloving. Such is the age in which we live. "For the time will come when they will not endure sound doctrine, but according to their own desires...will turn their ears away from the truth."[35]

---

35. 2 Timothy 4:3–4

CHAPTER SEVENTEEN

A Most Costly Gift

Being justified freely by His grace through the redemption that is in Christ Jesus.

—Romans 3:24

In the last several chapters, we have considered the moral condition of fallen man, his universal rebellion against God, and the dire consequences of divine judgment: all men stand condemned before God. However, in the text before us, we will discover that a radical change has taken place in the Christian's standing before God—he is no longer counted as a sinner, but he has been justified by faith in the Lord Jesus Christ.

JUSTIFICATION

From the Scriptures we learn that God is a righteous God.[1] His works are perfect, and all His ways are just. He is a God of faithfulness who will not pervert what is right.[2] Being righteous, He cannot be morally neutral or apathetic. He loves righteousness and hates evil.[3] His eyes are too pure to approve evil, and He cannot look upon wickedness with favor.[4] He has established His throne for judgment, and He will judge the world in righteousness.[5] He is a God who has indignation every day. If a man does not repent, He will sharpen His sword and make His bow ready for judgment.[6]

---

1. Psalm 7:9
2. Deuteronomy 32:4; Job 8:3
3. Psalms 11:7; 5:5
4. Habakkuk 1:13
5. Psalm 9:7
6. Psalm 7:11–12

The Scripture's testimony concerning the righteousness of God and the evil of man leads us to a great theological and moral problem: How can sinful man stand before the righteousness of God? How can a righteous God have fellowship with wicked men? The psalmist described the problem in this way: "Who may ascend into the hill of the LORD? Or who may stand in His holy place? He who has clean hands and a pure heart, who has not lifted up his soul to an idol, nor sworn deceitfully. He shall receive blessing from the LORD."[7]

Right standing in the presence of God requires absolute, or unmitigated, moral perfection. Every thought, word, and deed from the moment of birth to the moment of death must be found in perfect conformity to the nature and will of God. The slightest flaw or smallest deviation from this standard results in an immediate disqualification. We only need to look to the sin and fall of Adam to learn that there is a great strictness and severity in God's righteousness. For this reason, when the moralist asks, "What must I *do* to be saved?" we must place before him the demand of perfect obedience. If, by the grace of God, he is confounded and brought to despair, then we point him to Christ.

The man who would seek to earn a right standing before God is the most pathetic and hopeless of all creatures. Since the fall of Adam, no man has ever fulfilled God's righteous demands. Our hands are unclean and our hearts impure.[8] We run to falsehood from the womb, and out of the abundance of the heart, we have spoken deceitful things.[9] We have no strength or right to stand before Him. We utterly disqualify ourselves. If anything is ever to be done to mend this breach, God must do it. Justification is a gift given by His grace.[10]

The word *justified* comes from the Greek verb *dikaióo*, which means to prove or declare someone to be righteous or as he ought to be. In the context of Scripture and the doctrine of salvation, the word *justified* is a forensic, or legal, declaration.[11] The man who believes God is justified, that is, righteousness has been credited to his account. He is reckoned, or declared, to

---

7. Psalm 24:3–5
8. Jeremiah 17:9
9. Psalm 58:3; Matthew 15:18–19
10. Romans 3:24
11. *Forensic* is from the Latin word *forensis*, pertaining to a market or forum. The term *forensic* denotes that which pertains to the courts or legal matters, such as forensic medicine, which applies medical facts to legal cases.

be right with God, and God treats him as such. In his letter to the church in Rome, the apostle Paul wrote, "For what does the Scripture say? 'Abraham believed God, and it was accounted to him for righteousness.'"[12]

It is important to note that the term *justified* does not mean that the moment a man believes God he is made righteous. If that were the case, the believing one would be transformed into a perfectly righteous being that no longer sins or is even capable of such. Nor does the term mean that the believing man is infused with a special grace that enables him to live a more righteous life and thus gain a right standing before God based upon his works. If that were the case, then salvation would no longer be by faith, and grace would no longer be grace.[13] Scripture and the most useful confessions and ministers throughout the history of the church testify that justification is a legal standing before the throne of God. The man who believes God's testimony regarding His Son is forgiven of all his sin and is declared right before the judgment throne of God.[14] The Westminster Confession (11.1) states it this way: "Those whom God effectually calls, He also freely justifies: not by infusing righteousness into them, but by pardoning their sins, and by accounting and accepting their persons as righteous, not for anything wrought in them, or done by them, but for Christ's sake alone...by imputing the obedience and satisfaction of Christ unto them."

BENEFITS OF JUSTIFICATION

So then, justification is a wonderful and multifaceted blessing received by faith in the person and work of Jesus Christ. Regarding the Christian who has been justified, we may say the following. First, all his sins past, present, and future have been forgiven and will never be taken into account before the bar of God. The apostle Paul quotes David as saying: "Blessed are those whose lawless deeds are forgiven, and whose sins are covered; blessed is the man to whom the LORD shall not impute sin."[15]

To those who think that God is not much different from themselves, this truth can evoke only a faint and patronizing appreciation.[16] To those

---

12. Romans 4:3; Galatians 3:6; James 2:23
13. Romans 11:6
14. 1 John 5:11
15. Romans 4:7–8
16. Psalm 50:21

who think a great deal of themselves and do not understand or believe the archaic and dreadful doctrine of total depravity, this truth is pleasant, but not surprising. However, to the man who has seen the depravity of his heart and the shame of his deeds before a holy God, this truth is beyond amazing. It is astounding, staggering, breathtaking, spectacular, phenomenal, extraordinary, mind-blowing, jaw-dropping, nearly unbelievable, and altogether wondrous. It calls for a ringing of bells, tears of joy, and shouts of glory! This demonstrates once again the need to teach on dark things so that when the light appears it is absolutely lovely.

Secondly, the righteousness of Christ imputed to the Christian means that the Christian is declared righteous before God. The word *impute* is an extremely important theological term translated from the Greek word *logízoma,* which means to reckon or credit. With regard to the believer, it means that the righteousness of Christ is reckoned or credited to his account. Thus, the believer is righteous before God—not by his own virtue or merit, but through the perfect life and atoning death of the Lord Jesus Christ. The apostle Paul writes: "But of Him you are in Christ Jesus, who became for us wisdom from God—and righteousness and sanctification and redemption."[17]

During His earthly life and ministry, the Lord Jesus Christ walked in perfect obedience before God. The apostle Paul testifies that Christ "knew no sin."[18] The writer of Hebrews tells us that He was tempted in all things as we are, and yet He was without sin.[19] This is one of the most astounding truths in the Scriptures regarding the person of Jesus. The best way to comprehend something of its magnitude is by way of comparison: there has never been one moment in our lives that we have loved the Lord our God in the manner He deserves. However, there was never one moment in the life of Jesus that He did not love the Lord His God with all His heart, soul, mind, and strength.[20] Again, there has never been one moment in our lives that we did what we did for the glory of God without one deviant motivation. However, there was not one moment in the life of Jesus that He failed to glorify God perfectly and completely, with every fiber of His being. For this reason, the testimony

17. 1 Corinthians 1:30
18. 2 Corinthians 5:21
19. Hebrews 4:15
20. Mark 12:30; Luke 10:27

of the Father regarding Him never wavered: "This is My beloved Son, in whom I am well pleased."[21]

The amazing thing about justification is that this perfect life Jesus lived is imputed to the believer—placed in his account. Furthermore, this is according to the will of the Father and the Son. Christ gives His righteousness freely, superabundantly, and with joy unmeasured. The patriarch Joseph, who was a type of Christ, possessed a splendid coat of many colors that he would not share with his brothers. However, Christ, the one greater than Joseph, delights in clothing His brothers in His multifaceted robe of indescribable righteousness. It is a coat of beauty that brings glory to the most impoverished wretch, and a coat of mail to stand against all the flaming arrows of the evil one.[22] Having been clothed in Christ, God now looks at each and every believer and declares without wavering, "This is My beloved Son, in whom I am well pleased."

Thirdly, having been declared righteous before the throne of God, the believer is now treated as righteous. The Scriptures declare that Christ became sin on our behalf so that we might become the righteousness of God in Him.[23] On the cross, God caused the iniquity of us all to fall upon Him,[24] and God treated Him severely, as though He were guilty of the sins He bore. He was forsaken of God, smitten of God and afflicted, crushed for our iniquities, and chastened for our well-being.[25] He bore the divine curse and suffered the wrath of God that we evoked with our sin, and yet, by His suffering, the debt we could not pay was paid in full.[26] Consequently, the believer is now declared righteous and receives the infinite and immeasurable benefit of that righteousness—God treats us as sons! This is an amazing truth that will transform the way in which the believer sees himself. We are the beneficiaries of the great exchange, "the just for the unjust."[27]

Fourthly and finally, the Christian has peace with God by faith in the atoning work of Christ. The apostle Paul writes, "Therefore, having been justified by faith, we have peace with God through our Lord Jesus

---

21. Matthew 3:17; 17:5; Mark 1:11; 9:7; Luke 3:22; 2 Peter 1:17
22. Ephesians 6:16
23. 2 Corinthians 5:21
24. Isaiah 53:6
25. Psalm 22:1; Matthew 27:46; Mark 15:34; Isaiah 53:5
26. John 19:30
27. 1 Peter 3:18

Christ."[28] In light of the former hostility that existed, this is an almost unimaginable blessing. Through the gift of justification, the Christian is no longer a child of wrath, but a son of God.[29] Having been justified by Christ's atoning death, we shall be saved from the wrath of God through Him.[30] It is this glorious truth that led the apostle Paul to describe the Christian in the following manner: "You turned to God from idols to serve the living and true God, and to wait for His Son from heaven, whom He raised from the dead, even Jesus who delivers us from the wrath to come."[31]

GRACE

Possibly the most amazing thing about justification is that it is by God's grace, or unmerited favor. With this truth, the whole of Scripture unanimously agrees: the believer has been "justified freely by His grace."[32]

The word *freely* comes from the Greek adverb *doreán*, which literally means "freely, undeservedly, or without a cause." It is the same word used by the Lord Jesus Christ to show His disciples that the world's hostility toward Him was entirely undeserved: "But this happened that the word might be fulfilled which is written in their law, 'They hated Me without a cause.'"[33]

Christ was without sin.[34] Even His enemies could not bring a just charge against Him.[35] He never gave anyone cause to hate Him. In the same way, we never gave God cause or reason to declare us right before Him. The slightest examination of our lives prior to conversion will prove the utter impossibility that we earned our justification by our merit or that our salvation was anything other than by grace. God did not declare us right with Him *because of us*, but rather *in spite of us*. Neither inherent worth nor personal merit moved God to save us. It was grace and grace alone!

---

28. Romans 5:1
29. Ephesians 2:3; Galatians 4:5
30. Romans 5:9
31. 1 Thessalonians 1:9–10
32. Romans 3:24
33. John 15:25
34. Hebrews 4:15; 2 Corinthians 5:21
35. John 8:46

This doctrine of justification by grace through faith distinguishes Christianity from all the other religions of the world. Imagine an interview between a secular reporter and representatives of the three major world religions—Judaism, Islam, and Christianity. First, the reporter draws near to the Orthodox Jew and asks, "If you died at this very hour, where would you go, and what is the reason for your hope?"

The Jew would reply, "I will go to heaven. I love and obey the Torah, or Law of God. I have walked in the way of the righteous. My works speak for me."

Next, the reporter turns to the Muslim with the same question: "If you died at this very hour, where would you go, and what is the reason for your hope?"

The Muslim would answer, "I will go to heaven. I love the Koran. I have followed the teachings of Allah's greatest prophet. I have made the holy pilgrimages, been faithful in prayer, and given alms to the poor. I am a righteous man."

Finally, the reporter makes his way to the Christian with the same question: "If you died at this very hour, where would you go, and what is the reason for your hope?"

The Christian would answer, "I will go to heaven." But then, with a look of both joy and contrition, he declares, "In sin my mother conceived me, and in sin was I brought forth. I have broken all the laws of God, and I deserve the greatest condemnation."

At this, the reporter stops him and exclaims, "I do not understand the reason for the hope that is within you. The Orthodox Jew and the devout Muslim, I understand. They are going to heaven and they will stand in the presence of God by virtue of their own merit and deeds, but you claim to be destitute of these necessary things. How can you be right with God? What is the foundation for your hope?"

The Christian smiles and replies, "My hope for entrance into the presence of God is founded upon the virtue and merit of another, Jesus Christ, my Lord."

This has been the personal testimony of every Christian who has walked upon this earth from the first day of the apostles until now, and it will remain the singular testimony of Christianity until the end of the age. The apostle Paul wrote, "I also count all things loss for the excellence of the knowledge of Christ Jesus my Lord, for whom I have suffered the loss of all things, and count them as rubbish, that I may gain Christ and be found in Him, not having my own righteousness, which is from the law, but that which is through faith in Christ, the righteousness which is from God by faith."[36]

The famed clergyman and hymn writer Augustus Toplady echoes the same strong sentiments of the apostle Paul in his renowned hymn "Rock of Ages":

> Not the labors of my hands
> Can fulfill Thy law's commands.
> Could my zeal no respite know;
> Could my tears forever flow,
> These for sin could not atone;
> Thou must save, and Thou alone.
>
> Nothing in my hand I bring;
> Simply to the cross I cling.
> Naked, come to Thee for dress;
> Helpless, look to thee for grace;
> Foul, I to the fountain fly;
> Wash me, Savior, or I die.

Those who boast of a right standing before God based upon personal virtue or merit do not understand who God is or who they are. The smallest glimpse of the righteousness of God or the moral depravity of man is enough to crush any hope of a salvation earned. Entrance into His presence demands absolute moral perfection. His holiness is such that He cannot behold evil or look upon iniquity.[37] The singular sin of Adam resulted in his exile and blanketed the world in condemnation and death. How then can we who have sinned beyond our ability to calculate present ourselves before Him with any hope of right standing? Each one of us has sinned enough to cast a thousand worlds into destruction. If we are to be saved, it is by Him. If a reason is to be found for our salvation, it must come from Him. If something is to be done, it must be accomplished by the gracious work of a saving God.

REDEMPTION

36. Philippians 3:8–9
37. Habakkuk 1:13

There are some words that ought to be spoken quietly, with reverence and a trembling lip. The word *redemption* is one of those words. It is translated from the Greek word *apolútrosis*, which refers to a release that has been made possible through the payment of a price or ransom. This word is often used in ancient literature with regard to the release of slaves or captives of war. In the New Testament, redemption refers to the liberation of men from the condemnation and slavery of sin through the blood sacrifice of Jesus Christ.

People often ask, "To whom was the ransom paid?" and, "From what we have been redeemed?" Although many ingenious and equally erroneous opinions have been put forth, the New Testament is clear: our sin offended God's justice and kindled His wrath. We were "shut up" to judgment and condemnation without the least recourse to gain our freedom.[38] The justice of God demanded satisfaction through the death of the culprit, for "the wages of sin is death" and "the soul who sins shall die."[39] "But God, who is rich in mercy, because of His great love with which He loved us," intervened and made payment for us by sending His only begotten Son to die our death and pay our debt.[40]

This would have been a noble work even if we had been loyal subjects of God's kingdom who had fallen captive through no fault of our own, but this was not the case. He redeemed us even though we were not victims but criminals. We carried the blame. We rushed headlong into rebellion against our God. Our condemnation and imprisonment under His justice and wrath was our own doing. Our sin formed the shackles and provoked the executioner's ax.

This grim reality of our guilt is what makes the truth of our redemption that much more spectacular. If He had died for noble servants, it would have been an incomprehensible act of grace, but He died for far less. As the apostle Paul writes: "For scarcely for a righteous man will one die; yet perhaps for a good man someone would even dare to die. But God demonstrates His own love toward us, in that while we were still sinners, Christ died for us."[41]

38. Romans 11:32 NASB
39. Romans 6:23; Ezekiel 18:4
40. Ephesians 2:4
41. Romans 5:7–8

The justification of the believer is a gift that comes through the redemption made possible through the person and work of Jesus Christ. Although freely given to the believer, we cannot comprehend the cost demanded and the price paid by Jesus. In fact, the saints in heaven may find their primary employment to be searching out the value of that sacrifice. There is no knowledge more splendid or worthy of pursuit than the knowledge of Christ's work of redemption on behalf of His people. The apostle Peter writes, "Knowing that you were not redeemed with corruptible things, like silver or gold, from your aimless conduct received by tradition from your fathers, but with the precious blood of Christ."[42]

Even the most meager knowledge of the price paid for our redemption should move both sinner and saint to respond in faith, devotion, and adoration. Those who do not presently believe should repent of their unbelief and run to Christ, for how shall they escape if they neglect so great a salvation?[43] Those of us who do believe should no longer live for ourselves, but for Him who died on our behalf. As the apostle Paul reasons, "For the love of Christ compels us, because we judge thus: that if One died for all, then all died; and He died for all, that those who live should live no longer for themselves, but for Him who died for them and rose again."[44]

Any real consideration of Christ's payment for the believer's redemption should move him to bow in appreciation and cry out, "How then shall I live?" As Christians, we do not do things simply because they are good or wise or lead to a prosperous life. We do them for Christ, because He shed His own blood for our souls. This is the great motivation of the Christian life and the reason we seek to conduct ourselves with reverence during our earthly pilgrimage.[45]

IN CHRIST ALONE

It would be difficult for the apostle Paul to make any mention of justification or redemption without including that it is all in Christ alone. In the first thirteen verses of Ephesians, he uses the phrase *in Christ* or its counterpart eleven times in order to prove that everything the believer

42. 1 Peter 1:18–19
43. Hebrews 2:3
44. 2 Corinthians 5:14–15
45. 1 Peter 1:17–18

has before God, he has in Christ. This truth cannot be overexaggerated or mentioned too often.

We often say that Jesus is all that we need, but it would be even more appropriate to say that He is all we have. Apart from Him, we have no part with God![46] It is the testimony of Scripture that all things were created in Him, through Him, and for Him, and the same may be said of our salvation.[47] Our release from captivity and right standing with God are only in Christ, by Him, and for Him. Every man on this planet is either in Adam and condemned, or in Christ and justified. A child may be in a godly home, and a man may be in a biblical church, but unless they are in Christ, they have no hope and are without God in the world.[48] Christ alone is the way, the truth, and the life, and no man comes to the Father except by Him.[49] There is salvation in no one else, for there is no other name under heaven that has been given among men by which we must be saved.[50]

It is this very truth that makes Christ precious to the believer while also being a "stone of stumbling and a rock of offense" to the world.[51] For us who believe, Christ is of greatest value and is worthy of our highest devotion. We are quick to renounce any claim of personal merit and to point to Christ with the joyful declaration, "But God forbid that I should boast except in the cross of our Lord Jesus Christ."[52] To make the slightest suggestion that we are justified by our own works or that we have added something to the work of Christ on our behalf should repulse us. We stand with the psalmist in declaring: "Not unto us, O LORD, not unto us, but to Your name give glory, because of Your mercy, because of Your truth.[53]

For those who refuse to believe, Jesus Christ is the epitome of arrogance and intolerance. How dare He stand before the world and claim

---

46. 1 John 5:12

47. Colossians 1:16: "For by Him all things were created." The phrase *by Him* is derived from the Greek phrase *en auto,* which may also be translated "in Him." If the meaning is "by Him," it indicates that the Son was the agent or instrument of creation. The more probable meaning is "in Him," and indicates that the Son was the sphere in which creation took place. Everything in heaven and earth has to do with Him; all things directly relate to Him and stand in relation to Him.

48. Ephesians 2:12
49. John 14:6
50. Acts 4:12
51. 1 Peter 2:7–8
52. Galatians 6:14
53. Psalm 115:1

to be the only Savior among us, especially in the midst of so many other sincere candidates vying for the position? How dare the church stand in opposition to the only absolute left in culture—the belief that no one is wrong, except the one who claims to be right? How dare the Christian believe that his way is the only way to the exclusion of everyone else? To a postmodern world, such a claim is nothing more than an atrocious demonstration of idiocy and bigotry.

For this reason, Christianity has always been a scandal to the world. The early Christians of the Roman Empire were accused and persecuted as atheists because they denied the existence of all other gods and claimed allegiance to Christ alone. The modern Christian follows in the same scandalous tradition when he stands upon Christ alone and declares Him to be the only hope for the world. Nevertheless, if the Christian message loses this exclusivity, it is no longer Christian, and it no longer has power to save.

CHAPTER EIGHTEEN

The Divine Dilemma

Whom God set forth as a propitiation by His blood, through faith.
—Romans 3:25

If Romans 3:23–27 is the acropolis of the Christian faith, then verse 25 is the very citadel of the city. This one text explains the cross of Jesus Christ like no other. Here, we can look beyond the veil to discover the reason for the cross. Here, we can know the nature of Christ's sufferings. Here, we come to understand what had to be accomplished, and was accomplished, through His death. It is the missing link in much of modern-day gospel preaching and the reason so few, even among God's people, understand the cross.

Many theologians and preachers down through the ages would agree that Roman 3:25 is one of the most important in all of the Scriptures. This high opinion stems from the fact that it contains the very heart of the gospel: Christ died as a propitiation. The entire Christian faith rests upon this truth, and yet it is all but unknown within contemporary evangelicalism. How many evangelicals have ever even heard of the word *propitiation*? Of those who have heard, how many understand its meaning or comprehend anything of its great significance? This lack of knowledge is an indictment against our age, and it proves how little we truly understand about the gospel. Countless gospel sermons are preached and thousands of gospel tracts and books are written every year, and yet this essential text is rarely, if ever, found among them. It is no wonder that there is so little power in the contemporary presentation of the gospel.

A PUBLIC DISPLAY

Romans 3:25 tells us that God "set forth," or "displayed publicly" (NASB) His Son as a propitiation. The word *displayed* comes from the Greek word *protíthemai*, which means to set forth in order to expose to public view. On the cross of Calvary, God literally "placarded His Son."[1] At that precise moment in history, He raised Him up on a tree at the very crossroads of the religious center of the universe for all to see.[2]

Although not explicit in Scripture, it would not be wrong to suppose that God could have put away sin in a closet, or that Christ could have died in a more private manner. The fact that He was publicly displayed before the world is proof that God intended His suffering and death to be instruments, or means, of revelation. Through the cross, God determined to reveal to men and angels certain truths about Himself that could not be revealed in any other way.[3] It is the long-standing testimony of the church that the cross of Jesus Christ is the greatest revelation of God and of reality itself. The cross is that great and final word from God to man that explains everything that must be explained and answers our long-standing questions about the purpose and work of God among men.

It is beyond the scope of this chapter even to attempt an overview of all that the cross of Christ reveals. Borrowing from the language of the apostle John, we may say that if everything revealed through the cross were recorded in detail, even the world itself could not contain the books that would be written.[4] Therefore, we must confine ourselves to the text and closely follow Paul's leading. Under the direct and infallible guidance of the Holy Spirit, he passes over all the other countless precious gems revealed through the cross and points us to one of the greatest truths of the gospel: God publicly displayed His Son in order to demonstrate that He is a righteous God.[5]

At first, this truth may not seem that remarkable or surprising to those who have studied the Scriptures. From front to back, the Scriptures testify that God is a righteous God, that all His works are perfect, and that all His ways are just.[6] Why then must God publicly demonstrate to both men and angels that He is righteous? What has He done to

---

1. A placard is a poster, sign, or notice. To placard something is to place it in public view so it can be seen.

2. Galatians 4:4

3. Ephesians 3:10; 1 Peter 1:12

4. John 21:25

5. The word *demonstrate* is derived from the Greek phrase *eís éndeixin*, literally: "for demonstration" or "for proof."

6. Deuteronomy 32:4

cast doubt upon His justice so that He should have to explain His ways or vindicate Himself? The apostle Paul explains that it was necessary that God once and for all time vindicate His justice and demonstrate His righteousness, "because in His forbearance God had passed over the sins that were previously committed."[7] In other words, God saw it necessary to prove His righteousness to men and angels because throughout human history He has forestalled His judgment of sinners and granted forgiveness to wicked men. Although this is good news for sinful man, it presents the greatest theological and moral problem in the Scriptures: How can God be just while at the same time restraining His judgment and offering forgiveness to those who ought to be condemned? How can God be just and yet justify ungodly people?

THE DIVINE DILEMMA

Webster's Dictionary defines the word *dilemma* as "a situation involving a choice between equally unsatisfactory alternatives," or "a problem seemingly incapable of a satisfactory solution." In the Scriptures, the greatest of all dilemmas is set before us on almost every page: How can a just God pardon the wicked?

In the last chapter, we worked at length to prove that God freely justifies even the most wicked men who turn to Him in faith. This truth is the church's greatest joy and the theme of her most glorious and beloved hymns. We rejoice with David: "Blessed is he whose transgression is forgiven, whose sin is covered."[8] Yet the problem remains—how can God be just and yet grant pardon to wicked men? Shall not the judge of all the earth do right?[9] Can a just God be apathetic toward sin or brush it under the rug as though it never happened? Can a holy God bring wicked men into fellowship with Himself and still be holy?

In the book of Proverbs, the Scriptures put forth a maxim that seems to negate any possibility of God's pardon or justification of sinful men. It declares, "He who justifies the wicked, and he who condemns the just, both of them alike are an abomination to the LORD."[10] According to this text, anyone who justifies wicked men is an abomination to the Lord. The

7. Romans 3:25
8. Psalm 32:1; Romans 4:7
9. Genesis 18:25
10. Proverbs 17:15

word *abomination* comes from the Hebrew word *tow`ebah*, which denotes something that is abominable, disgusting, or loathsome. It is one of the strongest words in the Hebrew Scriptures! The truth communicated is that God abhors and loathes any person, especially any authority or judge, who justifies or acquits a guilty person. Yet this is the very theme of the gospel message! Throughout history, God has done this very thing. He has justified wicked men, forgiven their lawless deeds, and covered their sins.

How then can He still be just? The following illustration may help to explain the problem more clearly: Suppose that a man returned home one evening to find his entire family murdered on the floor of his living room, and the assassin was still standing over them with blood on his hands. Suppose that the man captured the assailant and turned him over to the authorities with all the evidence against him. Suppose that on the day of the murderer's sentencing, the judge made the following declaration: "I am a very loving judge, full of compassion and mercy. I therefore declare you 'not guilty' before the bar of justice and free from every penalty of the law."

What would the victim's response be to such a verdict? Would he agree that justice had been served? Not at all! He would be appalled at the judge's justification of this wicked man and call for his immediate removal. He would write his congressional representative, put editorials in the newspaper, and tell everyone who would listen that there is a judge on the bench who is far more corrupt and abominable than the very criminals he sets free! We would probably all agree with his assessment; however, therein lies the problem. If we demand such justice from our earthly judges, should we expect less from the Judge of all the earth? Borrowing from the discourse of Elihu, "Surely God will never do wickedly, nor will the Almighty pervert justice."[11]

FORGIVE AND FORGET?

Still, one might ask, "Why can't God simply forgive man's sin and be done with it? The Scriptures command us to forgive freely, so why would it be wrong for God to do the same?" There is a threefold answer to this question.

First, God is not like us, but is of infinitely greater worth than all of His creation combined. Therefore, it is not only right but also necessary

---

11. Job 34:12

for Him to seek His own glory and defend it. Given who He is, even the slightest form of rebellion is a grotesque offense to His person, a crime of highest treason worthy of the strictest censure. For Him to allow any offense against His person to go unpunished would be a twofold injustice. He would do injustice to His own deity by denying Himself the glory that rightfully belongs to Him. He would also do injustice to His creation by allowing it to deny the very reason for its own existence (i.e., the glory of God) and to run headlong into futility. If this is too difficult for modern man to accept, it is only because he has such a low view of God.

Secondly, God cannot simply forgive man's sin and be done with it because there are no contradictions in His character. He cannot simply deny His justice in order to manifest His love by granting forgiveness to the wicked. He must be both just and loving, and He cannot be one at the expense of the other. Many well-intentioned evangelists have wrongly declared to the lost multitudes that instead of being just with sinful man, God has determined to be loving. The logical conclusion is that God's love is unjust or that He is able to turn His back on His own justice in the name of love. Such a statement betrays ignorance of the gospel and of the attributes of God. The marvel of the gospel is not that God chose love over justice but that He was able to remain just while granting forgiveness in love.

Thirdly, God is the Judge of all the earth. It is His place to enforce justice, punish evil, and vindicate right. It would not be appropriate for the heavenly Judge to pardon the wicked any more than it would be for an earthly judge to pardon the criminal who stands before him in a court of law. It is our frequent complaint that our justice system is corrupt, and we cringe when convicted criminals are pardoned. Should we expect less justice from God than we do from our own judges? It is a well-founded truth that without the enforcement of justice, all nations, peoples, and cultures would run headlong into anarchy and self-destruction. If God ignored His own righteousness, granted pardon without the satisfaction of justice, and rendered no final judgment of evil, creation simply could not bear it.

THE PROPITIATION

Having demonstrated the absolute necessity of God's justice and His judgment of the wicked, the question remains, "How can God be just and yet justify ungodly people?" The answer is found in one of the greatest words of Scripture—*propitiation*. The word is derived from the Latin word *propicio,* which means "mercy." In the New Testament, it is translated from the Greek word *hilastérion,* which refers to a thing that propitiates, appeases, or placates.

The only other place in the New Testament where the word *hilastérion* occurs is in the book of Hebrews where it refers to the mercy seat that covered the ark of the covenant.[12] The cherubim overshadowed the mercy seat, and it was made of gold.[13] In the Old Testament dispensation, God's presence appeared in a cloud above the mercy seat in the Holy of Holies, and it was there that God promised to meet with His people and give them His commandments.[14] Most importantly, it was upon and before the mercy seat that once a year on the Day of Atonement the high priest sprinkled the blood of the bull seven times.[15] It was from this same mercy seat that God pronounced pardon upon His people and declared Himself reconciled through the bloody death of the sacrifice. It is for this reason that the covering over the ark was called the mercy seat, for it was there that sin was atoned for and mercy was made possible.

In our text, the word *propitiation* refers specifically to the sacrifice of Jesus Christ on the cross of Calvary.[16] It explains that Jesus' death took our sin away, satisfied God's divine justice, and appeased His wrath. Because Jesus Christ once and for all paid for the sins of His people, God can justly extend mercy to the guilty and be both "just and the justifier" of anyone who has faith in His Son.[17]

According to the Scriptures, man has sinned, and the wages of sin is death.[18] God is just, and the guilty cannot be pardoned until the demands of His law are satisfied.[19] In the fullness of time, the Son of God became a

---

12. Hebrews 9:5: "Above it were the cherubim of glory overshadowing the mercy seat [*hilastérion*]. Of these things we cannot now speak in detail." It is important to note that the same Greek word is also used with reference to the mercy seat in the Septuagint (the Greek translation of the Hebrew Scriptures).

13. Exodus 25:17–18

14. Leviticus 16:2; Exodus 25:22

15. Leviticus 16:14–15

16. 1 John 2:2: "And He Himself is the propitiation (*hilasmós*) for our sins, and not for ours only but also for the whole world."

17. Romans 3:26

18. Romans 3:23; 6:23

19. Proverbs 17:15

man and walked on this earth in perfect obedience to the law of God.[20] At the end of His life, and according to the will of the Father, He was cruci-fied by the hands of wicked men.[21] On the cross, He stood in the place of His guilty people, and their sin was imputed to Him.[22] As the Sin-Bearer, He became accursed of God, forsaken of God, and crushed under the weight of God's wrath.[23] His death paid the debt for sin, satisfied the demands of God's justice, and appeased His wrath. In this manner, God solved the great dilemma. He has justly punished the sins of His people in the death of His only Son and therefore may freely justify all who place their hope in Him. We will spend the next several chapters investi-gating this great truth.

---

20. Galatians 4:4
21. Acts 2:23
22. 2 Corinthians 5:21
23. Galatians 3:13; Matthew 27:46; Isaiah 53:10

CHAPTER NINETEEN

A Qualified Redeemer

And the Word became flesh and dwelt among us.
—John 1:14

Whom God set forth as a propitiation by His blood, through faith.
—Romans 3:25

Before we turn our attention to a more in-depth study of Christ as our propitiation, it will help to consider the requirements demanded for such a role. To put it plainly, the death of the sacrifice is utterly meaningless unless the one offering His life as a propitiation is truly qualified to do so. In other words, the value of the act is dependent upon the character of the one performing it. Most evangelicals regard the cross of Christ with great emphasis on what He did, and rightly so, but we often place too little emphasis on who He is. Jesus was both God and man, both impeccable (without sin) and of infinite value. If He did not meet all of these qualifications, then His offering on our behalf would have accomplished nothing. Yet, we will see that He was all these things and more. Therefore, Jesus was uniquely qualified to offer His life as an atoning sacrifice and to be the Savior of the world.[1]

A WORD OF CAUTION

We must always take great caution whenever we speak or write about the person of Jesus Christ. We cannot fully comprehend the mystery of the incarnate God and the exact role of His divine and human natures in our redemption. As the apostle Paul writes, "And without controversy great is the mystery of godliness: God was manifested in the flesh, justified in

---

1. John 4:42; 1 John 4:14

the Spirit, seen by angels, preached among the Gentiles, believed on in the world, received up in glory."[2]

Throughout the history of the church, there have been many heresies regarding the exact relationship between the divine and human natures in the person of Jesus Christ. Some of these false teachings have come from heretics who sought to deny either Christ's deity or His humanity. However, other erroneous teachings have also come from sincere Christians who simply took it upon themselves to explain the matter and leave no room for mystery. Therefore, we must endeavor to speak and write with caution. In this matter, it is better to say too little than too much, to relegate too much to the category of mystery rather than attempt to remove all mystery by adding to the Scriptures. As Moses cautions us: "The secret things belong to the LORD our God, but those things which are revealed belong to us and to our children forever, that we may do all the words of this law."[3]

TWO NATURES AND THE WORK OF SALVATION

It is the abiding testimony of Scripture that God alone is Savior and He shares this glorious divine prerogative with no one. Speaking through the prophet Isaiah, God declared, "I, even I, am the LORD, and besides Me there is no savior."[4] Even in this secular age, there is no shortage of gods or saviors. However, against the tide of this smorgasbord of deities and deliverers, the Scriptures stand alone in declaring salvation to be the exclusive work of the one true God who made heaven and earth. As the prophet Jonah declared from the belly of a great fish, "Salvation is of the LORD."[5] Therefore, to ascribe the work of salvation or grant the title of "Savior" to any being other than God is a great blasphemy.

This biblical truth presents a problem for anyone who considers the New Testament claims regarding the person and work of Jesus Christ. In light of what we know about salvation as the exclusive work of God, and in light of the countless references to Jesus as Savior, the following conclusions remain: If Jesus is Savior, then He is God in the strictest sense

2. 1 Timothy 3:16
3. Deuteronomy 29:29
4. Isaiah 43:11; see also Hosea 13:4
5. Jonah 2:9

of the term. If Jesus is not God in the strictest sense of the term, then He is no Savior.

Those who would deny Christ's deity and yet claim to benefit from His death are a great contradiction. He cannot save if He is not God. However, if Jesus is true deity, then there is no contradiction when the prophet Isaiah declares there to be no savior besides Yahweh, and the apostle Peter proclaims that there is salvation in no one else but Jesus.[6] Also, Isaiah can rightly admonish the ends of the earth to turn to God alone for salvation, and the apostle Paul can cry out that "whoever calls on the name of the LORD shall be saved."[7]

To be the Savior of the world it was necessary that Christ be God, and yet it is also true that the justice of God required sin to be punished in the same nature in which it had been committed.[8] Therefore, the one who died had to be a man. It was man who broke God's law, and it was a man who must die. As God spoke through the prophet Ezekiel, "The soul who sins shall die."[9] For such a soul to be free from God's righteous sentence, it was necessary that another soul of like nature die in its place. The writer of Hebrews supports this truth with the statement that it is impossible for the blood of bulls and goats to take away the sins of a higher-ranking humanity.[10] Only a man who was truly one with Adam's race could take the place of the guilty and make atonement for their sin.

Scripture teaches that Jesus of Nazareth was that man. The writer of Hebrews tells us that since He came to "give aid" to the descendants of Abraham, it was necessary that He be made like His brethren in all things, and since the children share in flesh and blood, He Himself likewise also partook of the same.[11] It was for this reason that when the apostle Paul wrote of Christ as the only mediator between God and men, he referred to Him as "the Man" Christ Jesus.[12] To be the Savior of God's people, it was necessary that the Word become flesh and dwell among us, and that, "being in the form of God," He be made in the likeness of

6. Acts 4:12

7. Isaiah 45:22; Romans 10:13

8. Francis Turretin, Institutes of Elenctic Theology (Phillipsburg, N.J.: P&R, 1994), 2:303.

9. Ezekiel 18:4

10. Hebrews 10:4

11. Hebrews 2:14–17

12. 1 Timothy 2:5

men.[13] Pilate's famous declaration *"Ecce Homo"* ("Behold the Man") is just one more reminder that Jesus Christ was that man![14]

TWO NATURES AND THE WRATH OF GOD

According to the Scriptures, the power of God's anger and fury is beyond all comprehension.[15] The earth itself quakes at His judgments, and not even the combined strength of the nations can endure His indignation.[16] It is not without reason that the mightiest of men will one day cry out for mountains to fall upon them to hide them from His wrath.[17] Even the psalmists and the prophets who dwelt in the presence of God were awestruck by the devastating power of His fury. On beholding it, they asked, "Who may stand in Your presence when once You are angry?"[18] "Who can stand before His indignation? And who can endure the fierceness of His anger?"[19] Finding no answer for their fearful musings, they could only conclude, "You, Yourself, are to be feared."[20]

In light of what we know about the wrath of God, it is right to conclude that if Jesus of Nazareth had been a mere man or created being, He never could have endured the wrath of God against the sins of His people. However, He was able to bear it to the very end and come forth victorious because He was God in the flesh and was sustained by His own divine omnipotence. The Westminster Larger Catechism agrees: "Question 38: Why was it requisite that the Mediator should be God? Answer: It was requisite that the Mediator should be God, that He might sustain and keep the human nature from sinking under the infinite wrath of God, and the power of death."

In light of the power of God's wrath, we must acknowledge the truth of Christ's deity, and yet we must be extremely careful not to deny or diminish an equally essential truth: Christ suffered the wrath of Almighty God as a man. We must take care to maintain that on the cross of Calvary, real wrath fell upon a real man and caused Him real

---

13. John 1:1, 14; Philippians 2:6–8
14. John 19:5
15. Psalm 90:11
16. Jeremiah 10:10
17. Revelation 6:16
18. Psalm 76:7
19. Nahum 1:6
20. Psalm 76:7

suffering of untold magnitude. Although Christ's deity sustained Him, it in no way provided a buffer against the wrath poured out upon Him. He suffered "in His own body"[21] the exact measure of divine wrath that was necessary to satisfy divine justice and bring peace between God and His people. For this reason, He was truly a *"Man* of sorrows and acquainted with grief."[22]

TWO NATURES AND THE VALUE OF THE SACRIFICE

Skeptics often ask, "How can one man suffering on a cross for a few hours pay for the sins of a multitude of men and save them from an eternity of suffering? How can the life of one man satisfy the justice due the many?" One of the most beautiful and precious doctrines of Scripture encases the answer to these questions: the infinite worth and perfect obedience of the Son of God.

The One who was nailed to the cross of Calvary was God, and the life He gave for the sake of His people was of infinite worth. The One who hung upon the tree was a man whose perfect obedience to the law of God gave merit to His sacrifice and provided a perfect righteousness to be imputed to His people. Therefore, we answer the skeptic's question of how the one can pay for the many by pointing to Jesus Christ, who was able to redeem a nearly countless multitude of men because of His infinite worth as God and His perfect obedience as Man.

Regarding the deity of Jesus Christ, we must again affirm that He was God in the very strictest and most complete use of the term. And it was this "fullness of deity" that gave infinite dignity to His person and infinite value to His sacrifice.[23] The great Genevan reformer Francis Turretin beautifully illustrates this truth: "Although money has no higher value in the hand of a king than in that of a captive, still the head and life of a king are of more value than the life of a vile slave (as the life of David was reckoned of more worth than that of half the Israelite army—2 Sam. 18:3). In this way, Christ alone ought to be estimated at a higher value than all

---

21. 1 Peter 2:24

22. Isaiah 53:3, emphasis added

23. Dabney writes, "Had there not been a divine nature to reflect an infinite dignity upon His person, His suffering the curse of sin for a few years would not have been a satisfaction sufficient to propitiate God for the sins of the world." Robert Lewis Dabney, *Systematic Theology* (Edinburgh: Banner of Truth, 1985), 201.

men together. The dignity of an infinite person swallows up and absorbs all the infinities of punishment due to us."[24] And John Newton echoes:

> If Messiah had been a sinless and perfect man, and no more, He might have yielded a complete obedience to the will of God, but it could have been only for Himself. The most excellent and exalted creature cannot exceed the law of His creation. As a creature, he is bound to serve God with his all, and his obligations will always be equal to his ability. But an obedience acceptable and available for others, for thousands and millions, for all who are willing to plead it, must be connected with a [divine] nature which is not thus necessarily bound.[25]

Again we ask, "How can the life of one Man satisfy the divine justice due the many? It is because He was true deity and His one life was worth more than the lives of all others combined! Imagine for a moment that the whole of creation is placed upon a scale—mountains and molehills, dust and stars, mice and men, all that has been or shall be. Then imagine that Christ steps on to the counterbalance. The scales immediately tip in His favor, for His worth infinitely outweighs the whole of all else.

If there had been a sinless man or an angel without blame who had been willing to die, his death would have not availed against our sin. Had all the countless myriads of angels offered their spotless lives upon that tree, their sacrifice would not amount to the payment demanded. Our salvation required a sacrifice of infinite value, and "our great God and Savior Jesus Christ" has such value.[26] We have not been redeemed with perishable things like silver and gold, but with precious blood, the blood of an unblemished and spotless lamb, the blood of Christ, the very blood of God![27]

Having shown the necessity of Christ's deity in giving infinite worth to His person and infinite merit to His sacrifice, we must again be extremely cautious that we do not neglect an equally essential truth: Christ was a man whose perfect obedience to the law of God enabled Him to die for the sins of His people and to impute a perfect righteousness to them.[28] First, we must understand that the man who died for the

---

24. Turretin, *Elenctic Theology*, 2:437.
25. John Newton, *The Works of John Newton* (Edinburgh: Banner of Truth, 1985), 4:60.
26. Titus 2:13
27. 1 Peter 1:18–19; Acts 20:28
28. The word *impute* means to reckon or credit. With regard to the believer, it means that the righteousness of Christ (His perfect obedience) is reckoned or credited to him.

sins of others must himself be a perfect man and without sin. Otherwise, his own life would be forfeited, and he would be under the condemnation of death and eternal punishment for his own misdeeds. Therefore, it was Christ's active obedience (His perfect obedience to the law of God) that made His passive obedience (the offering of Himself as a sacrifice for sins) acceptable to God. To put it simply, a sinner cannot offer his life for the sins of another but is obliged to die for his own guilt. Since Jesus Christ was a sinless man, He was able to offer Himself freely for the sins of His people.[29]

Secondly, we must understand that the salvation of man requires more than merely the removal of guilt; it also demands the imputation of righteousness. For a man to be at peace with God, he must be more than pardoned or acquitted—he must be righteous before God. David clearly illustrates this truth when he answers the age-old question regarding who may ascend into the hill of the Lord and who may stand in His holy place: "He who has clean hands and a pure heart, who has not lifted up his soul to an idol, nor sworn deceitfully."[30]

The one great requirement for entrance into the presence of God is righteousness—absolute conformity to the law of God, perfect obedience without one deviation in heart or deed. This truth presents an insurmountable obstacle to fallen man. Scripture clearly testifies that no one is righteous, that all have sinned, and that our constant moral failure has made righteousness through the law an impossibility.[31] To put it simply, we are thoroughly unrighteous creatures who are morally bankrupt and utterly disqualified to stand in the presence of God. We are without strength and without hope in ourselves.[32]

The good news of the gospel is that Jesus of Nazareth lived a life of perfect righteousness before God. His every thought, word, and deed conformed to the will of God without the slightest deviation. Every moment of His life, He loved the Lord His God with all His heart, soul, mind, and strength.[33] Everything He did, even the most menial tasks of eating and

---

In other words, Christ's righteousness is credited into the believer's account. Thus, God considers the believer righteous.

29. Hebrews 4:15
30. Psalm 24:4
31. Romans 3:10, 20–23; Galatians 2:16
32. Romans 5:6; Ephesians 2:12
33. Mark 12:30

drinking, He did for the glory of His God.[34] Thus, the Father could always testify of Him, "This is My beloved Son, in whom I am well pleased."[35]

What we must understand is that Christ not only died for His people, He also lived a perfect life for them. And this perfect life is imputed to, or placed in, the account of everyone who believes.[36] It is for this reason that the apostle Paul tells us we are "the righteousness of God in Him."[37] Paul explains it this way: "But now the righteousness of God apart from the law is revealed, being witnessed by the Law and the Prophets, even the righteousness of God, through faith in Jesus Christ, to all and on all who believe. For there is no difference."[38]

This beloved doctrine of imputation clearly demonstrates the relationship between the first and the last Adam.[39] The first Adam stood as the head of his race. In the garden, he both lived and fell for himself and his descendants. Thus, the apostle Paul concludes that "by one man's disobedience many were made sinners," and "by the one man's offense many died."[40] In a similar but greater way, the second Adam, Jesus Christ, stood as the head of His people, and He not only died for them but also lived for them so that His perfect life of obedience might be imputed to them as a gift by faith. For this reason, the apostle Paul concludes that through the obedience of the One the many are made righteous.[41]

It was necessary that Christ be God so that His deity might give infinite value to His sacrifice on behalf of His people. Likewise, it was also necessary that Christ be man so that He might live a perfect life of obedience, die in the place of sinners, and then impute His righteous life to all who believe.

TWO NATURES AND A PROPER MEDIATOR

Webster's Dictionary defines *mediator* as one who is qualified and able to interpose between two parties in order to reconcile them or to interpret

---

34. 1 Corinthians 10:31
35. Matthew 3:17; 17:5
36. Romans 4:22–24; 5:1
37. 2 Corinthians 5:21
38. Romans 3:21–22
39. Scripture portrays Adam and Christ as the first and last Adam. See Romans 5:14 and 1 Corinthians 15:45.
40. Romans 5:15–19
41. Romans 5:19

them to one another. To be a proper mediator between God and man, it was necessary that Jesus of Nazareth be both God and man in one person. True humanity was necessary that He might lay His hand upon man for his salvation and comfort. True deity was required that He might lay His hand upon God and have dealings with Him—what mere creature could or would attempt such a thing and survive it? From the Scriptures, we understand that the mightiest seraphim would not dare extend his hand and touch the One who is a consuming fire and who dwells in unapproachable light.[42] It takes all the seraphims' strength simply to stand in the presence of God with head bowed and face covered.[43] This is further proof that though our mediator must be a man, He must also be more than the mightiest of angels or the greatest of created beings. He must be God so that He might have dealings with God on our behalf.

Jesus of Nazareth meets both of these qualifications. He is a man like us in that He partook of our flesh and blood and is not ashamed to call us brothers.[44] "For we do not have a High Priest who cannot sympathize with our weaknesses, but was in all points tempted as we are, yet without sin."[45] At the same time, He is the Son of God, holy, innocent, undefiled, separated from sinners, and exalted above the heavens.[46] Having made purification for our sins, He sat down at the right hand of the Majesty on high.[47] On our behalf, He passed through the heavens and laid His hand on the Almighty.[48]

What these few pages described concerning the person of Christ represents not even the foothills of a much greater mountain. However, the purpose of saying what has been said is to urge ministers and laymen to explore the glories of Christ's person and to make them known through the gospel. We must always remember and treasure in our hearts the fact that we are not saved merely by what Christ has done for us, but by who He was, is, and will be forever!

---

42. Hebrews 12:29; 1 Timothy 6:16
43. Isaiah 6:2–3
44. Hebrews 2:11, 14
45. Hebrews 4:15
46. Hebrews 7:26
47. Hebrews 1:3
48. Hebrews 4:14

CHAPTER TWENTY

The Cross of Jesus Christ

At the ninth hour Jesus cried out with a loud voice, saying, "Eloi, Eloi, lama sabachthani?" which is translated, "My God, My God, why have You forsaken Me?"

—Mark 15:34

He was withdrawn from them about a stone's throw, and He knelt down and prayed, saying, "Father, if it is Your will, take this cup away from Me; nevertheless not My will, but Yours, be done." Then an angel appeared to Him from heaven, strengthening Him. And being in agony, He prayed more earnestly. Then His sweat became like great drops of blood falling down to the ground.

—Luke 22:41–44

So when Jesus had received the sour wine, He said, "It is finished!" And bowing His head, He gave up His spirit.

—John 19:30

Before us is the most important chapter in this book, or as most Christians would agree, the most important chapter of human history. This theme cannot be broken apart into smaller portions, even for the convenience of the reader. This is the heart of the gospel, and if we must labor through it, it is worthy labor indeed!

One of the greatest maladies of contemporary gospel preaching is that it rarely explains the cross of Christ. It is not enough to say that He died—all men die. It is not enough to say that He died a noble death—martyrs do the same. We must understand that we have not fully proclaimed the death of Christ with saving power until we have cleared away the confusion that surrounds it and expounded its true meaning to our hearers: He died bearing the transgressions of His people and suffering the divine penalty for their sins. He was forsaken of God and crushed under the wrath of God in our place.

FORSAKEN OF GOD

One of the most disturbing, even haunting passages in the Scriptures is Mark's account of the Messiah's great inquiry as He hangs upon the Roman cross. In a loud voice, He cried out, "Eloi, Eloi, lama sabachthani?" which is translated, "My God, My God, why have You forsaken Me?"[1]

In light of what we know about the impeccable nature of the Son of God and His perfect fellowship with the Father, the Messiah's words are difficult to comprehend, yet they lay bare the meaning of the cross and the reason for which He died. The fact that His words are also recorded in the original Hebrew tells us something of their great importance. The author did not want us to misunderstand a thing!

In these words, Christ is not only crying out to God, but as the consummate teacher, He is also directing His onlookers and all future readers to one of the most important messianic prophecies of the Old Testament: Psalm 22. Though the entire psalm abounds with detailed prophecies of the cross, we will concern ourselves with only the first six verses:

> My God, My God, why have You forsaken Me? Why are You so far from helping Me, and from the words of My groaning? O My God, I cry in the daytime, but You do not hear; and in the night season, and am not silent. But You are holy, enthroned in the praises of Israel. Our fathers trusted in You; they trusted, and You delivered them. They cried to You, and were delivered; they trusted in You, and were not ashamed. But I am a worm, and no man; a reproach of men, and despised by the people.

In Christ's day, the Hebrew Scriptures were not laid out in numbered chapters and verses as they are today. Therefore, when a rabbi sought to direct his hearers to a certain psalm or portion of Scripture, he would do so by reciting the first lines of the text. In this cry from the cross, Jesus directs us to Psalm 22 and reveals to us something of the character and purpose of His sufferings.

In the first and second verses, we hear the Messiah's complaint: He considers Himself forsaken of God. Mark uses the Greek word *egkataleípo*,

---

1. Mark 15:34

which means to forsake, abandon, or desert.[2] The psalmist uses the Hebrew word *azab,* which means to leave or forsake.[3] In both cases, the intention is clear. The Messiah Himself is aware that God has forsaken Him and turned a deaf ear to His cry. This is not a symbolic or poetic forsakenness. It is real! If ever a person felt the forsakenness of God, it was the Son of God on the cross of Calvary!

In the fourth and fifth verses of this psalm, the anguish suffered by the Messiah becomes even more acute as He recalls the covenant faithfulness of God toward His people. He declares, "Our fathers trusted in You; they trusted, and You delivered them. They cried to You, and were delivered; they trusted in You, and were not ashamed." The apparent contradiction is clear. There had never been one instance in the history of God's covenant people that a righteous man cried out to God and was not delivered. However, now the sinless Messiah hangs upon a tree utterly forsaken. What could be the reason for God's withdrawal? Why did He turn away from His only begotten Son?

Jesus weaves the answer to these disturbing questions into His complaint. In verse 3, He makes the unwavering declaration that God is holy, and then in verse 6, He admits the unspeakable: He had become a worm and was no longer a man. Why would Christ direct such demeaning and derogatory language toward Himself? Did He see Himself as a worm because He had become "a reproach of men, and despised by the people" or was there a greater and more awful reason for His self-deprecation?[4] After all, He did not cry out, "My God, my God, why have the people forsaken Me?" but rather He endeavored to know why God had done so. The answer can be found in one bitter truth alone: God had caused the iniquity of us all to fall on Him, and like a worm, He was forsaken and crushed in our stead.[5]

A SERPENT AND A SCAPEGOAT

This dark metaphor of the Messiah dying as a worm is not alone in Scripture. There are others that take us even deeper into the heart of the cross and lay open for us what He must suffer in order to accomplish the

---

2. Mark 15:34
3. Psalm 22:1
4. Psalm 22:6
5. Isaiah 53:5–6

redemption of His people.[6] If we shudder at the words of the psalmist, we will be further taken aback to read that the Son of God is also likened to a serpent lifted up in the wilderness, and to two sin-bearing goats—one slaughtered and the other driven out.

The first metaphor occurs in the book of Numbers. Because of Israel's nearly constant rebellion against the Lord and their rejection of His gracious provisions, God sent "fiery serpents" among the people and many died.[7] However, as a result of the people's repentance and Moses's intercession, God once again made provision for their salvation. He commanded Moses to "make a fiery serpent, and set it on a pole." He then promised, "Everyone who is bitten, when he looks at it, shall live."

At first, it seems contrary to reason that "that which was cured was shaped in the likeness of that which wounded."[8] However, it provides a powerful picture of the cross. The Israelites were dying from the venom of the fiery serpents. Men die from the venom of their own sin. God commanded Moses to place the cause of death high upon a pole. God placed the cause of our death upon His own Son as He hung high upon a cross. He had come "in the likeness of sinful flesh," and was made to be sin on our behalf.[9] The Israelite who believed God and looked upon the brazen serpent would live. The man who believes God's testimony concerning His Son and looks upon Him with faith will be saved.[10] As it is written: "Look unto me, and be ye saved, all the ends of the earth: for I am God, and there is none else."[11]

The priestly book of Leviticus contains the second metaphor. Since it was impossible for a single offering to fully typify or illustrate the Messiah's atoning death, God required of the people an offering involving two sacrificial goats.[12] The first goat was slain as a sin offering before the Lord, and its blood was sprinkled on and in front of the mercy seat behind the veil in the Holy of Holies.[13] It typified Christ, who shed His blood on the cross to make atonement for the sins of His people. It is a wonderful

---

6. Luke 24:26

7. Numbers 21:5–9

8. Matthew Henry, *Matthew Henry's Commentary on the Whole Bible* (Peabody, Mass.: Hendrickson, 1991), 1:665.

9. Romans 8:3; 2 Corinthians 5:21

10. 1 John 5:10–11

11. Isaiah 45:22 KJV

12. Leviticus 16:5–10

13. Leviticus 16:9, 15, 20

illustration of Christ's death as a propitiation—He shed His blood to satisfy the justice of God, appease His wrath, and bring peace. The high priest presented the second goat before the Lord as the scapegoat.[14] The high priest had to lay "both his hands on the head of the live goat, [and] confess over it all the iniquities of the children of Israel, and all their transgressions, concerning all their sins."[15] The priest then sent the scapegoat away into the wilderness, bearing on itself all the iniquities of the people into a solitary land. There, it would wander alone, forsaken of God and cut off from God's people. The scapegoat typified Christ, who "bore our sins in His own body on the tree" and suffered and died alone "outside the camp."[16] It is a wonderful illustration of Christ's death as an expiation— He carried our sin away. The psalmist wrote, "As far as the east is from the west, so far has He removed our transgressions from us."[17]

THE MESSIAH IS MADE SIN

How can we not think it astounding that a worm, a venomous serpent, and a goat should be symbols of Christ? To identify the Son of God with such loathsome things would be blasphemous had they not come from the Old Testament Scriptures themselves, and had they not been confirmed by the authors of the New Testament who go even farther in their dark portrayal of His sacrificial death. Guided by the Holy Spirit, they tell us that the Messiah who knew no sin was "made...to be sin," and He who was the beloved of the Father became "a curse" before Him.[18]

All of us have heard these truths before, but have we ever given them enough consideration to actually understand them and be broken by them? On the cross, the One declared "holy, holy, holy" by the seraphim choir, was "made" to be sin.[19] The journey into the meaning of this phrase seems almost too dangerous to take. We balk at the very first step. What does it mean that the One in whom "all the fullness of the Godhead bodily" dwell was made sin?[20] We must not explain the

---

14. Leviticus 16:10
15. Leviticus 16:21
16. 1 Peter 2:24; Hebrews 13:11–12
17. Psalm 103:12
18. 2 Corinthians 5:21; Galatians 3:13
19. Isaiah 6:2–3
20. Colossians 2:9

truth away in an attempt to protect the reputation of the Son of God, and yet we must be careful not to speak terrible things against His impeccable and immutable character. How was it that He was made sin? From the Scriptures we conclude that Christ was made sin in the same way that the believer "become[s] the righteousness of God" in Him.[21] In his second letter to the church in Corinth, the apostle Paul writes, "For He made Him who knew no sin to be sin for us, that we might become the righteousness of God in Him."[22]

In this present life, the believer is the "righteousness of God"—not because of some purifying work upon his character through which he becomes a perfectly righteous or sinless being, but rather as a result of imputation, by which he is considered righteous before God through the work of Christ on his behalf. In the same way, Christ was made sin not because of some moral degeneration in His character through which He actually became corrupt or unrighteous, but as a result of the imputation that made Him guilty before the judgment seat of God in our place. On the cross, Christ did not become sinful; rather our sins were imputed to Him, and God considered Him to be guilty of our crimes and treated Him with the judgment we deserved. He did not become sin by partaking in our corruption but by bearing our guilt. We must not forget that even while He bore our sins, He remained the unblemished and spotless Lamb of God, and His sacrifice was a fragrant aroma to His Father.[23]

We must be careful to understand that this truth does not diminish the horrifying nature of Christ being made sin on our behalf. Although it was an imputed guilt, it was real guilt, bringing unspeakable anguish to His soul. He truly stood in our place, bore our sin, carried our guilt, and experienced the full measure of the wrath of God that our sin deserved.

The great contrast between what He truly was and what He was "made" to be further reveals the agony Christ experienced. It is dreadful for the sinner to come face-to-face with his own sin and feel the weight of his own guilt. It is quite another thing for the "One who knew no sin" to bear a filth that was totally foreign to Him and to feel the guilt of a countless multitude of sinners. It is an unspeakable terror for the sinner to be treated as guilty before the bar of God, but it is quite another

---

21. I owe this thought to John Calvin and his commentary on 2 Corinthians 5:21.
22. 2 Corinthians 5:21
23. 1 Peter 1:19; Ephesians 5:2

thing for One who is "harmless, undefiled, separate from sinners" to be so treated.[24] It is one thing for the sinner to be condemned by a God with whom he has no relations and toward whom he possesses no affections. It is quite another thing for the beloved Son of God to be judged and condemned by His own Father, with whom He had shared the most intimate communion throughout eternity and toward whom He possessed a love beyond definition and measure.

THE CHRIST BECOMES A CURSE

That Christ was made sin is a truth as terrible as it is incomprehensible, and yet, just when we think that no darker words can be uttered against Him, the apostle Paul lights a lamp and takes us further down into the abyss of Christ's humiliation and forsakenness. We enter the deepest cavern to find the Son of God hanging from the cross and bearing His most infamous title: "Accursed of God"!

The Scriptures declare that all humankind lay under the curse of God for violating the precepts of divine law. As the apostle Paul writes to the church in Galatia: "Cursed is everyone who does not continue in all things which are written in the book of the law, to do them."[25] The word *cursed* comes from the Greek word *katára*, which denotes an execration, imprecation, or malediction. In the New Testament, it refers to the state of being under divine disapproval or reprobation leading to judgment and condemnation. The divine curse is the antonym of divine blessing; therefore, by using the Beatitudes as our standard, we can learn something of what it means to come under the curse of God.

The blessed are granted the kingdom of heaven. The cursed are refused entrance.

The blessed are recipients of divine comfort. The cursed are objects of divine wrath.

The blessed inherit the land. The cursed are cut off from it.

The blessed are satisfied. The cursed are miserable and wretched.

The blessed receive mercy. The cursed are condemned without pity.

The blessed shall see God. The cursed are cut off from His presence.

24. Hebrews 7:26
25. Galatians 3:10; Deuteronomy 27:26

The blessed are sons and daughters of God. The cursed are disowned in disgrace.[26]

From heaven's perspective, those who break God's law are vile and worthy of all loathing. They are a wretched lot, justly exposed to divine vengeance and rightly devoted to eternal destruction. It is not an exaggeration to say that the last thing that the accursed sinner should and will hear when he takes his first step into hell is all of creation standing to its feet and applauding God because He has rid the earth of him. Such is the vileness of those who break God's law, and such is the disdain of the holy towards the unholy.

Such language is a gross offense to the world and much of the contemporary evangelical community. Nevertheless, it is biblical language and it must be said. If for etiquette's sake we refuse to explain and illustrate the dark sayings of Scripture, then God will not be regarded as holy, men will not understand their dreadful predicament, and the price paid by Christ will never be calculated or appreciated. Unless we comprehend what it means for man to be under the divine curse, we will never comprehend what it meant for Christ to "become a curse for us." We will never fully understand the horror and beauty of what He did for us on that tree! "Christ has redeemed us from the curse of the law, having become a curse for us (for it is written, 'Cursed is everyone who hangs on a tree.')"[27]

The truth conveyed in Galatians 3:10 is what made Jesus Christ and His gospel such a scandal to the Jews of the first century. They were all familiar with the terrifying truth of Scripture that "he who is hanged is accursed of God."[28] How then could the Messiah be the Deliverer and King of Israel and yet die in such a degrading and accused fashion? To entertain such an idea was more than scandalous—it was outright blasphemy! Yet the Jews failed to see that it was an "exchanged curse" and that it was necessary for the Christ to become what they were in order to redeem them from what they deserved.[29] He became a worm and no man, the serpent lifted up in the wilderness, the scapegoat driven outside

---

26. paraphrase of Matthew 5:3–12
27. Galatians 3:13
28. Deuteronomy 21:23
29. Richard N. Longenecker, *Galatians*, vol. 41 of Word Biblical Commentary (Waco, Tex.: Word Books, 1990), 122–23.

the camp, the bearer of sin, and the One upon whom the curse of God did fall. And He did it all in the place of His people!

In Deuteronomy 27–28, God divided the nation of Israel into two separate camps, placing one on Mount Gerizim and the other on Mount Ebal. Those on Mount Gerizim were to pronounce the blessings that would come to all who diligently obey the Lord their God.[30] Those on Mount Ebal were to pronounce the curses that would fall upon all who refused such obedience.[31] Though Christ had every right to the blessings of Gerizim, it was from Mount Ebal that His own Father thundered against Him as He hung from Calvary's tree. From behind the closed doors of heaven, the Father crushed His only Son with every terror that should befall those for whom He died. When He raised His eyes to heaven to find God's countenance, His Father turned away. When He cried out, "My God, My God, why have you forsaken Me?" His Father, as His judge, replied, as it were, "The Lord, the Lord your God, damns you."[32] Christ bore the curses of Deuteronomy 28 for His people.

> The LORD will send on you cursing, confusion, and rebuke...until you are destroyed and until you perish quickly.[33]

> The LORD will strike you with madness and blindness and confusion of heart. And you shall grope at noonday, as a blind man gropes in darkness...and no one shall save you.[34]

> The LORD will rejoice over you to destroy you and bring you to nothing.[35]

> Cursed shall you be in the city, and cursed shall you be in the country.[36]

> Cursed shall you be when you come in, and cursed shall you be when you go out.[37]

---

30. Deuteronomy 28:1
31. Deuteronomy 28:15
32. I owe this thought to R.C. Sproul and his sermon on Galatians 3:13 preached at the 2008 Together for the Gospel Conference.
33. Deuteronomy 28:20
34. Deuteronomy 28:28–29
35. Deuteronomy 28:63
36. Deuteronomy 28:16
37. Deuteronomy 28:19

And your heavens which are over your head shall be bronze, and the earth which is under you shall be iron.[38]

And you shall become an astonishment, a proverb, and a byword among all nations where the LORD will drive you.[39]

Moreover all these curses shall come upon you and pursue and overtake you, until you are destroyed, because you did not obey the voice of the LORD your God, to keep His commandments and His statutes which He commanded you.[40]

As Christ bore our sin upon Calvary, He was cursed as a man who makes an idol and sets it up in secret.[41] He was cursed as one who dishonors his father or mother, who moves his neighbor's boundary mark, or misleads a blind person on the road.[42] He was cursed as one who distorts the justice due an alien, orphan, or widow.[43] He was cursed as one who is guilty of every manner of immorality and perversion, wounds his neighbor in secret, or accepts a bribe to strike down the innocent.[44] He was cursed as one who does not confirm the words of the law by doing them.[45] The sage of Proverbs wrote, "Like a flitting sparrow, like a flying swallow, so a curse without cause shall not alight."[46] However, the curse did alight upon the Branch, not because of some flaw in His character or error in His deeds, but because He bore the sins of His people and carried their iniquity before the judgment bar of God.[47] There He stood uncovered, unprotected, and vulnerable to every repercussion of divine judgment. David cried out, "Blessed is he whose transgression is forgiven, whose sin is covered. Blessed is the man to whom the LORD does not impute iniquity, and in whose spirit there is no deceit."[48] Yet on the cross, the sin imputed to Christ was exposed before God and the host of heavens. He was placarded before men and made a spectacle to angels

---

38. Deuteronomy 28:23
39. Deuteronomy 28:37
40. Deuteronomy 28:45
41. Deuteronoomy 27:15
42. Deuteronomy 27:16–18
43. Deuteronomy 27:19
44. Deuteronomy 27:20–25
45. Deuteronomy 27:26
46. Proverbs 26:2
47. Isaiah 11:1
48. Psalm 32:1–2

and devils alike.[49] The transgressions He bore were not forgiven Him, and the sins He carried were not covered. If a man is counted blessed because iniquity is not imputed to Him, then Christ was cursed beyond measure because the iniquity of us all fell upon Him.[50] For this reason, He was treated as the covenant breaker spoken of at the renewal of the Mosaic covenant in Moab:

> The LORD would not spare him; for then the anger of the LORD and His jealousy would burn against that man, and every curse that is written in this book would settle on him, and the LORD would blot out his name from under heaven. And the LORD would separate him from all the tribes of Israel for adversity, according to all the curses of the covenant that are written in this Book of the Law.[51]

At Calvary, the Messiah was singled out for adversity, and every curse written in the book of the law fell upon Him. In this Seed of Abraham, all the families of the earth are blessed, but only because He was cursed more than any man who ever walked upon the earth.[52] The book of Numbers contains one of the most beautiful promises of blessing that has ever been given by God to man. It is referred to as the priestly or Aaronic blessing: "The LORD bless you and keep you; the LORD make His face shine upon you, and be gracious to you; the LORD lift up His countenance upon you, and give you peace."[53] Though beautiful and gracious, this blessing presents us with a great theological and moral problem. How can a righteous God grant such blessing to a sinful people without compromising His righteousness? Again, we find the answer in the cross. The sinner can be blessed only because the Holy and Righteous One was cursed.[54] Any and every blessing from God that has ever been granted or ever will be granted to His people is only because, on the tree, Christ received the very opposite of this priestly blessing.[55] To us, it is said, "The Lord bless you," only because to Him it was said, "The Lord curse You, and give You over to destruction; the Lord take the light of His

---

49. Romans 3:25: "displayed publicly."
50. Isaiah 53:6
51. Deuteronomy 29:20–21
52. Genesis 12:3
53. Numbers 6:24–26
54. Acts 3:14
55. Numbers 6:22–27. I owe this thought to R. C. Sproul and his sermon on Galatians 3:13 preached at the 2008 Together for the Gospel Conference.

presence from You and condemn You; the Lord turn His face from You and fill You with misery."

The psalmist describes the blessed as those who are made joyful with gladness in God's presence, who know the joyful sound of the festal shout, and who walk in the light of His countenance.[56] For our sakes, Christ was made sorrowful with the absence of His Father's presence, He came to know the terrifying sound of judgment's trumpet, and He hung in the darkness of God's unbearable frowning countenance. Because of Adam's fateful choice, corruption and futility enslaved the entire creation as it groaned under the curse.[57] To liberate creation, the last Adam took upon Himself the sins of His people and groaned under the dreadful yoke: "Christ has redeemed us from the curse of the law, having become a curse for us."[58]

It is the greatest travesty that the true meaning of the Christ's "cry from the cross" has often been lost in romantic cliché. It is not uncommon to hear a preacher declare that the Father turned away from His Son because He could no longer bear to witness the suffering inflicted upon Him by the hands of wicked men. As we have learned, such interpretations are a complete distortion of the text and of what actually transpired on the cross. The Father did not turn away from His Son because He lacked the fortitude to witness His sufferings but because "He made Him who knew no sin to be sin for us, that we might become the righteousness of God in Him."[59] He laid our sins upon Him and turned away, for His eyes are too pure to approve evil and He cannot look upon wickedness with favor.[60]

It is not without good cause that many gospel tracts picture an infinite abyss or separation between a holy God and sinful man. With such an illustration, the Scriptures fully agree. As the prophet Isaiah cried out: "Behold, the LORD's hand is not shortened, that it cannot save; nor His ear heavy, that it cannot hear."[61] According to this text, and countless others, all men should live and die separated from the favorable presence of God and under divine wrath. For this reason, the Son of God stood in our place, bore our sin, and was "forsaken of God." For the breach to be

---

56. Psalms 21:6; 89:15
57. Romans 8:20–22
58. Galatians 3:13
59. 2 Corinthians 5:21
60. Isaiah 53:6; Habakkuk 1:13
61. Isaiah 59:1

closed and fellowship restored, "Ought not the Christ to have suffered these things and to enter into His glory?"[62]

CHRIST SUFFERS THE WRATH OF GOD

To obtain the salvation of His people, Christ suffered the terrifying abandonment of God, drank down the bitter cup of God's wrath, and died a bloody death in the place of His people. Only then could divine justice be satisfied, the wrath of God be appeased, and reconciliation be made possible.

In the garden, Christ prayed three times for the cup to be removed from Him, but each time His will submitted to that of His Father.[63] We must ask ourselves, what was in the cup that caused Him to pray so fervently? What terrible thing did it contain to cause Him such anguish that His sweat was mingled with blood?[64]

It is often said that the cup represented the cruel Roman cross and the physical torture that awaited Him—that Christ foresaw the cat-o'-nine-tails coming down across His back, the crown of thorns piercing His brow, and the primitive nails driven through His hands and feet. However, those who believe these things to be the source of His anguish do not understand the cross or what happened there. Although the tortures heaped upon Him by the hands of men were all part of God's redemptive plan, there was something much more ominous that evoked His cry for deliverance.

In the first centuries of the primitive church, thousands of Christians died on crosses. It is said that Nero crucified them upside down, covered them with tar, and set them aflame to provide streetlights for the city of Rome. Throughout the ages since then, a countless stream of Christians have experienced the most unspeakable tortures, and yet it is the testimony of friend and foe alike that many of them went to their deaths with great boldness. Are we to believe that the followers of the Messiah met such cruel physical death with joy unspeakable while the captain of their salvation cowered in a garden, fearing the same torture?[65] Did the Christ of God dread whips and thorns, crosses and spears, or did the cup represent a terror infinitely beyond the greatest cruelty of men?

---

62. Luke 24:26
63. Luke 22:41–44
64. Luke 22:44
65. Hebrews 2:10

To understand the ominous contents of the cup, we must refer to the Scriptures. There are two passages in particular that we must consider—one from the Psalms and the other from the Prophets: "For in the hand of the LORD there is a cup, and the wine is red; it is fully mixed, and He pours it out; surely its dregs shall all the wicked of the earth drain and drink down."[66] And, "For thus says the LORD God of Israel to me: 'Take this wine cup of fury from My hand, and cause all the nations, to whom I send you, to drink it. And they will drink and stagger and go mad because of the sword that I will send among them.'"[67]

As a result of the unceasing rebellion of the wicked, the justice of God had decreed judgment against them. He would rightly pour forth His indignation upon the nations. He would put the cup of the wine of His wrath to their mouths and force them to drink it down to the dregs.[68] The mere thought of such a fate awaiting the world is absolutely terrifying, yet this would have been the fate of all—except that the mercy of God sought for the salvation of a people, and the wisdom of God devised a plan of redemption even before the foundation of the world.[69] The Son of God would become a man and walk upon the earth in perfect obedience to the law of God. He would be like us in all things, tempted in all ways like us—but without sin.[70] He would live a perfectly righteous life for the glory of God and for the benefit of His people. Then at the appointed time, He would be crucified by the hands of wicked men, and on that cross He would bear His people's guilt and suffer the wrath of God against them. The true Son of Adam, who was also the true Son of God, would take the bitter cup of wrath from the very hand of God and drink it down to the dregs. He would drink until *it was finished*, and the justice of God was fully satisfied.[71] The divine wrath that should have been ours would be exhausted upon the Son, and by Him, it would be extinguished.

Imagine an immense dam that is filled to the brim and straining against the weight behind it. All at once, the protective wall breaks away and the massive destructive power of the deluge is unleashed. As certain destruction races towards a small village in the nearby valley, the ground

---

66. Psalm 75:8
67. Jeremiah 25:15–16
68. Dregs are the residue or sediment left at the bottom of the wine flask.
69. Matthew 25:34; Ephesians 1:4; 1 Peter 1:20; Revelation 13:8; 17:8
70. Hebrews 2:17; 4:15
71. John 19:30

suddenly opens up before it and drinks down that which would have carried it away. In similar fashion, the judgment of God was rightly racing toward every man. Escape could not be found on the highest hill or in the deepest abyss. The fleetest of foot could not outrun it, nor could the strongest swimmer endure its torrents. The dam was breached and nothing could repair its ruin. But when every human hope was exhausted, at the appointed time, the Son of God interposed Himself between divine justice and His people. He drank down the wrath that we ourselves had kindled and the punishment we deserved. When He died, not one drop of the former deluge remained. He drank it all on our behalf!

Imagine two giant millstones, one turning on top of the other. Imagine that caught between the two is a single grain of wheat pulled under the massive weight. First, the stones crush its hull beyond recognition, and then its inward parts pour out and are ground into dust. There is no hope of retrieval or reconstruction. All is lost and beyond repair. Thus, in a similar fashion, it pleased the Lord to crush His only Son and put Him to grief unspeakable.[72] Thus, it pleased the Son to submit to such suffering that God might be glorified and His people might be redeemed.

We should not think that God found some gleeful pleasure in the suffering of His beloved Son, but through His death, the will of God was accomplished. No other means had the power to put away sin, satisfy divine justice, and appease the wrath of God against us. Unless that divine grain of wheat had fallen to the ground and died, it would have abided alone without a people or a bride.[73] The pleasure was not found in the suffering, but in all that such suffering would accomplish: God would be revealed in a glory yet unknown to men or angels, and a people would be brought into unhindered fellowship with their God.

The beloved Puritan writer John Flavel once wrote a dialogue between the Father and the Son regarding fallen humanity and the great price that would be required to obtain our redemption. It beautifully illustrates the true agony of the cross and the love of the Father and the Son which moved them to embrace it. Flavel writes:

Here you may suppose the Father to say, when driving His bargain with Christ for you—

72. Isaiah 53:10
73. John 12:24

Father: My Son, here is a company of poor miserable souls, that have utterly undone themselves, and now lie open to my justice! Justice demands satisfaction for them, or will satisfy itself in the eternal ruin of them: What shall be done for these souls?

And thus Christ returns.

Son: O my Father, such is my love to, and pity for them, that rather than they shall perish eternally, I will be responsible for them as their Surety; bring in all thy bills, that I may see what they owe Thee; Lord, bring them all in, that there may be no after-reckonings with them; at my hand shall thou require it. I will rather choose to suffer their wrath than they should suffer it: upon me, my Father, upon me be all their debt.

Father: But, my Son, if thou undertake for them, thou must reckon to pay the last mite, expect no abatements; if I spare them, I will not spare thee.

Son: Content, Father, let it be so; charge it all upon me, I am able to discharge it: and though it prove a kind of undoing to me, though it impoverish all my riches, empty all my treasures, yet I am content to undertake it![74]

People sometimes think and even preach that the Father looked down from heaven, witnessed the suffering that was heaped upon His Son by the hands of men, and counted such affliction as payment for our sins. This is heresy of the worst kind. Christ satisfied divine justice not merely by enduring the affliction of men but by enduring the wrath of God. It takes more than crosses, nails, crowns of thorns, and lances to pay for sin. The believer is saved—not simply because of what men did to Christ on the cross, but because of what God did to Him: He crushed Him under the full force of His wrath against us.[75] Rarely does our gospel preaching make this truth clear enough.

GOD WILL PROVIDE

In one of the most epic narratives in the Old Testament, God commands the patriarch Abraham to carry his son Isaac to Mount Moriah and to

---

74. John Flavel, *The Fountain of Life: A Display of Christ in His Essential and Mediatorial Glory*, in *The Works of John Flavel* (London: Banner of Truth, 1968), 1:61.

75. Isaiah 53:10

offer him as a sacrifice there. "Then He said, 'Take now *your son, your only son Isaac, whom you love,* and go to the land of Moriah, and offer him there as a burnt offering on one of the mountains of which I shall tell you.'"[76]

What a burden Abraham carried! We cannot even begin to imagine the sadness that filled the old man's heart and tortured him every step of his journey. The Scriptures are careful to tell us that he was commanded to offer "your son, your only son Isaac, whom you love." The specificity of the language seems designed to catch our attention and make us think that there is more meaning hidden in these words than what first glance can tell. This man and this boy are simply types, or shadows, of a greater Father, a greater Son, and a greater sacrifice!

On the third day, the two reached the appointed place, and the father bound his beloved son with his own hands. Finally, in submission to what must be done, he laid his hand upon his boy's brow and "took the knife to slay him."[77] At that very moment, the mercy of God intervened, and the old man's hand was stayed. God called out to him from heaven and said: "Abraham, Abraham!… Do not lay your hand on the lad, or do anything to him; for now I know that you fear God, since you have not withheld your son, your only son, from Me."[78]

At the sound of the Lord's voice, Abraham raised his eyes and found a ram caught in the thicket by its horns. He took the ram and offered it up in the place of his son.[79] He then named that place *YHWH-jireh* or "The-Lord-Will-Provide." Thus, it is a faithful saying that remains until this day: "In the Mount of the LORD it shall be provided."[80]

As the curtains draw to a close on this epic moment in history, not only Abraham but also everyone who has ever read this account breathes a sigh of relief that the boy is spared. We think to ourselves, "What a beautiful ending to the story," but it was not an ending—it was a mere intermission!

Two thousand years later, the curtain opens again. The background is dark and ominous. The Son of God is on center stage at Mount Calvary. Loving obedience binds Him to the will of His Father. He hangs there bearing the sin of His people. He is accursed—betrayed by His

---

76. Genesis 22:2, emphasis added
77. Genesis 22:10
78. Genesis 22:11–12
79. Genesis 22:13
80. Genesis 22:14

creation and forsaken of God.[81] Then the horrifying thunder of God's wrath breaks the silence. The Father takes the knife, draws back His arm, and slays "His Son, His only Son, whom He loves," fulfilling the words of Isaiah the prophet: "Surely He has borne our griefs and carried our sorrows; yet we esteemed Him stricken, smitten by God, and afflicted. But He was wounded for our transgressions, He was bruised for our iniquities; the chastisement for our peace was upon Him, and by His stripes we are healed…. Yet it pleased the LORD to bruise Him; He has put Him to grief."[82]

The curtain draws to a close on a slain Son, a crucified Messiah, in order to open for hell-worthy sinners. Unlike the account of Isaac, there was no ram to die in His place. He is the Lamb who died for the sins of the world.[83] He is God's provision for the redemption of His people. He is the fulfillment of that which Isaac and the ram only foreshadowed. In Him, that dreadful Mount called Golgotha is now renamed *YHWH-jireh* or "The Lord will provide." And it is a faithful saying that remains until this day: "In the Mount of the LORD it shall be provided."[84]

Calvary is the mount, and salvation is the provision. God once called out to Abraham: "Abraham, Abraham!… Now I know that you fear God, since you have not withheld your son, your only son, from Me."[85] Those of us who believe now cry out to God with a similar prose: "God, my God, now I know that You love me since You have not withheld Your Son, Your only Son, whom You love, from me."[86]

The Messiah is dead, but it is still not the end. One more scene remains…a resurrection and a great coronation!

---

81. John 1:11; Acts 3:14; Matthew 27:46
82. Isaiah 53:4–5, 10
83. John 1:29
84. Genesis 22:14
85. Genesis 22:11–12
86. Genesis 22:12; Romans 8:32

CHAPTER TWENTY-ONE

The Vindication of God

Whom God set forth as a propitiation by His blood, through faith, to demonstrate His righteousness, because in His forbearance God had passed over the sins that were previously committed, to demonstrate at the present time His righteousness, that He might be just and the justifier of the one who has faith in Jesus.
                                                      —Romans 3:25–26

The very beginning of Romans 3:25–26 tells us that it was God's will to set forth, to publicly display, or placard, His Son on the cross of Calvary. As we have already stated, at the precise moment in history, God raised Him up on a tree at the very crossroads of the religious center of the universe for all to see.[1] According to our text, God chose this most public place for the sacrifice of His Son so that He might vindicate Himself by demonstrating once and for all that He is a righteous God. Yet we must ask, why was such a vindication necessary?[2] The text above sets the reason before us: "because in His forbearance God had passed over the sins that were previously committed."[3]

According to the apostle Paul, it was necessary that God vindicate Himself, or prove His righteousness, because in His forbearance He had passed over the sins of His people and not administered the justice or punishment that was due them. Throughout human history, He had shown grace and granted forgiveness to a countless multitude of men He had called from the world and declared to be His people. However, in doing so, He had opened Himself up to multiple accusations of injustice:

---

1. Galatians 4:4
2. *Webster's Dictionary* defines *vindication* as the defense of anything; a justification against denial or censure, or against objections or accusations.
3. Romans 3:25

How can a righteous God grant forgiveness to the wicked, and how can a truly holy God call them into fellowship with Himself? If God is righteous, why did He not administer justice? On what basis did He grant forgiveness to that great multitude of Old Testament saints? It is the clear testimony of the Scriptures that the ancient bloody sacrifices of bulls and goats had no power to take away sin.[4] How then, could God forgive them? Does His forbearance of their sin prove that He is not righteous? Does it demonstrate that He is so apathetic toward evil that He can pass over sin with a nod or grant forgiveness on a whim? Has the God of heaven compromised His justice by granting pardon to those who should justly be condemned?[5] Shall not the Judge of all the earth do right?[6]

The cross of Calvary provides the answer to all these questions. There, God laid the sins of His people upon the head of His only Son. There, the justice of God that was due the people of God in all ages—past, present, and future—was poured out upon Jesus of Nazareth. From the first man pardoned in the Old Testament dispensation to the last man forgiven at the very ending of the world, they all owe their pardon to the fact that Christ died for their sins. Through the cross, it is as though God declares to His accusers:

> Do you question how I could call forth a people even from the wicked antediluvian age and claim them as Mine? Do you demand an explanation because I spared Noah, when in reality he too should have died in the flood? Do you call Me to account because I called pagan Abram from that vile city of Ur, credited righteousness to him, and made him My friend? Do you wonder because I saved a remnant from the nation of Israel and embraced them as my special treasure even though their sins called for their rejection? Do you endeavor to know how I could forgive the multitude of David's sins and call him My son?
>
> Your accusations have gone on long enough. I have now answered you in the cross of My beloved Son, who was destined to die for the sins of My people even before the foundation of the world. Throughout the long ages of my forbearance, My eye was fixed upon that tree where He would suffer for them. Everything I have done for them in the past was based upon what My Son has

4. Hebrews 10:4
5. Proverbs 17:15
6. Genesis 18:25

done for them now. Yes, I have freely pardoned a great multitude of wicked men, their lawless deeds I forgave, their sins I covered, and their transgressions I did not take into account, but it was because I had determined to satisfy every demand of justice against them through the atoning work of my beloved Son!"

The cross of Calvary stops every mouth and shows every accusation against God to be false. On that tree, He condemned the sins of His people with perfect justice and atoned for their crimes with a love that cannot be measured. On that altar of wood, "mercy and truth have met together; righteousness and peace have kissed."[7] God has vindicated Himself. He has proven to be both just and the justifier of the one who has faith in Jesus Christ.[8] The cross abolishes any uncertainties regarding His righteousness or intolerance toward sin. The cross proves that any doubts regarding His love are unfounded and should no longer be entertained in the hearts of His people.

GOD HAS PROVEN HIS HATRED OF SIN

There are countless passages in the Old and New Testaments that demonstrate the hatred of God toward sin and the reality of His wrath toward the wicked. However, the greatest demonstration of God's hatred and holy violence against any form of unrighteousness is found in the cross of His dear Son. How much does God hate sin, and what will be His reaction against it? His hatred of sin is such that when His own Son bore our sin, He crushed Him and did not spare Him, but graciously gave Him up.

In the midst of all the evangelical romanticism surrounding the cross of Christ, we have forgotten (if we ever even knew) that Calvary was terrifying! It was an unspeakable horror beyond description. The nails that held the feet and hands to post and beam; the crown of twisted thorns gouging the brow; the broad, crude lance buried in the side; the brutal treatment of the body by wicked and disgusting men—these things were not even the beginnings of the horror that occurred upon that skull-shaped hill called Golgotha.[9] Instead, they were only the backdrop of a

7. Psalm 85:10

8. Romans 3:26

9. The name *Golgotha* is of Aramaic origin and is translated *skull*. It is the name of the place outside of Jerusalem where Jesus was crucified. It was given this name because it bore the shape of a skull.

much greater terror. It was not the will of a man that blotted out the sun and made the day as dark as pitch.[10] It was not the power of the Roman army that shook the earth and split the rocks into pieces like dry clods of clay.[11] It was the wrath of Almighty God focused in its full strength upon His only begotten Son! Compared to the measure of divine wrath that was poured out on Christ, the great deluge in the day of Noah was like a drop of dew on a blade of grass, and the fire that fell from heaven upon Sodom and Gomorrah was a harmless spark that could not have kindled the driest wood. The day of Calvary was a day of wrath, a day of trouble and distress, a day of destruction and desolation, a day of darkness and gloom.[12] On that day, the consuming fire and continual burning of the Almighty fell from heaven upon Christ.[13] On that tree, God blew upon Him with the fire of His wrath that melts mountains like wax before a flame and like water rushing down a steep slope.[14] For this reason, Christ cried out: "I am poured out like water, and all My bones are out of joint; my heart is like wax; it has melted within Me."[15]

The Lord Jesus Christ was singled out for adversity from the vast multitude of humanity, and every curse written in the law was made to rest upon Him. As He hung upon the cross, the full measure of divine wrath against the people of God was focused upon Him alone, and the full measure of God's anger burned against Him.[16]

How much does God hate sin? When His own Son bore our sin, God crushed Him. In light of this terrible truth, we should be careful to heed the warnings of the writer of Hebrews, "How shall we escape if we neglect so great a salvation?"[17] If we go on rejecting the gospel after having received a right knowledge of it, there no longer remains for us a sacrifice for sin. We can search through heaven and earth until they both pass away, but we will find no other remedy for our sin, no other medium for cleansing, and no other name by which we might be saved.[18] What we will find is a terrifying expectation of judgment and the fury of a fire that

---

10. Luke 23:44–45
11. Matthew 27:51
12. Zephaniah 1:15
13. Isaiah 33:14
14. Ezekiel 22:18–22; Micah 1:4; Nahum 1:4
15. Psalm 22:14
16. Deuteronomy 29:20–21
17. Hebrews 2:3
18. Acts 4:12

will consume us as adversaries. The Scriptures warn that anyone who has set aside the law of Moses will die without mercy. How much more severe will the punishment be for neglecting Christ and His sacrifice? Though we do not see our apathy and unbelief to be a great crime, God sees it differently. In His estimation, we have trampled His Son underfoot, regarded the blood He shed as unclean, and insulted the Spirit of grace who made these things known to us. For this reason, He warns, "Vengeance is Mine" and "I will repay." For this reason, we must hold to the gospel and plead with all men to repent and turn to Christ before it is too late. For it is a "fearful thing to fall into the hands of the living God."[19]

GOD HAS PROVEN HIS LOVE FOR HIS PEOPLE

If the sinner ever doubts the righteousness of God, he only needs to look to the cross. However, it is equally true that if the Christian ever doubts the love of God, he only needs to look to the same tree. There, our salvation was accomplished.[20] There, the enmity was removed and peace was made with God.[21] There, God proved His love for His people in a way that puts an end to doubt forever! For this reason, the apostle John writes: "In this the love of God was manifested toward us, that God has sent His only begotten Son into the world, that we might live through Him. In this is love, not that we loved God, but that He loved us and sent His Son to be the propitiation for our sins."[22]

From John's pen, we understand that the greatest manifestation of the love of God toward His people is that He sent His Son to be a propitiation for their sins.[23] This singular act reveals both the character and the magnitude of the love of God in an unprecedented manner. On the cross, the Father proved His love toward us in that He caused the iniquity of us all to fall upon His beloved Son and crushed Him under the divine wrath that should have been ours.[24] On the cross, the Spirit proved His love toward us in that He orchestrated and directed all that was necessary for

---

19. This paragraph is adapted from Hebrews 10:26–31.
20. John 19:30
21. Romans 5:1
22. 1 John 4:9–10
23. Translated from the Greek noun *hilasmos,* which denotes an appeasing or propitiating; the means of appeasing or a propitiation.
24. Isaiah 53:4–10

the Son's execution.[25] On the cross, the Son proved His love toward us in that He laid down His life for His friends.[26] For though He was rich, yet for our sake, He became poor—so that we, through His poverty, might become rich.[27] For though He existed in the form of God, He emptied Himself, taking the form of a bond servant, and He humbled Himself by becoming obedient to the point of death, even death on a cross.[28] For though He knew no sin, He bore our sin and became a curse for us—for it is written, "Cursed is everyone who hangs on a tree."[29]

The terrible cost that an infinitely good God paid for our sins should move us to mourning and the rending of our hearts. As the prophet Zechariah foretold, we look upon Him whom we have pierced, and we mourn for Him, as one mourns for an only son, and we weep bitterly over Him like the bitter weeping for a firstborn.[30] Yet at the same time, God is able to take the dark strokes of the cross and paint His most beautiful picture. At Calvary, He reveals His love to men and angels in a way that transcends the beauty and power of all other revelations combined. Our sin and the incomprehensible sufferings of Christ on our behalf act as a pitch-black night against which the stars of God's mercy and grace shine in the most glorious manner possible.

If the value of a gift demonstrates love, then Calvary proves that God's love for His people cannot be calculated. Who can measure the worth of Christ? It would be easier to count the stars in the heavens and every grain of sand in the sea. His value is infinitely greater than all of creation combined. Who can measure the love of the Father for the Son? Although the world disdains the Son, and even His own people do not properly esteem Him, He is chosen by God and precious in His sight.[31] Men and angels cannot comprehend the worth that the Father ascribes to Him and the esteem that He has for Him. The Son has always been the Father's Beloved in whom He was well pleased.[32] He has always been His

---

25. The Holy Spirit orchestrated all that was necessary for our redemption, from Christ's conception (Luke 1:35; Matthew 1:20) to His crucifixion at the hands of godless men (Acts 2:23).

26. John 15:13

27. 2 Corinthians 8:9

28. Philippians 2:6–8

29. Galatians 3:13; 2 Corinthians 5:21; Deuteronomy 21:23

30. Zechariah 12:10

31. 1 Peter 2:4

32. Matthew 3:17; 17:5; Mark 1:11; 9:7; Luke 3:22

supreme delight.[33] Therefore, when the Father gave His Son, He gave us everything and withheld nothing.

God's love, manifested in the giving of His Son as a propitiation for our sins, is even further magnified when we realize that this love is entirely unmerited. It comes forth from the character and purpose of God and is entirely independent of the virtue and merit of His people. He does not love us *because of us*, but *in spite of us*. The apostle John writes: "In this is love, *not that we loved God,* but that He loved us and sent His Son to be the propitiation for our sins."[34]

God's love is not a response to us; rather, it is contrary to all that we deserve. He loves us even though we possess no virtue or merit to earn or obligate such love.[35] He loves us even though we have been hostile to Him in mind and deed.[36] He loves us even though we have hated Him without a cause![37]

It is this aspect of God's love that most captivated the heart of the apostle Paul and should captivate ours. Paul considered himself the foremost of sinners, a blasphemer, and a violent aggressor of the church.[38] Therefore, the only explanation he could find for Christ's death on his behalf was the unmerited love of God. It was a love from which he could not free himself. It constrained him, obliged him, drove him, and prevailed upon him in every way.[39] The unmerited nature of God's love was the great theme of his heart, and he labored with the greatest intent to make it known to all men. He knew that the love of God could only be comprehended and appreciated to the degree that we understand how undeserving we are of that love. For this reason, he wrote to the church in Rome: "For scarcely for a righteous man will one die; yet perhaps for a good man someone would even dare to die. But God demonstrates His own love toward us, in that while we were still sinners, Christ died for us."[40]

As we learn to calculate more accurately the Father's love for the Son and the magnitude of our sins against God, we can begin to decipher

33. Proverbs 8:30
34. 1 John 4:10, emphasis added
35. Isaiah 64:6
36. Romans 8:7; Colossians 1:21
37. Romans 1:30; John 15:25
38. 1 Corinthians 15:9; 1 Timothy 1:13–15
39. 2 Corinthians 5:14–15
40. Romans 5:7–8

the Father's love toward us. It must be immense beyond measure if He gave His only Son to us while we deserved nothing but His wrath. If the Father had given us a thousand perfect worlds for each day of eternity, the combined worth of these gifts would not compare to the singular gift of His Son. They would not reflect even a fraction of the love that was manifested when He gave His Son as a propitiation for our sins! If we think this is hyperbole or even the slightest exaggeration, we are blind to the glories of Christ and do not understand His worth. In the words of John Flavel:

> But let me tell you, the whole world is not a theatre large enough to show the glory of Christ upon, or unfold the one half of the unsearchable riches that lie hid in Him. These things will be far better understood, and spoken of in heaven, by the noon-day divinity, in which the immediately illuminated assembly do there preach his praises, than by such a stammering tongue, and scribbling pen as mine, which doth but mar them. Alas! I write his praises but by moon-light; I cannot praise him so much as by halves. Indeed, no tongue but his own (as Nazianzen said of Bazil) is sufficient to undertake that task. What shall I say of Christ? The excelling glory of that object dazzles all apprehension, swallows up all expression. When we have borrowed metaphors from every creature that hast any excellency of lovely property in it, till we have stripped the whole of creation bare of all its ornament, and clothed Christ with all that glory; when we have even worn out our tongues, in ascribing praises to him, alas! We have done nothing, when all is done.[41]

---

41. Flavel, *The Fountain of Life Opened Up*, 1:xviii.

CHAPTER TWENTY-TWO

The Resurrection of Jesus Christ

Why do you seek the living among the dead? He is not here, but is risen!
—Luke 24:5–6

And declared to be the Son of God with power according to the Spirit of holiness.
—Romans 1:4

Who was delivered up because of our offenses, and was raised because of our justification.
—Romans 4:25

In chapter 21, the curtains closed on the Son of God with His execution on a Roman cross. He had carried the sins of His people, suffered the wrath of God, and given up His spirit.[1] But this was not the end. We join with the primitive Christians of centuries past in joyfully and confidently proclaiming: "He has risen! He has risen indeed!"

The historical resurrection of Jesus Christ is one of the great pillars of the Christian faith. Without belief in this fact, a person is not a Christian. Without proclaiming this fact, the gospel has not been preached. Therefore, any preacher, theologian, scribe, or so-called prophet who does not hold unwaveringly to the physical, historical resurrection of Jesus has nothing to say to the church. We need not learn from them, understand them, or bring them into fellowship. They are not Christian.

There may have been a golden age in Christianity when there was no need to give such stern warnings regarding Christ's resurrection, but sadly, that is no longer the case. The resurrection stands on the frontlines of the gospel war and receives the greatest force of the enemy's

---

1. Luke 23:46

onslaught. The devil rightly understands that the whole of Christianity rises or falls upon this one doctrine.[2] Therefore, his primary goal is its denial. If this cannot be achieved, the enemy is content when those who seek to be more ecumenical treat the resurrection as a nonessential, and he also likes to see those who truly believe neglect the resurrection in their gospel proclamation.

The great doctrines of Christianity have always been under attack from all sides, and the resurrection is no exception. However, the uniqueness of our age is that the most dangerous attacks now come from those who claim to be thoroughly Christian and even evangelical. They do not deny the resurrection outright, and they may even strongly affirm it for themselves. But they do not require such conviction of others, nor do they hold it to be an essential doctrine for entrance into Christianity. They have chosen a false form of tolerance over truth and a twisted compassion for humanity over the fear of God and fidelity to the Scriptures. Like Judas, they kiss the Savior under the pretense of homage, and yet they betray Him.[3]

Denying Christ's resurrection—or even treating it as a nonessential—devastates genuine Christianity. However, those of us who believe the doctrine and seek to faithfully proclaim the gospel can also practice something of a lesser evil: neglecting to give the resurrection its rightful place in our preaching. This great doctrine is not something that we should merely tag on to the end of a lengthy sermon on the cross, but it should be given equal prominence with the cross. A thorough survey of the apostles' preaching in the book of Acts will demonstrate that the resurrection of Jesus Christ was the primary theme of their gospel. It was not a message brought out of the closet one Sunday a year at Easter. It was the unrelenting victory chant of the early church!

It is important to keep in mind that the debate that rages around Christianity and the gospel is not the historicity of the death of Christ. Only the pseudo-intellectual fraught with postmodern delirium who is oblivious to the historical method would deny that there was a man named Jesus of Nazareth who lived in Palestine and died under the reign of Pontius Pilate. The dispute occurs concerning the resurrection. Thus, the resurrection is just as much a scandal as the cross and must

---

2. 1 Corinthians 15:14
3. Matthew 26:49–50

be proclaimed with equal thoroughness and intensity. If we will give greater emphasis to the proclamation of the resurrection, we will have a more biblical gospel and will witness a greater demonstration of the gospel's power.

THE BIBLICAL ACCOUNT

Before we consider the exact meaning and significance of Christ's resurrection, it will be helpful to have at least a general understanding of the historical account as Scripture reveals it to us.

It is early morning on the third day. The women make their way timidly to the garden where the body of Christ has been entombed. Theirs is not an errand of hope but of pity. Their only desire is to honor the body of their beloved Jesus with a proper burial. Their conversation is limited to what would become a minor technicality: "'Who will roll away the stone?'... For it was very large."[4] Resurrection is the farthest thing from their minds.

However, pity turns to fear; fear to hope unquenchable; and hope to joy unspeakable, full of glory. They find a displaced stone, an opened door, an empty tomb, and an angelic proclamation of good news: "Why do you seek the living among the dead? He is not here, but is risen! Remember how He spoke to you when He was still in Galilee, saying, 'The Son of Man must be delivered into the hands of sinful men, and be crucified, and the third day rise again.'"[5]

The women quickly depart from the tomb "with fear and great joy." They run to bring His disciples the word, but their testimony appears as idle talk and nonsense to the very ones who should have believed them.[6] Then, hoping against hope, Peter and John run to the empty tomb. After a brief and perplexing investigation, they return to the others without a sure word: "For as yet they did not know the Scripture, that He must rise again from the dead."[7]

In their quick departure, they leave behind the weeping Mary Magdalene who becomes the first to see the risen Lord. He commissions her to return once more to the unbelieving disciples with still another

---

4. Mark 16:2–4
5. Luke 24:5–8
6. Luke 24:11
7. John 20:9

confirmation of His resurrection.[8] This is followed by a second appearing to the women returning from the tomb, and then by a third to Cleopas and another disciple on the road to Emmaus.[9] Finally, Jesus appears to Peter, and then to the Eleven.[10] He even appears to His unbelieving half brother James in an encounter that so alters James, he becomes part of the apostolic band and a pillar in the church of Jerusalem.[11] Finally, He appears "as by one born out of due time" to Saul of Tarsus on the road to Damascus.[12] It is unnecessary to write about this encounter or the effect of it. The very man who had pledged himself to the destruction of Christianity becomes its most ardent propagator and defender.[13] In summary, we have the sure word of Scripture that before His ascension, our Lord appeared to a great number of witnesses, to individuals and was seen "by over five hundred brethren at once."[14]

THE UNIQUENESS OF CHRIST'S RESURRECTION

All too often, men use terminology that they are unable to define and do not fully understand. This is very dangerous, especially for Christians who are called to live by the will of God that has been revealed to them in words. This is particularly true with regard to the work of Christ and the resurrection. What does it truly mean?

The English word *resurrection* is derived from the Latin verb *resurgere* (*re*: again; *surgere*: to rise). The New Testament word is translated from the Greek noun *anástasis* (*ana*: up, again; *stasis*: stand). Thus, the word literally means to stand up or rise again. In both ancient and modern literature, the word describes a dead being coming back to life. However, when applied to Christ, the term takes on a meaning unique to Him.

It is absolutely essential that we recognize that Christ's resurrection was not a mere revivification. In the Old Testament, the son of the widow of Zarephath and the Shunammite's son were raised to life by the power of God working through the prophets Elijah and Elisha.[15] The

---

8. John 20:11–18
9. Matthew 28:9–10; Luke 24:13–32
10. Luke 24:34–43
11. 1 Corinthians 15:7; Acts 1:14; 15:13
12. 1 Corinthians 15:8; Acts 9:3–19
13. Acts 9:1–2; 1 Corinthians 15:10
14. 1 Corinthians 15:6
15. 1 Kings 17:17–24; 2 Kings 4:18–37

New Testament teaches that Lazarus was raised from the dead, as well as Jairus's daughter, a young boy, Tabitha, and Eutychus.[16] However, although they were truly revived from the dead, they were still subject to death. As Paul explained to the church in Corinth, their bodies were still mortal and perishable.[17] They would once again die and be subject to the dishonor of the grave.

Christ's resurrection was unique in that He was raised from the dead never to die again. As He declared to John on the Isle of Patmos: "I am He who lives, and was dead, and behold, I am alive forevermore."[18] In his letter to the church in Rome, Paul set forth this truth with the greatest clarity: "Knowing that Christ, having been raised from the dead, dies no more. Death no longer has dominion over Him. For the death that He died, He died to sin once for all; but the life that He lives, He lives to God."[19]

An equally powerful truth that demonstrates the uniqueness of Christ's resurrection is that He was raised by His own authority and power. Although the Scriptures teach that the resurrection was equally a work of the Father and the Holy Spirit, it is also attributed to Christ Himself.[20] When asked for a sign proving His authority to cleanse the temple, Jesus responded, "Destroy this temple, and in three days I will raise it up."[21] He declared to the Pharisees, "I lay it down of Myself. I have power to lay it down, and I have power to take it again."[22]

The resurrection of Jesus Christ was unique to Him. It was not a mere revivification that would only extend life until the next bout with death. Rather, He has triumphed over death, hell, and the grave. He lives to die no more!

THE RESURRECTION AS A VINDICATION OF CHRIST

We have surveyed the historical account of Christ's resurrection and considered its uniqueness. Now we will turn our attention toward its significance. Although the subject is far-reaching and worthy of several

16. John 11:23–25, 43; Mark 5:41–42; Luke 7:14–15; Acts 9:36–43; 20:7–12
17. 1 Corinthians 15:53
18. Revelation 1:18
19. Romans 6:9–10
20. Romans 6:4; Galatians 1:1; Romans 1:4; 8:11
21. John 2:19
22. John 10:18

volumes, we will consider only two of its most important implications: the resurrection vindicated Christ, and it confirmed our faith.

In previous chapters, we learned that the death of Christ vindicated God from any accusation of injustice for His past forbearance and justification of the wicked.[23] In the following, we will discover that God also vindicated Jesus by raising Him from the dead. Through the resurrection, God publicly and powerfully declared Jesus to be the Son of God and the promised Messiah of Israel. The empty tomb was, and remains to this day, a sign to the world of Jesus' divine sonship. The apostle Paul wrote to the church in Rome that Jesus was "declared to be the Son of God with power according to the Spirit of holiness, by the resurrection from the dead."[24] The word *declared* comes from the Greek word *horízo*, which means to determine, establish, appoint, designate, or mark out. The word does not suggest that Christ became or was first appointed the Son of God at the resurrection, but rather that He was publicly and irrefutably marked out to be the Son of God by this miraculous event.

The Father had affirmed the divine sonship of Jesus throughout the full course of His ministry by the miracles He worked in His Father's name, by an audible voice from heaven at His baptism, and even by His transfiguration in the presence of Peter, James, and John.[25] However, none of these compare to the great and final declaration of sonship that occurred when the Father raised His dearly Beloved from the dead. Through the empty tomb, He was declared the Son of God in a "mighty, striking, and triumphant manner."[26] Regarding the use and meaning of the word *horízo*, John MacArthur writes, "The Greek word, from which the English word 'horizon' comes, means 'to distinguish.' Just as the horizon serves as a clear demarcation line, dividing earth and sky, the resurrection of Jesus Christ clearly divides Him from the rest of humanity, providing irrefutable evidence that He is the Son of God."[27]

To view Christ's resurrection as the great proof or sign of both His sonship and messiahship is not a foreign theme to the gospels. When

---

23. Romans 3:25–26

24. Romans 1:4

25. John 10:37–38; Matthew 3:17; 17:5

26. Marvin Richardson Vincent, *Word Studies in the New Testament* (Peabody, Mass.: Hendrickson), 3:4.

27. *The MacArthur Study Bible: New King James Version* (Nashville: Word Bibles, 1997), 1691.

the unbelieving Jews asked Jesus for a sign or proof of His authority to cleanse the temple, He pointed to His future resurrection: "Destroy this temple, and in three days I will raise it up."[28] When the scribes and Pharisees asked Him for further proof of His messiahship, He again pointed to His power over death: "For as Jonah was three days and three nights in the belly of the great fish, so will the Son of Man be three days and three nights in the heart of the earth."[29]

The resurrection of Jesus is that one great and invincible proof of who He is and what He has accomplished on behalf of His people. It is Christ's great vindication even before His enemies. The scribes dismissed Jesus as a man who had not studied, the rulers spurned Him as a misfit prophet from Galilee, and the Pharisees derided Him as an associate of Beelzebub and a friend of sinners.[30] However, all their assaults came to nothing and their argument fell apart when the One they crucified was "declared to be the Son of God with power according to the Spirit of holiness, by the resurrection from the dead."[31] The soldiers mocked Jesus on His way to Calvary saying, "Hail, King of the Jews!"[32] But they shook with fear and became as dead men when the angel rolled the stone away.[33] The chief priests, scribes, and elders heaped insults upon Him saying, "He saved others; Himself He cannot save."[34] But they stood in awe when He saved three thousand on the day of Pentecost.[35] They cut Him with their tongues in His darkest hour, saying, "If He is the King of Israel, let Him now come down from the cross, and we will believe Him."[36] But they trembled when the fisherman, empowered by the resurrection of his Lord, declared to them: "Therefore let all the house of Israel know assuredly that God has made this Jesus, whom you crucified, both Lord and Christ."[37]

---

28. John 2:19
29. Matthew 12:40
30. John 7:15, 52; Mark 3:22; Matthew 11:19; Luke 7:34
31. Romans 1:4
32. Matthew 27:29
33. Matthew 28:4
34. Matthew 27:42
35. Acts 2:41
36. Matthew 27:42
37. Acts 2:36

THE RESURRECTION AS A CONFIRMATION OF OUR FAITH

The empty tomb was not only a vindication of Jesus Christ before the world, but it was also a confirmation of the Christian's faith. The fact that God raised Him from the dead is proof that God has accepted His atoning sacrifice for the sins of His people. The apostle Paul described this to the church in Rome: "[He] was delivered up because of our offenses, and was raised because of our justification."[38] The key to understanding this text is found in the repetition of the Greek preposition *día*, which is accurately translated "because." Christ was handed over to death *because* He bore our transgressions, and God raised Him from the dead *because* He accepted His death as the atoning sacrifice for our sins. Therefore, Christ's resurrection is the confirmation that the sins of His people have been atoned for and their justification secured. Thomas Schreiner writes: "To say that Jesus was raised because of our justification is to say that His resurrection authenticates and confirms that our justification has been secured. The resurrection of Christ constitutes evidence that His work on our behalf has been completed."[39]

It is important to note that Christ was not raised so that we *would be* justified or because the atonement was not accomplished on the cross. According to Christ's own words His redemptive work on behalf of His people "was finished" at the moment of His death.[40] Nor were we justified the moment Christ was raised. The Scriptures clearly teach that justification is granted to a person the moment that he or she believes—we are justified by a personal faith in the person and work of Christ.[41] This text teaches that Christ was raised because He truly is the Messiah and His death was accepted by God as payment for the sins of His people. In the resurrection we have the divine pledge that by faith in His sacrifice we are justified before God.

God raised Jesus of Nazareth from the dead because He was exactly who He said He was, and His death accomplished exactly what He said it would. Christ vindicated His Father when He died upon Calvary and proved that the God who justifies the wicked is just beyond all reproach. The Father vindicated His Son when He raised Him from the dead and

---

38. Romans 4:25
39. Thomas R. Schreiner, *Romans: Baker Exegetical Commentary on the New Testament* (Grand Rapids: Baker Books, 1998), 244.
40. John 19:30
41. Romans 5:1

demonstrated that He was beyond all doubt the Son of God and the Savior of the world.

Prior to Christ's crucifixion, the disciples had hoped that "it was He who was going to redeem Israel."[42] However, all their hopes were crushed as death seemed to have the final word. How could Jesus of Nazareth be the fulfillment of the promises of God if He lay dead in a borrowed tomb? But then how could Isaac be the promised seed through which Abraham's descendants would be named if he was to die on an altar by his father's own hand?[43] Could Abraham dare believe that God would raise him from the dead?[44] And how could all of Joseph's dreams come true if he lay as good as dead in an Egyptian prison?[45] Could God bring him forth in a day and set him over all the land of Egypt?[46] The Scriptures answer our questions with a question: "Is there anything too hard for Me?"[47]

Isaac was unbound and given back to his father. Joseph was freed from prison and exalted to the right hand of Pharaoh. Christ was raised from the dead and exalted to the right hand of God. He was raised because He is the Son of God, and His Father had accepted His death as the atoning sacrifice for our sins.

---

42. Luke 24:21
43. Genesis 21:12; Romans 9:7
44. Hebrews 11:19
45. Genesis 37:5–10
46. Genesis 41:41
47. Jeremiah 32:27

CHAPTER TWENTY-THREE

The Foundation of Faith
in the Resurrection

Why should it be thought incredible by you that God raises the dead?
—Acts 26:8

The enemies of Christianity are right about concentrating their attack on the historical resurrection of Christ because the entirety of our faith depends upon it. If Christ has not been raised then our faith is utterly worthless.[1] Those of us who believe are still in our sins, and those who have died have perished forever.[2] Furthermore, we who preach the resurrection are false witnesses of God because we testify that He has raised Christ when He has not.[3] Finally, if Christ has not risen, our lives are a pathetic waste. We suffer hardship for no reason, and people hate us for the sake of a false prophet who has no power to save. As the apostle Paul writes, "If in this life only we have hope in Christ, we are of all men the most pitiable."[4]

By our own admission, the resurrection is everything to the Christian faith. If Christ has not been raised, our religion is false. Therefore, we would do well to ask ourselves a very important question: "How do we know that He has been raised?" Why do we believe? In the following pages, we will consider two very important but different mediums that confirm and make known the reality of the resurrection. First, the Holy Spirit reveals this reality by His illuminating and regenerating work, and, second, the historical-legal evidences that surround the event itself confirm the resurrection. The former is absolutely essential. The latter provides strong confirmation of the Christian faith and is an effective tool for dialogue with the unbelieving world.

---

1. 1 Corinthians 15:14, 17
2. 1 Corinthians 15:17–18
3. 1 Corinthians 15:15
4. 1 Corinthians 15:19

THE WORK OF THE HOLY SPIRIT

The evangelical church often attempts to validate its faith in the resurrection by pointing to the empty tomb, the inability of Christ's enemies to present a body, the transformation of the disciples, and many other pieces of historical and legal evidence. However, although these pieces of evidence do demonstrate that the Christian faith is not illogical or contra-historical, they are not the basis or foundation of the Christian's faith. The following facts demonstrate why.

First, the apostles did not use this form of apologetic in their preaching.[5] They did not strive to prove the resurrection but to proclaim it.[6] Their confidence did not rest in their powerful arguments but in the power of the gospel to save! This is evident in Paul's letter to the Corinthians:

> And I, brethren, when I came to you, did not come with excellence of speech or of wisdom declaring to you the testimony of God. For I determined not to know anything among you except Jesus Christ and Him crucified. I was with you in weakness, in fear, and in much trembling. And my speech and my preaching were not with persuasive words of human wisdom, but in demonstration of the Spirit and of power, that your faith should not be in the wisdom of men but in the power of God.[7]

Secondly, the overwhelming majority of those who have converted to Christianity throughout church history, including its greatest intellectuals, were not brought to faith by studying the historical and legal evidence of the resurrection, but by sitting under the proclamation of the gospel. Thirdly, if our faith in the resurrection is founded upon the historical and legal evidences of the event, how can we explain the faith of countless believers who lived and died for their faith without the slightest knowledge of such evidence? How do we explain the tribal Christian, who can barely read and is unable to offer one historical argument for the resurrection? He will endure the most despicable persecutions, even martyrdom, rather than deny the faith that he is unable to defend logically. In light of these truths, we must conclude that although the historical and

---

5. Apologetics is a discipline of the Christian faith which employs logical or reasoned arguments to defend the faith and to demonstrate the errors in arguments of those who would oppose it.

6. Acts 4:2, 33; 17:18; 24:21

7. 1 Corinthians 2:1–5. See also Romans 1:16 and 1 Corinthians 1:18–24.

legal evidences for the resurrection are helpful in many ways, they are not the foundation of our faith in the resurrection.

What then is the foundation of the believer's faith in the resurrection? How does he know that Christ has been raised? The answer from the Scriptures is clear. We owe our knowledge and unwavering faith in the resurrection to the regenerating and illuminating work of the Holy Spirit. At the moment of new birth, God supernaturally imparts our conviction regarding the reality of the resurrection of Jesus Christ and the validity of the Christian faith.[8] We know that Christ has risen from the dead because the Holy Spirit has illumined our minds to the truth of the Scriptures as they bear witness to Christ.[9] Consequently, we also believe because the Spirit regenerates our hearts, imparting faith and new affections for the Christ who has been revealed to us. The apostle Paul describes this miraculous work of the Spirit in the following manner: "For it is the God who commanded light to shine out of darkness, who has shone in our hearts to give the light of the knowledge of the glory of God in the face of Jesus Christ."[10]

Those who have been born again can no more deny the resurrection of Jesus Christ than they can deny their own existence. By God's sovereign decree and the witness of the Holy Spirit, it has become an incontestable reality to them.[11] As the persecutors of the Christian faith quickly learn, "For those infected with the religion of Jesus, there is no cure."[12]

The truths we have learned serve as both a warning and a directive. Although apologetics has its place, the kingdom of heaven advances through the proclamation of the gospel. Men will come to faith—not through our eloquence or logical arguments, but through our faithful preaching of the life, death, and resurrection of Jesus Christ. We must never forget that our mission is a fool's errand, and our labor is a waste of time and effort unless the Spirit of God is working to illuminate the minds and regenerate the hearts of our hearers. For this reason, we must

8. John 3:3

9. John 5:39; 1 John 5:6–10

10. 2 Corinthians 4:6

11. Matthew 11:25: "At that time Jesus answered and said, 'I thank You, Father, Lord of heaven and earth, that You have hidden these things from the wise and prudent and have revealed them to babes.'"

12. This is said to be the testimony of the Soviet soldiers who sought to turn Christians from their faith in the living Christ.

refuse to lean upon the broken staff of human wisdom, and we must cling to the truth that the gospel alone is the power of God unto salvation for all who believe.[13]

HISTORICAL OR LEGAL EVIDENCE

An individual's faith in Christ is not dependent upon his or her ability to recite the historical or legal evidence of Christ's resurrection. Nor does it stand or fall according to the believer's ability to defend it through the use of apologetics or classical logic.[14] Nevertheless, it is important to recognize and proclaim that the Christian faith is not contrary to history or to the highest and most pristine use of reason. True Christianity finds no virtue in seeking to transform myth into a useful narrative in order to promote some moral good in the world. Rather, the Christian faith and the resurrection of Jesus Christ are grounded in actual events of history that can be abundantly substantiated through the same types and kinds of evidences used by the secular historian.

Those who do reject the claims of Christianity as unhistorical or mythological do so because of biased presuppositions that will not allow the evidence to speak for itself.[15] Their logic is perilous: they have already decided that the resurrection is an impossibility; therefore every evidence in favor must be fallacious, and every claim must be the deduction of a fool or the invention of a charlatan.

The adversity of sinful men toward the gospel is one more reason to assert that apart from the grace of God and the regenerating work of the Holy Spirit, no man will accept the claims of Christ. Man will ignore the claims he can ignore, distort the claims he cannot ignore, and resist the claims he cannot distort. In other words, he will expend more energy denying the truth than he would have expended by simply submitting to it. Although it is beyond our scope to explore all the pieces of evidence which substantiate Christ's resurrection, in the following pages we will consider a few that benefit both the believer's faith and the seeker's inquiries.

---

13. Isaiah 36:6; Romans 1:16

14. I owe this insight to Pastor Charles Leiter.

15. Robert Reymond writes that those who do reject the claims of Christianity as unhistorical or mythological do so on "highly questionable critical and philosophical grounds with which they are simply more comfortable psychologically and religiously" (*A New Systematic Theology of the Christian Faith*, 581).

A PREDICTED EVENT

The death and resurrection of Jesus Christ were not sudden events that caught Him unaware; each was clearly predicted as a necessary fulfillment of the will of God. This is evident in Jesus' instruction to His doubting disciples after His resurrection: "O foolish ones, and slow of heart to believe in all that the prophets have spoken! Ought not the Christ to have suffered these things and to enter into His glory?"[16]

Hundreds of years before His coming, important Old Testament prophecies clearly revealed the resurrection of the Messiah. David predicted that God would not abandon the Messiah to the grave, nor allow His body to undergo decay.[17] The prophet Isaiah looked ahead and saw that God would greatly reward the Messiah after He had suffered the sins of His people unto death.[18] Christ Himself predicted His death and resurrection long before His crucifixion. When the unbelieving Jews asked Him for a sign of His authority to cleanse the temple, He declared, "Destroy this temple, and in three days I will raise it up."[19] When the scribes and Pharisees asked Him for further proof of His messiahship, the promise of His future resurrection accompanied His rebuke: "An evil and adulterous generation seeks after a sign, and no sign will be given to it except the sign of the prophet Jonah. For as Jonah was three days and three nights in the belly of the great fish, so will the Son of Man be three days and three nights in the heart of the earth."[20]

These prophecies prove that Christ's disciples did not invent the resurrection as a desperate attempt to keep the messianic dream alive. Christ declared it so clearly and so often that even His enemies knew of His predictions that He would rise again.[21] "On the next day, which followed the Day of Preparation, the chief priests and Pharisees gathered together to Pilate, saying, 'Sir, we remember, while He was still alive, how that deceiver said, "After three days I will rise."'"[22]

16. Luke 24:25–26
17. Psalm 16:8–11
18. Isaiah 53:12
19. John 2:19
20. Matthew 12:39–40
21. Matthew 16:21
22. Matthew 27:62–63

THE EMPTY TOMB

With all the attention given to the body of Jesus after His death—not only by His disciples, but also by his enemies—an empty tomb and an undiscovered body present strong evidence of a resurrection. From the very first day, all that was needed to destroy Christianity was to produce the dead body of the man Jesus. The Jewish leaders who called for His death and the Roman authorities who crucified Him knew the exact location of the tomb and had ample opportunity to exhume the body. With one bold move they could have proven to the world that the Easter message was a hoax and the apostles were devious perpetrators of a myth. Christianity would have died at its very infancy. Why was the body never produced?

Skeptics have invented three theories in response to this question. All are equally absurd. The first is that Jesus did not die upon the Roman cross; He only lost consciousness and the authorities wrongly pronounced Him dead.[23] Later, when placed in the cool tomb, He regained consciousness and escaped. We find the arguments against such a theory in the nature of crucifixion itself—He was pierced through the heart with a Roman spear and declared dead after a thorough examination by experts.[24] Even if He had survived the ordeal, He would have hardly been in any condition to move the heavy stone that blocked the tomb's entrance. Furthermore, it seems highly unlikely that such a personality would have been able to escape into some unknown region of Palestine and live out the rest of His life in anonymity.

The second theory is that the disciples stole the body and reburied it in some unknown location. The arguments against such a theory come from two sources. The first is the fierce reputation of the Roman guard, whose character and efficiency are legendary. The second is the New Testament's account of the disciples' fear during and after Christ's death. The Scriptures tell us that immediately after the death of Christ, the chief priest and Pharisees asked Pilate to secure the tomb with a trained Roman guard in order to prevent the disciples from stealing His body and perpetrating the myth that Christ had risen.[25] It is highly improbable that a handful of frightened disciples overpowered an entire Roman guard to steal away the body of Jesus. The disciples had already shown

---

23. This is often referred to as the "Swoon Theory" for obvious reasons.
24. John 19:31–34
25. Matthew 27:64

their lack of courage by deserting Christ during the crucifixion, and the leader among them, Simon Peter, could not even stand up to a servant girl when she identified him as one of Christ's followers.[26] It is also equally improbable that an entire Roman guard would fall asleep on duty as the chief priest suggested.[27] In fact, it takes more faith to believe this theory than it does to accept the resurrection!

The third theory is that the disciples simply went to the wrong tomb. This is also highly unlikely in light of the fact that the tomb belonged to Joseph of Arimathea, a member of the Sanhedrin council.[28] Both he and Nicodemus, "a man of the Pharisees…[and] a ruler of the Jews," were the very men who prepared the body of Jesus for burial and placed it in the tomb.[29] Furthermore, the Scriptures tell us that the women who had followed Jesus from Galilee also knew the exact location of the tomb.[30] If the disciples had gone to the wrong tomb, it is certain that friend and foe alike would have corrected their mistake by carrying them to the correct tomb, unwrapping the body, and pointing out the physical remains of Jesus.[31] Again, this theory joins the others in their absurdity.

CREDITABLE WITNESSES

For an event to be confirmed as historical or real, three things are required: there must be eyewitnesses, they must be sufficient in number, and they must demonstrate integrity and trustworthiness.[32] It is significant that the Scriptures' testimony regarding the resurrection of Jesus Christ meets all of these requirements.

First, eyewitness accounts of Christ's ministry, resurrection, and ascension provide the basis of Scripture's testimony. Every author of the New Testament stands with the apostle Peter in his declaration: "For we did not follow cunningly devised fables when we made known to you the power and coming of our Lord Jesus Christ, but were eyewitnesses of His

26. Mark 14:27; Matthew 26:56; Luke 22:55–62
27. Matthew 28:11–15
28. Matthew 27:57–61; Mark 15:42–47; Luke 23:50–56; John 19:38–42
29. John 3:1; Luke 23:50–53; John 19:38–42
30. Matthew 27:61, Mark 15:47; Luke 23:55
31. Reymond, *A New Systematic Theology*, 566.
32. Henry Thiessen, *Introductory Lectures in Systematic Theology* (Grand Rapids: Eerdmans, 1961), 246.

majesty."[33] The writers of the New Testament clearly recognize the importance of firsthand eyewitness testimony. To join the Eleven, Matthias had to be an eyewitness of Christ's life and ministry beginning with the baptism of John, through the resurrection, and until the day Christ ascended into heaven.[34] In writing his gospel, Luke took great pains to emphasize that he was writing an orderly account of things that were handed down by those who "from the beginning were eyewitnesses."[35] The apostle John begins his first epistle by powerfully and eloquently affirming the personal relationship with the Son to which all the apostles were privileged, a relationship that also formed the basis for both their doctrine and proclamation to others:

> That which was from the beginning, which we have heard, which we have seen with our eyes, which we have looked upon, and our hands have handled, concerning the Word of life—the life was manifested, and we have seen, and bear witness, and declare to you that eternal life which was with the Father and was manifested to us— that which we have seen and heard we declare to you, that you also may have fellowship with us; and truly our fellowship is with the Father and with His Son Jesus Christ. And these things we write to you that your joy may be full.[36]

It should be clear to any unbiased examiner that the apostles not only possessed a personal, firsthand knowledge of Christ's life, death, and resurrection, but they also recognized the importance of affirming the nature of their knowledge as such. They wanted the world to know that they had not been misled by hearsay, but had touched the hands, feet, and side of the resurrected Christ.[37] They had fellowshipped with Him and been instructed by Him.[38] Finally, they had worshiped Him as He passed from their view into heaven.[39]

Secondly, for an event to be confirmed as real and historical, there must be a sufficient number of eyewitnesses. To put it plainly, the greater the number of eyewitnesses, the greater the credibility of the event. This

33. 2 Peter 1:16
34. Acts 1:21–26
35. Luke 1:1–4
36. 1 John 1:1–4
37. Luke 24:39; John 20:27
38. Luke 24:13–32, 41–49; John 21:12–14
39. Acts 1:9–11

same principle is even found in the law of Old Testament and in the New Testament commands to the church where an event can be confirmed only by the testimony of two or three witnesses.[40]

Christ's resurrection also satisfies this requirement. The Scriptures report that there were hundreds of credible witnesses who encountered the risen Christ in a variety of situations and circumstances. On Resurrection Sunday, He appeared to Mary Magdalene in the garden, and then to the small group of women who were returning from the tomb.[41] On the same day, He joined Cleopas and another disciple as they walked together on the road to Emmaus.[42] Before the day had passed, He appeared also to Peter, and then to ten disciples in the upper room.[43] On the following Sunday, He appeared to the Eleven and had his famous discourse with Doubting Thomas.[44] After that, He appeared to more than five hundred witnesses at one time, and to His half brother James.[45] At some undisclosed time, He appeared again to Peter, John, and five other disciples when they were fishing on the Sea of Galilee.[46] Finally, He ascended into heaven in the presence of His disciples on the Mount of Olives.[47]

In light of the testimony of Scripture, it is impossible to discredit the account of the Christ's resurrection based upon some false notion that it lacked a sufficient number of eyewitnesses. To this truth, the great English preacher Charles Spurgeon eloquently testifies:

> Does it not strike you that very many events of the greatest importance recorded in history, and commonly believed, could not in the nature of things have been witnessed by one-tenth as many as the resurrection of Christ? The signing of famous treaties affecting nations, the births of princes, the remarks of cabinet ministers, the projects of conspirators, and the deeds of assassins. Any and all of these have been made turning points in history, and are never questioned as facts, and yet but few could have been present to witness them.... If this fact is to be denied, there is an end to all witness, and we have said deliberately what David said in haste: "All men are

40. Deuteronomy 17:6; 19:15; Matthew 18:16
41. Mark 16:9–11; John 20:11–19; Matthew 28:9–10
42. Mark 16:12–13; Luke 24:13–32
43. Luke 24:34–43; John 20:19–25
44. Mark 16:14; John 20:26–31; 1 Corinthians 15:5
45. 1 Corinthians 15:6–7
46. John 21:1–23
47. Luke 24:44–49; Acts 1:3–8

liars"; and from this day forth every man must become so skeptical of his neighbor, that he will never believe anything which he has not himself seen; the next step will be to doubt the evidence of his own senses; to what further follies men may then rush, I will not venture to predict.[48]

Thirdly and finally, for an event to be confirmed as historical or real, the eyewitnesses must demonstrate their integrity. In other words, they must prove themselves trustworthy. It is no secret that throughout the history of Christianity, countless skeptics have done their best to discredit the New Testament witnesses; however, they have never been able to disprove their sincerity or disqualify them on ethical or moral grounds. This forces skeptics to focus their attacks on the possibility of self-delusion and mass hysteria.

It has been argued that the disciples and many of the first-century Jews were predisposed to believe in the resurrection, and therefore they simply saw what they wanted to see. First, the Jewish nation struggled under the unbearable oppression of the Roman Empire. Because of this, the Jews of Jesus' day were longing for the coming of the Messiah and would have been convinced easily. Many among the Jews had already followed several false messiahs who had arisen among the people, proving they were disposed to believe anything.[49] Secondly, Jesus made many predictions regarding His future resurrection. When combined with the disciples' great love for their beloved teacher, such prophecies would have been perfect soil for the sprouting of self-delusion and mass hysteria.

Several facts stand against these popular theories. First, the vast majority of the Jewish nation rejected Jesus of Nazareth as the Messiah. His earthly ministry and death were a stumbling block to them.[50] Adding the resurrection to the already scandalous message of the cross would not have made Jesus' claims to messiahship any more compelling to the Jew. Furthermore, this theory does not take into account the fact that within a few decades the vast majority of believers were Gentiles who had no predisposition to believe anything about the gospel. As Lewis and Demarest write, "The event occurred in sharp antithesis to what they [the Jews] had expected theologically, and it was in genuine conflict with the framework

---

48. Spurgeon, *The Metropolitan Tabernacle Pulpit*, 8:218–19.
49. Acts 5:36–37
50. 1 Corinthians 1:23

of the secular world view at the time. To the Jew it was a stumbling block and to the Greek nonsense because the evidence required a Copernican revolution in their theology and cosmology."[51]

Secondly, the Jews and Gentiles were not predisposed to believe in the resurrection, and the same can definitively be said about the disciples. Mary Magdalene was the first to see Christ after the resurrection, and yet, when she first encountered the empty tomb, she believed that someone had stolen the Lord's body and moved it to an unknown location.[52] Even after reports of Christ's resurrection began to filter in, the disciples did not believe. Luke records that the news of Christ's resurrection "seemed to them like idle tales," and Mark writes that they "did not believe."[53] In their first encounters with the resurrected Christ, they thought He was a gardener, a ghost, and a mere traveler on the road to Emmaus.[54] These gross and rather comical misinterpretations were only resolved by further appearances of Christ and His careful exposition of the Law and the Prophets.[55] Before Thomas's doubt could be removed, he had to see in Christ's hands the imprint of the nails, put his finger into the wound, and put his hand in His side![56] For this reason, Christ reproached them for their unbelief and hardness of heart, and He scolded them as foolish men who were slow of heart to believe in all that the prophets had spoken.[57] These facts hardly substantiate the claim that the disciples were predisposed to believe the resurrection!

Thirdly and finally, a specific delusion or hallucination is usually confined to a single individual. To think that the hundreds of people who claimed to be eyewitnesses all shared the same hallucination is extremely improbable. Furthermore, mass hysteria usually requires the

---

51. Bruce Demarest and Gordon Lewis, *Integrative Theology* (Grand Rapids: Baker Academic, 1990), 2:466. Nicolaus Copernicus (1473–1543) was the first to suggest a heliocentric cosmology—a model of the solar system in which the sun replaced the earth as the center of the planets. His theory was a radical departure from the status quo and became a landmark in the history of modern science now known as the Copernican Revolution. Thus, any equally radical theory is often referred to as a "Copernican Revolution."

52. John 20:2, 13, 15
53. Luke 24:9–11; Mark 16:11
54. John 20:15; Luke 24:13–31, 37
55. Luke 24:25, 44–46
56. John 20:24–29
57. Luke 16:14; 24:25–26

aid of powerful political or religious institutions which hold sway over the masses. However, in the case of Christ's resurrection and the gospel, the powerful institutions of the day were united in their opposition to the message and did everything in their power to discredit it. The propagators were mostly uneducated, untrained men with no political, religious, or economic power to promote their cause.[58]

A LIE WITHOUT A MOTIVE

An often overlooked yet extremely convincing argument for the historical reality of the resurrection is the apostles' lifelong dedication to the gospel, regardless of the suffering and loss it imposed upon them. If Christ had not been resurrected and the disciples had simply invented the story, then we should be able to discover a motive for the deception. What did they hope to achieve by perpetrating the lie? It is a historical fact that the apostles and the great majority of the early disciples died poor, defamed, persecuted, and hated. As the apostle Paul declared, "We have been made as the filth of the world, the offscouring of all things until now," and "If in this life only we have hope in Christ, we are of all men the most pitiable."[59]

If these men had invented the resurrection story for the typical reasons that men usually create such lies and propagate them—wealth, fame, and power—then they would have recanted or denounced the story when they saw that it was not achieving their desired goal. Nevertheless, history proves that most of them died as martyrs under terrible persecution rather than renounce their belief in the gospel or the resurrection of Christ upon which the gospel stands. The only explanation for such tenacity and persistence in the face of such suffering and death is that the resurrection is true—a historical reality—and the apostles and other Christians were simply communicating what they had truly witnessed. As the apostle John wrote, "That which we have seen and heard we declare to you."[60] James Montgomery Boice writes, "What accounts for a belief in the resurrection on the part of Christ's disciples? Nothing but the resurrection itself. If we cannot account for the belief of the disciples this way, we are faced with the greatest enigma in history. If

---

58. Acts 4:13
59. 1 Corinthians 4:13; 15:19
60. 1 John 1:3

we account for it by a real resurrection and real appearances of the risen Lord, then Christianity is understandable and offers a sure hope to all."[61]

Another important factor in the equation is the use of women as witnesses. Fraudulent men hoping to propagate a lie for their own gain never would have done this. In the time and culture of the New Testament, women were not considered legitimate witnesses in legal proceedings. Nevertheless, in all four Gospels, women take a prominent role as the first witnesses to the resurrection of Jesus Christ.[62] Mary Magdalene was the first person to see the Lord after the resurrection, and she is the first to bear witness of His resurrection to others. In fact, she is portrayed as something of a heroine in that she believed and obeyed in the face of the apostles' unbelief.[63] The women who had accompanied Mary Magdalene to the tomb on Sunday morning were the next to see the Lord, and they were the first He actually commissioned to take the news to others.[64] If the writers of the New Testament had been attempting to perpetrate a fraud, they would not have used such women as their primary witnesses; instead, they would have selected men, the more credible witnesses in the eyes of others.

THE TRANSFORMATION OF THE DISCIPLES

One of the greatest hurdles that the skeptic must overcome in his denial of Christ's resurrection is the obvious transformation of the disciples. If the resurrection is not a historical reality, or worse, it is a hoax, then the seemingly miraculous transformation that occurred in the character and deeds of the apostles and the other eyewitnesses is inexplicable.

Prior to the resurrection, the disciples were timid, fearful, and driven by self-preservation. They abandoned Him during His arrest, denied Him during His trial, and hid themselves in unbelief and were engulfed in despair for three days following His death.[65] The women among them showed far greater moral fortitude and hope than the very men who had been personally commissioned by Christ to be His apostles. It was

---

61. James Montgomery Boice, *Foundations of the Christian Faith: A Comprehensible and Readable Theology* (Downers Grove, Ill.: InterVarsity Press, 1986), 358.

62. Matthew 28:1–10; Mark 16:1–8; Luke 24:1–12; John 20:1–18

63. Mark 16:9–11; John 20:11–18

64. Matthew 28:8–9

65. Matthew 26:56, 69–75; Mark 16:14; John 20:19; Luke 24:17

the women who went to the tomb on Sunday morning while the men cowered in the upper room. And it was the women who first believed and proclaimed the resurrection while the men were muted by doubt.

However, after the resurrection, these same men and women became valiant and indomitable defenders of the faith. From the book of Acts, we learn that they stood against the world and "turned [it] upside down" with the message of the gospel and the resurrection of Jesus Christ.[66] When the most powerful religious and political institutions among Jews or Gentiles commanded them "not to speak at all nor teach in the name of Jesus," they defied their authority with unflinching and unrelenting commitment to Christ's person and message.[67] The apostles Peter and John demonstrate this in their declaration to the Sanhedrin: "Whether it is right in the sight of God to listen to you more than to God, you judge. For we cannot but speak the things which we have seen and heard."[68]

Although they were threatened, beaten, imprisoned, and martyred, the disciples of Christ refused to deny or to cease proclaiming what they had "seen and heard."[69] In one generation, these men and women, emboldened by the truth of the resurrection of Jesus, spread the gospel throughout the entire known world.[70] They had no political, religious, or economic power. They had no academic credentials, yet they changed the world to a degree that no political or military machine has ever equaled. If Christ had not risen, how can such a transformation in their lives be explained, and how can the success of their mission be accounted for? R. A. Torrey writes, "Something tremendous must have happened to account for such a radical and astounding moral transformation as this. Nothing short of the fact of the resurrection, of their having seen the risen Lord, will explain it."[71]

THE CONVERSION OF ENEMIES

The radical transformation of the followers of Jesus Christ after His resurrection is not the skeptic's only problem. He must also explain the

---

66. Acts 17:6
67. Acts 4:18
68. Acts 4:19–20
69. 1 John 1:1, 3
70. Colossians 1:5–6
71. R. A. Torrey, *The Bible and Its Christ* (Old Tappan, N.J.: Fleming H. Revell, n.d.), 92.

subsequent conversion of those who opposed Jesus and persecuted the movement that followed Him. Apart from the resurrection, how did Christianity affect some of its earliest and greatest opponents—especially the half brothers of Jesus and the infamous Saul of Tarsus?

The Scriptures clearly state that during Jesus' life and ministry, neither James nor Jude believed in Him, but both were openly antagonistic toward His person and ministry.[72] In fact, Jesus' family once traveled from Nazareth to Capernaum in order to take custody of Him because they thought He was "out of His mind."[73] However, after the resurrection, both brothers were radically converted and became leaders in the early church.[74] We can see their devotion to Christ and submission to His lordship in the introductions of their epistles, where they refer to themselves as bond servants of the Lord Jesus Christ.[75] They had been transformed from unbelieving antagonists into faithful bond servants who willingly submitted their lives to His lordship. How was such a transformation possible apart from accepting the testimony of Scripture? They had seen the risen Christ![76]

Another enemy of the early church whose conversion adds weight to the apostolic proclamation of the resurrection is Saul of Tarsus. In the book of Acts and by his own accounts, Saul stands out as the greatest and fiercest enemy of primitive Christianity. In his ignorance and unbelief, he saw Jesus of Nazareth as nothing more than an impostor and a blasphemer, and he thought that all who followed Him were worthy of imprisonment and death.[77] The book of Acts first introduces him to us as he gives his hearty approval to the martyrdom of Stephen.[78] Afterwards, we see him going to the high priest, "breathing threats and murder against the disciples of the Lord" and asking for letters so that "if he found any who were of the Way, whether men or women, he might bring them bound to Jerusalem."[79] However, on the road to Damascus, Saul undergoes a radical transformation. He becomes convinced that Jesus is the Messiah of

---

72. John 7:3–4

73. Mark 3:21

74. James: Acts 1:14; 12:17; 15:13; 1 Corinthians 9:5; 15:7; Galatians 1:19; 2:9; James 1:1; and Jude: Jude v. 1; Acts 1:14; 1 Corinthians 9:5

75. James 1:1; Jude 1:1

76. 1 Corinthians 15:7

77. 1 Timothy 1:13; 2 Corinthians 5:16

78. Acts 7:58; 8:1

79. Acts 9:1–2

Israel, receives baptism in His name, and immediately begins to proclaim Jesus in the synagogues, saying, "He is the Son of God."[80] His fellow Jews respond in amazement, saying, "Is this not he who destroyed those who called on this name in Jerusalem, and has come here for that purpose, so that he might bring them bound to the chief priests?"[81]

The news quickly spread throughout all the churches of Judea that he who once persecuted the faith was now preaching that same faith he once tried to destroy.[82] However, Saul had been such a violent adversary to the church that no believer dared associate with him. All were afraid of him until Barnabas brought him to the apostles and they confirmed his testimony.[83] In this way, Saul of Tarsus, the greatest enemy of the Christian faith, became its greatest defender and propagator. William Neil writes: "What is beyond question historically is that the fanatical oppressor of the Nazarenes, who left Jerusalem 'breathing threats and murder,' entered Damascus mentally shattered and physically blinded and became on his recovery the foremost protagonist of the beliefs he set out to extirpate."[84]

Since the skeptic cannot deny the historic realities of Saul's conversion and radically transformed life, he is therefore obliged to offer a reasonable explanation for it. After two thousand years, the church is still waiting!

THE MULTITUDES THROUGHOUT HISTORY

In the first year of Christianity, the respected teacher and Pharisee Gamaliel addressed the Sanhedrin with great wisdom regarding the followers of Jesus. This address is worth quoting at length:

> Men of Israel, take heed to yourselves what you intend to do regarding these men. For some time ago Theudas rose up, claiming to be somebody. A number of men, about four hundred, joined him. He was slain, and all who obeyed him were scattered and came to nothing. After this man, Judas of Galilee rose up in the days of the census, and drew away many people after him. He also perished, and all who obeyed him were dispersed. And now I say to you, keep away from these men and let them alone; for if this plan or this work

---

80. Acts 9:18–20
81. Acts 9:21
82. Galatians 1:22–23
83. Acts 9:26–27
84. William Neil, *The Acts of the Apostles* (London: Oliphants, 1973), 128.

is of men, it will come to nothing; but if it is of God, you cannot over-throw it—lest you even be found to fight against God.[85]

Prior to the coming of Jesus Christ, two false messiahs had appeared to the nation of Israel. Both of them drew a following, yet after the death of both, their followers quickly dispersed and nothing was ever heard of their movements again. Therefore, Gamaliel reasoned that if Jesus of Nazareth were just a man and His resurrection a hoax, then the same fate would befall His followers. However, Gamaliel also wisely reasoned that if the resurrection story was true, then Jesus was the Messiah, the movement would continue, and those who opposed it would be fight-ing against God. The last two thousand years of history seem to confirm Gamaliel's argument.

One of the greatest proofs of the resurrection of Jesus Christ is the continuation of the Christian faith throughout history and throughout the nations, tribes, and peoples of the world. To the present, there have been untold millions or even billions of people who testify to having a personal relationship with Jesus Christ and who claim that He has dra-matically changed the course of their lives. It is important to note that this group of people is not confined to some ethnic, political, economic, or academic subgroup, but includes individuals from every ethnicity, economic stratum, and academic level. The early church consisted of individuals who would never have come together in any other circum-stances. There were Greeks and Jews, circumcised and uncircumcised, barbarians, Scythians, slaves and freemen, but Christ was all, and in all.[86] The same may be said of Christianity today.

It is also important to note that a countless multitude of men, women, and children who have followed Christ have done so at great personal sacrifice. Some statisticians estimate that the number of martyrs has reached more than fifty million believers. Still others claim the number to be much higher. All of this leads us back to one unrelenting ques-tion: What is the rationale behind such devotion and sacrifice, and what could explain the continuation of the church in the midst of enemies who have vowed to exterminate it? It does make one trust that some-thing truly happened on that Sunday morning when the women found the stone rolled away!

---

85. Acts 5:35–39
86. Colossians 3:11

CHAPTER TWENTY-FOUR

Christ's Ascension as the High Priest of His People

Lift up your heads, O you gates! And be lifted up, you everlasting doors! And the King of glory shall come in. Who is this King of glory? The LORD strong and mighty, the LORD mighty in battle. Lift up your heads, O you gates! Lift up, you everlasting doors! And the King of glory shall come in. Who is this King of glory? The LORD of hosts, He is the King of glory.
—Psalm 24:7–10

Seeing then that we have a great High Priest who has passed through the heavens, Jesus the Son of God, let us hold fast our confession. For we do not have a High Priest who cannot sympathize with our weaknesses, but was in all points tempted as we are, yet without sin.
—Hebrews 4:14–15

Forty days after the resurrection, the Scriptures affirm that Christ ascended into heaven in the presence of a large company of His disciples. In the book of Acts, we read, "He was taken up, and a cloud received Him out of their sight."[1] The gospel of Luke testifies, "Now it came to pass while He blessed them, that He was parted from them and carried up into heaven."[2] Mark declares, "He was received up into heaven, and sat down at the right hand of God."[3] The apostle Paul described it this way: "God was manifested in the flesh, justified in the Spirit, seen by angels, preached among the Gentiles, believed on in the world, received up in glory."[4]

---

1. Acts 1:9
2. Luke 24:51
3. Mark 16:19
4. 1 Timothy 3:16

Christ's resurrection and ascension were the precursors and proofs of His coronation and enthronement at the right hand of God. According to the Scriptures, the Father has glorified the Son together with Himself with the glory that He had with Him before the foundation of the world.[5] However, the glory that has been regained is greater than the glory that He had set aside when He came into the world.[6] For now, He sits at the right hand of the Father not only as the fullness of deity but also as the glorified Man; not only as Ruler but as Redeemer and High Priest. He is God the Son and the second Adam; He is the lionhearted King and the Lamb that was slain; He is the Judge of all the earth and the Great High Priest who offered Himself as a propitiation for the sins of His people.

THE ASCENSION OF CHRIST

To begin our consideration of this majestic theme of ascension, we will turn our attention first to the Old Testament Scriptures. David's Psalm 24 is a processional liturgy that celebrates the Lord's entrance into Zion. The church has long interpreted this psalm as a celebration of Christ's ascension into the heavenly Jerusalem and into "the greater and more perfect tabernacle not made with hands."[7] Although the extent to which this psalm should be applied to Christ has been debated in recent years, the Reformers, Puritans, and some of the greatest theologians and expositors throughout church history interpreted it christologically. Here, we will follow their lead and find within this psalm the glory of Christ as He ascends to the right hand of God.

The first six verses of Psalm 24 address an extremely important question: Who may enter into the presence of the Lord? As we will see, the requirements are strict and unyielding: "Who may ascend into the hill of the LORD? Or who may stand in His holy place? He who has clean hands and a pure heart, who has not lifted up his soul to an idol, nor sworn deceitfully."[8] Upon reading this text, we should immediately recognize that we do not qualify to ascend into the hill of the Lord or stand in His holy place. Our hands are unclean, our hearts are impure, our souls are full of idolatry, and our lips are defiled by deceit. Our sins have made a

5. John 17:5
6. Philippians 2:6–8
7. Hebrews 9:11, 24
8. Psalm 24:3–4

separation between us and our God and closed the entrance to heaven as tightly as Jericho, so that none might go out and none might come in.[9] The verdict against us is just: there is none righteous, not even one.[10] Left to ourselves, we have no recourse except to close our mouths and await our condemnation.[11] Although we wash ourselves with snow and cleanse our hands with lye, the stain of our iniquity is before Him.[12] We cannot enter in or draw near.

In every way, humanity is utterly disqualified, and yet there is One among our race who has passed through the heavens and stands before God as an advocate on behalf of His people—Jesus Christ the righteous.[13] He is a descendant of Adam and therefore truly of our stock. During His earthly pilgrimage, He was like us in every way, except without sin.[14] He glorified God in every thought, word, and deed, and He loved the Lord His God with all His heart, soul, mind, and strength.[15] An uninterrupted obedience marked the entire course of His life.[16] He was blameless in regard to the law, and in the blazing white light of God's holiness that exposes every darkness, He stood without shadow or spot. The Scriptures declare that God charges error even against His angels, but in Jesus, He found only perfect holiness and an infinite store of righteousness.[17] He was holy, innocent, undefiled, and separated from sinners—the only member of Adam's race who stood approved of God by virtue of His own merit.[18] He was the only one of whom God has testified, "This is My beloved Son, in whom I am well pleased."[19]

In Psalm 24:7, we see this impeccable Man, Jesus of Nazareth, ascended and standing before the very gates of heaven. It is there that He lifts His voice and cries out, "Lift up your heads, O you gates! And be lifted up, you everlasting doors! And the King of glory shall come

---

9. Isaiah 59:2; Joshua 6:1
10. Romans 3:10
11. Romans 3:19
12. Job 9:30–31; Jeremiah 2:22
13. Hebrews 4:14; 1 John 2:1
14. Hebrews 4:15
15. 1 Corinthians 10:31; Matthew 22:37; Mark 12:30; Luke 10:27
16. John 8:29
17. Job 4:18
18. Hebrews 7:26
19. Matthew 3:17; 17:5; Mark 1:11; 9:7; Luke 3:22

in."[20] How our esteem for Jesus Christ would increase if only we could catch a glimpse of what is happening here! By virtue of His own merit, He stands before the gates of heaven and commands them to open to Him. At the sound of His voice, the angels run to the battlement and peer over the wall to catch a glimpse of Him.[21] They ask, "Who is this King of glory that the very gates of heaven should yield to Him? Who is this Man who comes in His own name and demands entrance by virtue of His own merit?" Even the great seraphim bow their heads and cover themselves in the presence of God to acknowledge that they have no righteousness of their own, to demonstrate that their virtue and glory derive from God and are the result of His grace.[22] They make no boast of merit and claim nothing in their own name. However, this Man not only lays claim to heaven but to the very throne of God! Who then is this King of glory? In response to the inquiry, Christ lifts up His voice a second time and cries out, "The LORD strong and mighty, the LORD mighty in battle. Lift up your heads, O you gates! Lift up, you everlasting doors! And the King of glory shall come in."[23]

This second command silences all further inquiries. The strength of His voice reveals His identity. It is the Word made flesh, the Son of Man ascending to where He was before.[24] Without delay, the ancient bolts break, the timbers tremble, and the gates yield to Jesus of Nazareth:

> The Son of God,[25]
>   the Son of Adam;[26]
> Conceived of the Holy Spirit,[27]
>   born of the lineage of David;[28]
> The fullness of deity,
>   in bodily form.[29]

---

20. Psalm 24:7
21. This thought came from Charles Spurgeon's comments on Psalm 24 in *The Treasury of David* (Grand Rapids: Zondervan, 1950), 1:377.
22. Isaiah 6:1–2
23. Psalm 24:8–9
24. John 1:1, 14; 6:62
25. John 1:34
26. Luke 3:23–38; 1 Corinthians 15:45
27. Matthew 1:20
28. Romans 1:3
29. Colossians 2:9

The Lion of the tribe of Judah,[30]
> the Lamb who takes away the sins of the world![31]
Unashamed before the throne of God,[32]
> not ashamed to call us brothers.[33]
The Judge of the living and the dead,[34]
> the Advocate of His people.[35]

Angels will retell the glory of that moment through the endless ages of eternity. The victorious Son returns bearing the very scars that prove His triumph. He has canceled out the certificate of debt consisting of decrees against His people and nailed it to the cross.[36] He has disarmed and made a public spectacle of the devil, who had enslaved His people under the penalty of death.[37] He has vindicated the righteousness of God, who justifies the wicked.[38] For this reason, all of heaven looks upon Him who was pierced and cries out with a loud voice: "Worthy is the Lamb who was slain to receive power and riches and wisdom, and strength and honor and glory and blessing!"[39]

As the victorious Christ passes through the eternal gates, the Father beckons Him to ascend the throne and take His rightful place at His side. There He sat down far above all rule and authority and power and dominion and every name that is named, not only in this age but also in the age to come, to the end that all might honor the Son even as they honor the Father.[40] In this way, David's prophecy was fulfilled finally and fully: "The LORD said to my Lord, 'Sit at My right hand.'"[41]

Jesus of Nazareth, our brother, is the King of glory. He is not an upstart god or a good creature recently promoted. He is the eternal Son of God, who did not consider equality with God a thing to be grasped, but laid aside His glory, clothed Himself in flesh, and died as a propitiation

---

30. Revelation 5:5
31. John 1:29
32. Hebrews 9:24
33. Hebrews 2:11
34. Acts 10:42; 2 Timothy 4:1
35. 1 John 2:1. Poem composed by author.
36. Colossians 2:14
37. Colossians 2:15; Hebrews 2:14–15
38. Romans 3:25–26
39. Revelation 5:12
40. Ephesians 1:21; John 5:23
41. Psalm 110:1

for the sins of His people.[42] On the third day He rose again from the dead, and after presenting Himself alive by many convincing proofs, He ascended into the heavens and took His seat at the right hand of the Majesty on high.[43] There He is enthroned as the High Priest and Forerunner of His people, and as the Lord and Judge of all.

CHRIST AS MEDIATOR

When the Man Christ Jesus ascended to the right hand of God, He took upon Himself the mediation of all things between God and creation. The Father's purpose in conferring this office upon Him is multifaceted, and each aspect demonstrates the supremacy of the Son and the boundless love of the Father toward Him. Christ's role as mediator is a manifestation in time and creation of a relationship between the Father and the Son that has existed throughout eternity. To begin, we must understand that it has always been the Father's purpose and good pleasure that the Son have preeminence in all things and that nothing be done independently of Him.[44] For this reason, God has always been pleased to deal with His creation through the Son's mediation. He created and sustains the world through His Son, He reveals Himself to the world through His Son, and He redeems the world through His Son.[45] One day He will judge the world through His Son.[46]

Secondly, we must also understand that the mediatorial work of the Son on Calvary will always be the epicenter of God's revelation to His creation. Its centrality and preeminence will not diminish throughout the endless ages of eternity, but rather it will increase as the redeemed creation continues its endless plight to search out the infinite glories of the gospel.

Thirdly, we must always remember and glory in the fact that every good and perfect gift from God that has ever graced creation has been through and for the sake of the Son.[47] Both those who worship God and those who curse Him owe every good they have ever known to the

---

42. Philippians 2:6–9; Romans 3:25; 1 John 2:1–2
43. Acts 1:3; Hebrews 1:3
44. Colossians 1:18; John 1:3
45. John 1:3; Colossians 1:16; Hebrews 1:3; John 1:1, 14, 18; 3:17; 12:41; Isaiah 61:1–3; Acts 4:12
46. John 5:22; Acts 10:42; 17:31; Romans 2:16
47. James 1:17

Son's mediation.[48] The church's right standing before God and the gifts lavished upon her are because of and for the sake of the Son.[49] The rain that falls upon the wicked and the sun that warms their faces are given through Him!

Fourthly, we must understand that the incarnation brought a new and marvelous aspect to the Son's mediatory work. The Man Christ Jesus, the eternal Son of God and a true Son of Adam, now sustains, governs, and mediates the universe, all because of His incarnation and final glorification in the flesh. The implications of this truth are mind-boggling. The apex of God's purpose for creation has been attained by and through Jesus of Nazareth.

CHRIST OUR FORERUNNER

The creation account of Genesis explains to us that God created man in His own image and intended him to rule over all the earth as His vice-regent.[50] That God conferred such a privileged title upon a mere creature of clay moved the psalmist to exclaim with wonder:

> When I consider Your heavens, the work of Your fingers, the moon and the stars, which You have ordained, what is man that You are mindful of him, and the son of man that You visit him? For You have made him a little lower than the angels, and You have crowned him with glory and honor. You have made him to have dominion over the works of Your hands; You have put all things under his feet.[51]

God put all things under the feet of our father, Adam. God made him to be the crown of creation, the head of his race, and the ruler over the works of God. Nevertheless, he quickly fell under the deceit of the serpent and joined him in his rebellion.[52] As a result, man forfeited his exalted place, throwing the whole creation into chaos, futility, and the slavery of corruption.[53] Furthermore, man had to leave the presence of God and became subject to divine justice, resulting in death.[54]

---

48. John 1:3–4
49. Ephesians 1:7–8
50. Genesis 1:26
51. Psalm 8:3–6
52. Genesis 3:1–7
53. Genesis 3:14–19; Romans 8:20–22
54. Genesis 3:24; 2:16–17; Romans 6:23

From the vantage point of man, Paradise was lost and recovery was an absolute impossibility. Yet in the mystery of God's providence, a great work drafted before the very foundation of the world would be unfolded![55] In the fullness of time, God sent forth His Son to join Adam's fallen race, to redeem a people for God, and to restore them to a glory that would far exceed that which was lost![56] This is the great argument of the second chapter of the book of Hebrews:

> For He [God] has not put the world to come, of which we speak, in subjection to angels. But one testified in a certain place, saying: "What is man that You are mindful of him, or the son of man that You take care of him? You have made him a little lower than the angels; You have crowned him with glory and honor, and set him over the works of Your hands. You have put all things in subjection under his feet." For in that He put all in subjection under him, He left nothing that is not put under him. But now we do not yet see all things put under him. But we see Jesus, who was made a little lower than the angels, for the suffering of death crowned with glory and honor, that He, by the grace of God, might taste death for everyone.[57]

According to the wisdom given to the writer of Hebrews, God has a plan for a new creation, for a world that is to come.[58] This new world will not be subject to angels, but to those who have been redeemed from Adam's fallen race. For this reason, the eternal Son of God was made for a little while lower than the angels so that He might taste death for every one of His people, redeem them from the penalty of death, and restore them to the glorious position that God has designated for them.

At the present, it is obvious to all that this design is yet to be fulfilled in its entirety, for we do not yet see all things subject to God's redeemed people.[59] However, we do see Jesus raised from the dead, ascended to the right hand of the Majesty on high, and crowned with glory and honor.[60] He has gone before His people as the Captain of their salvation.[61] He is

---

55. 1 Peter 1:20; Isaiah 46:9–10
56. Galatians 4:4
57. Hebrews 2:5–9
58. Hebrews 2:5
59. Hebrews 2:8
60. Hebrews 2:9; 1:3
61. Hebrews 2:10. "Captain of their salvation" (NKJV); "Author of their salvation" (NASB); "Founder of their salvation" (ESV).

the Pledge of a present hope and the Forerunner who will bring many sons to glory! The Scriptures declare that the creation itself longs anxiously for the revealing of the sons of God and groans for its freedom from slavery to corruption into the freedom of the glory of the children of God. Because of this one Man, Jesus, creation will not be disappointed, and neither will we!

CHRIST OUR HIGH PRIEST

Throughout history, the great problem of fallen man has been the need for a mediator who would be able to deal with God on equal terms and also deal with man in his fallen and wretched state. To qualify as the mediator between God and man, it was necessary that both natures of this mediator, divine and human, be "inseparably joined together in one person, without conversion, composition, or confusion."[62] Being the fullness of deity and possessing equality with God, such a person would be able to have dealings with God.[63] Being a true man and having been tempted in all things yet remaining without sin, he would also be able to sympathize with man's weakness and intercede on his behalf.[64] These are the qualities required in a mediator, and to the glory of God and the consolation of our souls, all of them and more have been met in the person of Jesus of Nazareth. He is God in the fullest sense of the term, and He shares equally in all the attributes, glories, and accolades of deity.[65]

Likewise, He is completely man.[66] In the incarnation, He was made like His brothers in all things and suffered temptation in all things, yet He was without sin.[67] For this reason, He is a faithful and merciful high priest who can deal with the ignorant and misguided and sympathize with their weaknesses.[68] By His own virtue and merit, He has passed through the heavens to advocate our cause in the very throne room of God.[69] He stands unashamed before God and yet is not ashamed to call

---

62. 1689 London Baptist Confession, chapter 8.2.
63. Colossians 2:9; Philippians 2:6
64. Hebrews 4:15
65. John 1:1, 14; Philippians 2:6
66. 1 Timothy 2:5
67. John 1:1, 14; Hebrews 2:14–18; 4:15; 2 Corinthians 5:21
68. Hebrews 2:17; 4:15; 5:1–4
69. Hebrews 4:14–15; 9:11–12

us brothers.[70] Robed in glorified flesh, He has become the Man "gone before us" into glory and the Man "for us" before the throne of God. There He sits enthroned as the representative of His people, and He lives forever to make intercession for them.[71]

The patriarch Job longed for a mediator who would be uniquely qualified to lay his hand upon God and man.[72] The one Job longed for is now firmly established at the right hand of God. At the end of the ages, He will finally put away sin by the accomplished sacrifice of Himself, and He has entered into heaven to appear in the presence of God for His people.[73] Through Him, we have an anchor of the soul, a sure and steadfast hope which enters within the veil.[74] He is able to save us "to the uttermost," because He lives forever to make intercession for us.[75]

Although Christ accomplished our atonement on Calvary and met every requirement for our justification, the Scriptures teach that Christ continues to intercede on behalf of His people.[76] It is one of the most beautiful doctrines in all the Scriptures, and yet it is often misunderstood. Eminent biblical scholar Charles Hodge wrote, "As to the nature of Christ's intercession, little can be said. There is error in pressing the representations of Scriptures too far; and there is error in explaining them away."[77] And John Murray wrote the following:

> The character of our Lord's intercession has at times been grotesquely misrepresented in popular Christian thought. He is not to be thought of 'as an *orante*, standing ever before the Father with outstretched arms, like the figures in the mosaics of the catacombs, and with strong crying and tears pleading our cause in the presence of a reluctant God; but as an enthroned Priest-King, asking what He will from a Father who always hears and grants His requests. Our Lord's life in heaven is His prayer.' His once self-offering is utterly acceptable and efficacious; His contact with the Father is immediate and unbroken; His priestly ministry on His people's behalf is

---

70. Hebrews 2:11
71. Hebrews 7:25
72. Job 9:28–35
73. Hebrews 9:24–26
74. Hebrews 6:19
75. Hebrews 7:25
76. John 19:30; Romans 4:25
77. Charles Hodge, *Systematic Theology* (New York: Scribner, Armstrong, and Co., 1871–1872), 2:593.

never-ending, and therefore the salvation which He secures to them is absolute.[78]

In light of these cautions from such renowned scholars, we must ask ourselves, "What does it really mean that Christ is our High Priest who always lives to make intercession for us?"[79] In the following, we will consider four related truths.

JESUS ATONED FOR HIS PEOPLE

First, Christ's intercession includes His once-and-for-all appearing before God on our behalf as the sacrifice for our sins. We must not think that Christ's ongoing intercession is necessary to complete something lacking in the atonement, or to procure forgiveness for the sins of His people. The Scriptures make it clear that Christ was manifested at the consummation of the ages to put away sin once and for all and obtain our eternal redemption by the sacrifice of Himself.[80] The writer of Hebrews states it in this way: "And every priest stands ministering daily and offering repeatedly the same sacrifices, which can never take away sins. But this Man, after He had offered one sacrifice for sins forever, sat down at the right hand of God, from that time waiting till His enemies are made His footstool. For by one offering He has perfected forever those who are being sanctified."[81]

The death of Christ once and for all resolves the matter of the believer's past, present, and future sins. For this reason, we should not think of Christ as standing or prostrating Himself before the Father, begging forgiveness for the ongoing sins of His people. His session at the right hand of God is the great and eternal memorial that atonement has been made.[82] It is the enduring monument that shall not be forgotten.

---

78. John Murray, *The Epistle to the Romans*, The International Commentary on the New Testament, 155. The text within the larger quotation was taken from H. B. Swete, *The Ascended Christ* (London, 1912), 95.

79. Hebrews 7:25

80. Hebrews 9:12, 26–28. (See also Hebrews 7:27; 10:10; 1 Peter 3:18.)

81. Hebrews 10:11–14

82. The word *session* is often employed by theologians to denote Christ being "seated" at the right hand of God.

JESUS PRAYS FOR HIS PEOPLE

Secondly, Jesus Christ's role as intercessor is not merely representative but also involves actual intercession, or the lifting of prayers and petitions to God on behalf of His people. To prove this, we will briefly consider three texts:

> Who is he who condemns? It is Christ who died, and furthermore is also risen, who is even at the right hand of God, who also makes intercession for us.[83]

> Therefore He is also able to save to the uttermost those who come to God through Him, since He always lives to make intercession for them.[84]

> Therefore I will divide Him a portion with the great, and He shall divide the spoil with the strong, because He poured out His soul unto death, and He was numbered with the transgressors, and He bore the sin of many, and made intercession for the transgressors.[85]

When the apostle Paul and the writer of Hebrews refer to the intercessory ministry of Christ, they use the same Greek word: *entugcháno*, which clearly denotes the act of prayer, entreaty, or intercession.[86] In his prophecy regarding the future intercessory ministry of the Messiah, Isaiah employs the Hebrew verb *paga*, which means to make entreaty or to interpose.[87] Therefore, to be faithful to the original meaning and context of these terms, we must conclude that Christ's intercession also includes His petitions to God on behalf of His people.

It is in this intercessory ministry that the power and majesty of Christ's dual nature shine forth. As the omniscient God, He knows every trial, temptation, and need of His people—immediately, effortlessly, simultaneously, and exhaustively.[88] As a man who has been tempted in all things, He is able to sympathize with His people and to come to their aid in the midst of their troubles.[89] As the God-man, He is able to enter

---

83. Romans 8:34

84. Hebrews 7:25

85. Isaiah 53:12

86. Romans 8:34; Hebrews 7:25. See Wayne A. Grudem, *Systematic Theology* (Grand Rapids: Zondervan, 1994), 627–28.

87. Isaiah 53:12

88. Paul David Washer, *The One True God* (Hannibal, Miss.: Granted Ministries Press, 2009), 40.

89. Hebrews 4:15; 2:16–18

into the very throne room of God and intercede on behalf of His people with a perfect knowledge of their need, a perfect sympathy toward them, and a perfect understanding of the will of God.

Although we might desire a more detailed description of the exact nature of Christ's heavenly intercession on behalf of His people, we must approach the matter with a great deal of caution. Scripture is nearly silent on the matter. However, we may be able to gain some insight by considering the nature of Christ's intercession during His earthly ministry. John Murray writes:

> The teaching and action of Jesus on earth must have encouraged His disciples to recognize in Him their all-prevailing intercessor. 'I have prayed for you,' He said to Simon Peter at the Last Supper, 'that your faith may not fail; and when you have turned again, strengthen your brethren' (Luke 22:32). If it be asked what form His heavenly intercession takes, what better answer can be given than that He still does for His people at the right hand of God what He did for Peter on earth? And the prayer recorded in John 17, also belonging to the same night in which He was betrayed, is well called His high-priestly prayer, and a careful study of it will help us considerably to understand what is intended here when our Lord is described as making intercession for those who come to God through Him.[90]

JESUS DEFENDS HIS PEOPLE FROM THE DEVIL

Thirdly, Christ's intercession includes His defense of the believer against the accusations of the devil and any who would align themselves with him. The Scriptures refer to the devil as the accuser of the brethren who accuses them before God day and night.[91] In fact, the name *devil* is translated from the Greek word *diábolos,* which denotes an accuser or one prone to accusation and slander. In this life, the devil constantly maligns and accuses the Christian, but Christ takes up the believer's defense before the throne of God. It is important to note that this defense does not rest upon the believer's innocence, merit, or the credibility of the devil's accusation. If it did, it might fail, for we are often guilty and the devil is often right in his prosecution of us. Instead, our defense rests upon Christ's perfect and immutable work on the believer's behalf. He

90. Murray, *The Epistle to the Romans,* 154–55.
91. Revelation 12:10

has fully paid for every crime that we have committed and thus nullifies every accusation the devil can rightly level against us. It is this confidence that led Paul to write: "Who is he who condemns? It is Christ who died, and furthermore is also risen, who is even at the right hand of God, who also makes intercession for us."[92] The apostle's question is, of course, rhetorical. He knows that the only One who truly has the right to condemn is the very One who died to free the believer from all condemnation. The accusations of the devil are no match for the blood of Christ. Even the weakest among God's people will overcome the greatest of devils because of the blood of the Lamb.[93] Furthermore, it is also important to point out that Christ not only intercedes for His people against the accusations of the devil, but He also intercedes for them in the midst of the devil's attacks upon them. The night before the crucifixion, Jesus told Peter that Satan had demanded permission to sift him like wheat, but Jesus promised that He had prayed that Peter's faith would not fail.[94] He has done the same for countless believers throughout the two-thousand-year history of the church and will do so until the end of the age.

JESUS COMFORTS HIS PEOPLE

Fourthly and finally, Christ's intercession is the greatest of comforts for His people. The believer has an immutable right standing before God through the atonement. Furthermore, the regenerating work and indwelling of the Holy Spirit gives him a new power over sin. Nevertheless, the believer is painfully aware of his many weakness and oft-repeated failures. These would leave him downcast and without hope if he did not have a merciful High Priest in heaven who is able to deal gently with the ignorant and misguided.[95]

The fourth and fifth chapters of the book of Hebrews clearly demonstrate this truth. There we learn that there are two powerful truths at work in the life of every believer. The first has to do with the power of the Word of God to expose even the most hidden thoughts and deeds in the believer's life. The Word of God is "living and powerful, and sharper

---

92. Romans 8:34
93. Revelation 12:11
94. Luke 22:31–32
95. Hebrews 5:1–2

than any two-edged sword, piercing even to the division of soul and spirit, and of joints and marrow, and is a discerner of the thoughts and intents of the heart."[96] The second truth has to do with the omniscience of God. He knows every thought, word, and deed of the believer—"there is no creature hidden from His sight, but all things are naked and open to the eyes of Him to whom we must give account."[97]

These two truths, the power of the Word of God to expose our sin and the omniscience of God from which no man can hide, would be enough to paralyze the believer and cast him into a sea of uncertainty and doubt. However, this is not the case, because the believer finds in Jesus a merciful and faithful high priest who can sympathize with his weaknesses, because He was tempted in all things yet was without sin.[98] For this reason, doubt and fear do not push believers away, but we have confidence to draw near to the throne of grace so that we may receive mercy and find grace to help in time of need.[99] The following hymn, written by Charitie L. Bancroft, powerfully portrays this glorious truth:

> Before the throne of God above
> I have a strong and perfect plea.
> A great high priest whose name is Love
> Who ever lives and pleads for me.
> My name is graven on His hands,
> My name is written on His heart.
> I know that while in heaven He stands
> No tongue can bid me thence depart.
>
> When Satan tempts me to despair
> And tells me of the guilt within,
> Upward I look and see Him there
> Who made an end of all my sin.
> Because the sinless Savior died
> My sinful soul is counted free.
> For God the just is satisfied
> To look on Him and pardon me.

---

96. Hebrews 4:12
97. Hebrews 4:13
98. Hebrews 2:16, 18; 4:14–15
99. Hebrews 4:16

Behold Him there the risen Lamb,
My perfect spotless righteousness,
The great unchangeable I AM,
The King of glory and of grace,
One in Himself I cannot die.
My soul is purchased by His blood,
My life is hid with Christ on high,
With Christ my Savior and my God![100]

---

100. Charitie L. Bancroft, "Before the Throne of God Above," 1863.

CHAPTER TWENTY-FIVE

Christ's Ascension as the Lord of All

Therefore God also has highly exalted Him and given Him the name which is above every name, that at the name of Jesus every knee should bow, of those in heaven, and of those on earth, and of those under the earth, and that every tongue should confess that Jesus Christ is Lord, to the glory of God the Father.

—Philippians 2:9–11

And seated Him at His right hand in the heavenly places, far above all principality and power and might and dominion, and every name that is named, not only in this age but also in that which is to come. And He put all things under His feet, and gave Him to be head over all things to the church.

—Ephesians 1:20–22

The ascension of Jesus Christ not only assures us that the church has a mediator, but also that the universe has a lord and judge. Psalm 24 refers to the ascended Christ as the King of Glory to whom even the gates of heaven are subject.[1] Since He is sovereign over the highest realm of creation, we can assume that He also reigns over every lesser realm, and that even the very gates of hell are subject to Him.[2]

The theme of Christ's lordship is prevalent in both the Old Testament prophecies concerning the Messiah and the New Testament proclamation of the apostles. Jesus is not only the Savior of the world, but He is also its absolute Sovereign. Therefore, we cannot be faithful to the New Testament's presentation of Christ or His gospel if we emphasize the former office to the exclusion of the latter. The reality of Christ's lordship

---

1. Psalm 24:7
2. Matthew 16:18; Revelation 1:18

is as essential to true gospel proclamation as the exclusivity of Christ's office as Savior. It is not coincidental that Peter concluded his first public proclamation of the gospel on the day of Pentecost with a declaration of the lordship of Jesus: "For David did not ascend into the heavens, but he says himself: 'The LORD said to my Lord, "Sit at My right hand, till I make Your enemies Your footstool."' Therefore let all the house of Israel know assuredly that God has made this Jesus, whom you crucified, both Lord and Christ."[3]

The ascension and exaltation of Christ as Lord is not to be treated as a minor doctrine to be tagged on to the end of a lengthy sermon on the cross, nor should it be downplayed in order to avoid offending a culture that has a hard time fitting a sovereign king into its worldview. Instead, it should be given its place among the most essential and prominent doctrines of the gospel. Along with the resurrection, Christ's exaltation to the right hand of God was a prominent theme in the proclamation of the apostles and the early church. Therefore, it should also be a prominent theme in the gospel that we preach today. We must preach Christ as the Savior who beckons the weary and heavy laden to come to Him without reservation.[4] We must preach Christ as Lord, the one who demands the allegiance of nations and rules over them with a rod of iron![5] Although we could fill volumes with the theme of Christ's lordship, we will attempt to address some truths related to this doctrine that have the greatest bearing on our understanding and proclamation of the gospel.

THE FOUNDATION OF CHRIST'S LORDSHIP

The first question to examine is, "What is the basis, or foundation, of Christ's lordship? From whom or through whom did His appointment come?" According to the Scriptures, it is His by divine decree. On the day of Pentecost, Peter declared that it was God who made this Jesus who was crucified to be both Lord and Christ.[6] In other words, the same God who said to Him, "You are a priest forever according to the order of Melchizedek," has also appointed Him as Lord and Sovereign of all.[7]

---

3. Acts 2:34–36
4. Matthew 11:28
5. Psalm 2:9–12
6. Acts 2:36
7. Psalm 110:4; Hebrews 5:6; 7:17, 21

In His final words to His disciples, Christ declared, "All authority *has been given* to Me in heaven and on earth."[8] From this, we understand that His title as absolute Sovereign was not something that He took for Himself, but rather God the Father conferred it upon Him.

David, writing under the inspiration of the Spirit, prophesied this truth: "The LORD said to my Lord, 'Sit at My right hand, till I make Your enemies Your footstool.'"[9] In His confrontation with the Pharisees and Sadducees, Jesus quoted this text in order to demonstrate that the Messiah would be more than a man and that His sovereignty would extend far beyond an earthly realm.[10] According to the Scriptures, God had granted that David should be the most prominent and powerful of Israel's kings, and yet David, in the Spirit, referred to his future messianic Son as his Lord who would sit at the very right hand of God. The apostle Paul confirmed the fulfillment of this prophecy in several of his epistles. He wrote to the church in Philippi that God had highly exalted Jesus and "given Him the name which is above every name."[11] To the church in Ephesus, he explained that God had seated Jesus at His right hand, far above all rule and authority and power and dominion.[12]

It is important to note that each text we have cited presents the conferment of authority from the Father to the Son as an accomplished event. Although the universal vindication of Christ and confession of His lordship is an event still in the future, it is nonetheless a present reality, an absolute certainty of which all men must be made aware and in which His people should trust. By virtue of who He is and as a reward for what He has accomplished, Jesus Christ has received from the Father all authority in every realm of creation. The Jews wanted to take Jesus by force and make Him king over Israel.[13] Satan offered Him all the kingdoms of this world if He would only fall down and worship him.[14] However, Christ overcame all of these temptations and devoted Himself in service to the only One who truly possessed the power to grant such authority. For this

---

8. Matthew 28:18, emphasis added
9. Matthew 22:44; Acts 2:34–35; Psalm 110:1
10. Matthew 22:43–45
11. Philippians 2:9
12. Ephesians 1:20–22
13. John 6:15
14. Matthew 4:8–9

reason, He was highly exalted by the Father. The apostle Paul explains it in this way:

> And being found in appearance as a man, He humbled Himself and became obedient to the point of death, even the death of the cross. Therefore God also has highly exalted Him and given Him the name which is above every name, that at the name of Jesus every knee should bow, of those in heaven, and of those on earth, and of those under the earth, and that every tongue should confess that Jesus Christ is Lord, to the glory of God the Father.[15]

THE INCONTESTABILITY OF CHRIST'S LORDSHIP

The truth that Jesus' universal lordship is founded upon divine decree has many implications, but one of the most important is that it guarantees that His lordship is immutable and incontestable. Psalm 2 powerfully demonstrates this truth, and both Jews and Christians alike have interpreted it as a royal psalm depicting the reign of the Messiah:

> Why do the nations rage, and the people plot a vain thing? The kings of the earth set themselves, and the rulers take counsel together, against the LORD and against His Anointed, saying, "Let us break Their bonds in pieces and cast away Their cords from us." He who sits in the heavens shall laugh; the LORD shall hold them in derision. Then He shall speak to them in His wrath, and distress them in His deep displeasure: "Yet I have set My King on My holy hill of Zion."[16]

In this psalm, we read of a Davidic king whose reign would have both absolute authority and unlimited jurisdiction. Furthermore, we learn that the king's installment upon the throne of the universe would be God's doing. The decision would be His divine prerogative and would be made independently of creation. It would not require the approval of men or angels, and its continuance would not depend upon their aid. In fact, if every creature in heaven, earth, and hell were to come together in one united force to fight against God's King, it would have no more effect than if the weakest among them were standing alone. Their rebellion would be as frivolous and comical as a mite beating its head against a

---

15. Philippians 2:8–11
16. Psalm 2:1–6

world of granite! This becomes glaringly apparent with only the slightest consideration of this royal psalm!

In the first three verses of the text, we witness the world's hostility toward Christ and the advancement of His kingdom. We are privy to the ancient battle between the malignant seed of the serpent and the seed of the woman.[17] A violent and hostile sea of humanity has set itself against the will of God and His King. Men consider Christ's righteous reign and will to be as fetters to their wickedness. They desire to tear the fetters apart and cast them away, and they are miserable unless they are free to do evil. For this reason, the nations are in an uproar. They are like a raging warhorse charging furiously into battle against God's appointed Sovereign. Even their greatest leaders are involved in the mutiny. The kings of the earth take their stand, and the rulers take counsel together against the Lord and His Anointed. Yet for all their plotting and scheming, their best-laid plans are vanity, and their greatest efforts accomplish nothing. They are like a tiny spider weaving a web in hopes of catching a charging lion. All their hostility, counsel, and warring are inconsequential. They have forgotten that there is no wisdom, no understanding, and no counsel against the Lord.[18] They fail to recognize that they are like a drop from a bucket, regarded as a speck of dust on the scales. In their collective power and glory, they are as nothing before Him, and He sees them as less than nothing and meaningless.[19] In their arrogance, they have refused the wise counsel of David, who gave the following warning to all nations and peoples everywhere: "Let all the earth fear the LORD; let all the inhabitants of the world stand in awe of Him. For He spoke, and it was done; He commanded, and it stood fast. The LORD brings the counsel of the nations to nothing; He makes the plans of the peoples of no effect. The counsel of the LORD stands forever, the plans of His heart to all generations."[20]

God has installed Jesus of Nazareth as His king, and the combined opposition of those who would oppose Him is insignificant, even comical, and worthy of divine ridicule. Writing under the inspiration of the Holy Spirit, David informs us that He who sits in heaven derides and

---

17. Genesis 3:15
18. Proverbs 21:30
19. Isaiah 40:15–17
20. Psalm 33:8–11

mocks his opponents. Their constant plotting and extravagant schemes amuse Him; He scoffs at their boasts and threats; He laughs at their greatest assaults and turns them back with nothing more than a word. Charles Spurgeon remarks: "Mark the quiet dignity of the Omnipotent One, and the contempt which He pours upon the princes and their raging people. He has not taken the trouble to rise up and do battle with them—He despises them, He knows how absurd, how irrational, how futile are their attempts against Him—He therefore laughs at them."[21] John Calvin also comments, "Let us, therefore, assure ourselves that if God does not immediately stretch forth his hand against the ungodly, it is now His time of laughter."[22]

The distance between God and the rebel nations is so great that He has no need to rise or even reposition Himself on His throne. When He is done with the amusement of their warring, He speaks to them with a minimal manifestation of His anger, and they are transfixed with horror. He declares to them His unalterable decree concerning His Son. It is as though He says to them: "Let the nations rage and let the rulers of the earth take their stand. But as for Me, I have enthroned My King upon My holy mountain. The die is cast by My hand, and all opposition is futile. His kingdom shall come and His will shall be done!"

Jesus Christ is the stone seen by the prophet Daniel.[23] This stone was cut out of the mountain by divine decree without the aid of human counsel or might; this stone crushes the competing kingdoms of the earth and brings them to an end; this stone became a great mountain and filled the whole earth; this stone's kingdom will endure forever and not be left to another people. For this reason, the nations are livid. They are beside themselves with fury. How dare God impose His king and His laws upon them! Yet their attitudes and actions have no strength against God's decree. There will never be an abdication of the throne, the office will never be open for reelection, there will never be a changing of the guard, and there is no possibility of revolt. The God of Scripture is an absolutely sovereign God, and He has granted to His Son an immutable and incontestable throne.

---

21. Spurgeon, *Treasury of David*, 1:11.

22. John Calvin, *Commentary on the Book of Psalms*, vol. 4 of Calvin's Commentaries (Grand Rapids: Baker, 1996), 4:14.

23. Daniel 2:34–35, 44–45

We live in an age and a culture that exalts human autonomy above the sovereignty of God and sets the individual's freedom of expression above the laws of God. In fact, human autonomy and freedom of expression are the twin sacred cows of modern man.[24] But consider these Scriptures: "But He is unique, and who can make Him change? And whatever His soul desires, that He does."[25] "All the inhabitants of the earth are reputed as nothing; He does according to His will in the army of heaven and among the inhabitants of the earth. No one can restrain His hand or say to Him, 'What have You done?'"[26] These biblical truths infuriate the great majority of mankind. Nevertheless, they are an essential part of the gospel and must not be hidden or minimized out of expediency or a desire to make the gospel inoffensive.

God has made this Jesus whom we crucified to be both Lord and Christ.[27] The Stone which the builders rejected has become the Chief Cornerstone.[28] By divine appointment, Christ now owns the throne of the universe. His installment is not open to criticism or debate. He will always be the Lord and Judge with whom every man must deal. This great truth must not be hidden from the preacher's public; it must be proclaimed to all without reservation. However, we must remember that we are not pleading with men to make Jesus Lord of their lives. Instead, we are pleading with them to acknowledge and submit to the Lord that God has made![29]

THE EXTENT OF CHRIST'S LORDSHIP

Having considered the foundation and incontestability of Christ's authority, we will now turn our attention toward the extent, or jurisdiction, of His authority. According to the Scriptures, it is both universal and absolute. In His final words to His disciples, Jesus declared, *"All authority has been given to Me in heaven and on earth."*[30] We should not allow the

---

24. The phrase *sacred cow* is a reference to the Hindu religion that considers cattle to be holy or even divine. To say that an idea, tradition, or custom is a sacred cow means that it is considered to be above any doubt or criticism—oftentimes, unreasonably.

25. Job 23:13

26. Daniel 4:35

27. Acts 2:36

28. Psalm 118:22; Matthew 21:42; Mark 12:10; Luke 20:17; Acts 4:11; 1 Peter 2:7

29. Acts 2:36

30. Matthew 28:18, emphasis added

brevity of His statement to cause us to doubt its significance. It is one of the most astounding claims that Jesus ever made. The word *authority* is translated from the Greek noun *exousia*, which denotes authority, right, and power. In the context of the ascension, it means that Christ has been given all authority in every jurisdiction or realm of creation, without limitation or exception. The reference to heaven and earth further proves the impossibility of anything being beyond His authority or power. Both the prophecies of the Old Testament and the teachings of the New Testament epistles confirm this as well. From the Old Testament:

> I was watching in the night visions, and behold, One like the Son of Man, coming with the clouds of heaven! He came to the Ancient of Days, and they brought Him near before Him. Then to Him was given dominion and glory and a kingdom, that all peoples, nations, and languages should serve Him. His dominion is an everlasting dominion, which shall not pass away, and His kingdom the one which shall not be destroyed.[31]

And in the New Testament: "He raised Him from the dead and seated Him at His right hand in the heavenly places, far above all principality and power and might and dominion, and every name that is named, not only in this age but also in that which is to come. And He put all things under His feet, and gave Him to be head over all things to the church."[32]

"God also has highly exalted Him and given Him the name which is above every name, that at the name of Jesus every knee should bow, of those in heaven, and of those on earth, and of those under the earth, and that every tongue should confess that Jesus Christ is Lord, to the glory of God the Father."[33]

Moses records how Pharaoh called for Joseph to be brought out of the dungeon and presented before him.[34] So Christ was brought forth from the grave and presented before the Ancient of Days.[35] Again, Moses records that Pharoah said to Joseph, "Without your consent no man may lift his hand or foot in all the land of Egypt."[36] So God the Father said to the exalted Christ, "Without your permission no one shall raise his

---

31. Daniel 7:13–14
32. Ephesians 1:20–22
33. Philippians 2:9–11
34. Genesis 41:14
35. Daniel 7:13
36. Genesis 41:44

hand or foot in all of heaven and earth." From Daniel's place in history, he looked far into the future and saw the promise of the exalted Christ as He was presented before the Ancient of Days and was given dominion, glory, and a kingdom so that all peoples of every language might serve Him.

From Paul's place in history, he looked back at Christ's exaltation as an accomplished fact and a present reality. He assures us that Christ is now seated at the right hand of God, far above all rule and authority and power and dominion. The psalmist saw only the fringes of Christ's glory when he wrote that the nations would be given to Him as an inheritance and the ends of the earth would be His possession to do with as He pleased.[37] The apostle Paul expands our view to include not only the earth and its inhabitants but also the entire universe. Everything that exists, visible and invisible, whether thrones or dominions or rulers or authorities, has been created through Him and for Him and is subject to Him.[38] From the axis of the universe to the farthest reaches of its expanse, Jesus of Nazareth is Lord! From the single cell of the most primitive life form to the seraphim of unimaginable complexity and power, Jesus of Nazareth is Lord. From the heart of His most devout follower to the fist of His most hostile enemy, Jesus of Nazareth is Lord! From the heights of heaven to the depths of hell, Jesus of Nazareth is Lord! His unlimited and unhindered sovereignty cannot be exaggerated!

CHRIST'S LORDSHIP AND MAN'S ALLEGIANCE

All moral creatures, human and angelic, friend and foe of Christ, have one final destiny: they will all bow their knee and confess with their tongue that Jesus Christ is Lord.[39] In light of this truth, and in light of the nature and extension of Christ's lordship, it should be clear to all reasonable creatures that their personal response to Him is absolutely critical. Since God has made this Christ to be both Lord and Judge of the universe, then every other concern for man is secondary, even trivial, in comparison. To be in right standing with the absolute Sovereign of the universe should be the greatest of all concerns for every man.

---

37. Job 26:14: "Indeed these are the mere edges of His ways, and how small a whisper we hear of Him! But the thunder of His power who can understand?" Also, Psalm 2:8–9.
38. Colossians 1:16
39. Philippians 2:9–11

It is the unapologetic determination and proclamation of the Scriptures that all men, without exception, owe Christ their complete allegiance, and there will be dire consequences for any and all who refuse Him.[40] To contemporary man this remark is beyond scandalous; it is outrageous, offensive, intolerable, even criminal. Therefore, without the least consideration of the possible validity of Christ's demands upon him, man takes the offensive and spews forth a barrage of questions to show his contempt toward any God who would demand his allegiance, or even suggest that he is not a fully autonomous creature. However, such ranting is not novel; it has been recorded in Scripture as the common response of rebellious men to the demands of a sovereign God:

"Who made you a prince and a judge over us?"[41]

"Who is the LORD, that I should obey His voice?"[42]

"Who is the Almighty, that we should serve Him?"[43]

In light of the majesty of Christ, the apostle Paul long ago penned the only reply that these objections merit: "But indeed, O man, who are you to reply against God?"[44] The Scriptures teach that God has made Jesus of Nazareth to be both Lord and Christ.[45] Who then is man that he should object or even demand an explanation? We learn from Job that those who question God darken counsel by words without knowledge; they put on the mantle of a fool and cross the most dangerous boundaries; they rush in where angels fear to tread.[46] Nevertheless, in spite of man's insolence, God has shown Himself to be a compassionate and gracious God, slow to anger and abounding in loving-kindness.[47] Therefore, He frequently condescends to such questions and instructs even the most rebellious among men as to why they should follow His directive and submit to His decree. We will consider a few reasons for honoring Christ in the following pages.

---

40. Psalm 2:10–12
41. Exodus 2:14; Acts 7:27, 35
42. Exodus 5:2
43. Job 21:15
44. Romans 9:20
45. Acts 2:36
46. Job 38:2
47. Exodus 34:6; Nehemiah 9:17; Psalms 86:15; 103:8; 145:8; Joel 2:13; Jonah 4:2

CHRIST, OUR CREATOR AND SUSTAINER

First, all men should honor the Son because He is their Creator and Sustainer. From the prologue of John we learn, "All things were made through Him, and without Him nothing was made that was made."[48] The writer of Hebrews and the apostle Paul confirm that what the Son created He also continues to sustain: "upholding all things by the word of His power," and "in Him all things consist."[49] From these truths, we can conclude that every creature in heaven and on earth owes its beginning and continued existence to the Son of God. For a man to refuse allegiance to the very One who gave him life and sustains his every breath is a great arrogance; for him to fight against the One upon whom his entire existence depends is insanity; for him to scorn the One who blesses him in spite of his sin is the epitome of ingratitude.

In an attempt to justify his neglect of God, fallen man will often ask, "If God is good, why does He allow bad things to happen to good people?" However, a more appropriate question should be, "Why does He allow good things to happen to bad people?" Or even, "Why does anything good happen at all?" We are a fallen and morally corrupt race that suppresses the truth of God in unrighteousness and categorically rejects His rule. For this reason, we should receive nothing but wrath and death. The whole world should be barren and lifeless. The fact that there is any goodness, beauty, joy, love, or purpose in the realm of human existence can only be explained in light of the grace and benevolence of the Son of God toward evil men. In Him, we live and move and exist.[50] He gives life and breath and all things.[51] He causes His sun to rise upon the evil, and He sends rain upon the unrighteous.[52] He satisfies the hearts of those who hate Him with food and gladness.[53] All this proves that we owe Him our greatest allegiance.

CHRIST, OUR REDEEMER

Secondly, all men should honor the Son because of His redemptive work on Calvary. Although it is beyond us here to sound the depths of God's

---

48. John 1:3
49. Hebrews 1:3; Colossians 1:17
50. Acts 17:28
51. Acts 17:25
52. Matthew 5:45
53. Acts 14:17

providence in redemption, we can declare without reservation that Christ's atoning work has benefited the entire universe, and that even those who refuse His offer of salvation have already benefited from it far more than words can tell. God gave His Son, and His Son willingly gave His life to make atonement for sin so that those who put their trust in Him might not perish but have everlasting life.[54]

Although the blessings of Calvary have been infinite, two benefits are most applicable to our present discussion. The first is the universal offer of pardon for sins, reconciliation with God, and the hope of eternal life. The gospel publishes a universal call for all men everywhere to believe in their heart and confess with their mouth that Jesus Christ is Lord.[55] It also sets forth the universal promise that none of those who come will be cast out.[56] This should be enough to secure the allegiance of all men. Our hearts were deceitfully wicked, our sins were over our heads, and our condemnation was just. And yet the Lord, who alone had the right to condemn us, willingly gave Himself over to death for our salvation. This is astounding beyond measure! The Scriptures remind us that one will hardly die for a righteous man, and yet while we were sinners, Christ died for us.[57] It is this love of Christ toward us that should win our hearts and move us to give Him our full allegiance. It should lead us to conclude that since He died for all, then all should no longer live for themselves but for Him who died and rose again on their behalf![58] On the day of judgment, a great shame will cover the faces of those who refused their allegiance to such a gracious Lord! They will have an eternity to ponder, "How could we have spurned so great a love? How could we have neglected so great a salvation?"

The second universal benefit of Calvary consists of the multiform blessings that have flowed from it to every corner of the globe: physical, material, economic, political, and cultural blessings, to name a few. All men, even those who continue in their rebellion against Christ, have benefited from the effects of the gospel upon themselves and their culture. Although Christ is much maligned because of the abominable deeds of those who have wrongly called themselves Christians, the true gospel

---

54. John 3:16
55. Acts 17:30; Romans 10:9–10
56. John 6:37
57. Romans 5:7–8
58. 2 Corinthians 5:14–15

has been the one shining light that has kept the world from total darkness and the salt that has kept it from total moral decay.[59] Although the secular mind may scoff at this claim, it will be fully vindicated on the day of judgment. On that day, real history will unfold, and all will see that every good thing from which they have ever benefited in every realm of human existence was intricately related to Christ's work on Calvary, the proclamation of His gospel, and the advancement of His kingdom. This vindication will be a great joy to the people of God as they see their Lord receive the honor that was long due Him. However, it will be a day of great shame to all those who saw no benefit in Christ and yet reaped the benefits of His revelation, His death, and His ongoing providence.

CHRIST, GOD'S CHOSEN KING

Thirdly, all men should honor and give the Son their allegiance because God would have it this way. God has determined that all should honor the Son even as they honor the Father. He who does not honor the Son does not honor the Father, and he will be subject to the appropriate judgment.[60] In short, there will be infinite benefit for those who obey the Lord Jesus Christ and believe in His name. However, there will be terrible consequences for those who refuse Him. It is for this reason that David gives the following solemn warning to the nations: "Now therefore, be wise, O kings; be instructed, you judges of the earth. Serve the LORD with fear, and rejoice with trembling. Kiss the Son, lest He be angry, and you perish in the way, when His wrath is kindled but a little. Blessed are all those who put their trust in Him."[61] In this text, we find three phrases that unite together in a singular voice to declare to all men what God demands of the world regarding His Son. First, there is the command for all mankind to worship the Lord with reverence. The phrase can also be translated "serve the Lord with fear." Worship and service are two sides of the same coin: one cannot exist without the other. God is not

---

59. Romans 2:24. This has been a common malady throughout redemptive history. Because of those who falsely identify themselves with Christ and His people, the way of truth is maligned (see Isaiah 52:5; Ezekiel 36:20; 2 Peter 2:2). Light references: John 1:4–5, 9; Matthew 4:16; 5:14. Salt has been used since the most ancient times to preserve food from decay (see Matthew 5:13).

60. John 5:23

61. Psalm 2:10–12

petitioning the tolerance of men or begging their sympathies for His Son. Instead, He is demanding that all men render unto Him their most reverent worship and service.

Secondly, there is the command for all mankind to rejoice before the Son with trembling. The mingling of these two opposing emotions—rejoicing and fear—seems foreign to contemporary man, but they are often found together in the Scriptures.[62] Rejoicing is the result of the graciousness and mercies of Christ toward those who submit to His lordship. Fear is the result of His majesty and power. His people rejoice because He is not ashamed to call them brothers, and yet they show Him their greatest reverence because of His supremacy and preeminence among them.[63] He alone has been given a name that is above every name.[64]

Thirdly, there is the command for all mankind to render homage to the Son. The phrase is translated literally, "Kiss the Son lest He become angry and you are destroyed." These words sound harsh to our contemporary ear; nevertheless, they are true. There are two extreme destinies set before every man: one of infinite bliss and the other of infinite terror. The determining factor between the two is our response to Jesus of Nazareth. God has established Him as the Lord of the universe and has demanded that all moral creatures, angelic and human, submit to His reign with joy, thanksgiving, and reverence. God has not set Christ's name before men as an option for them to review and debate. He has not requested that they weigh His worth and render an opinion. God has weighed Christ's worth and rendered His own opinion concerning Him. On earth, He publicly vindicated Christ by raising Him from the dead. In heaven, He made known His regard for Christ by seating Him at His right hand. Now all

---

62. Psalm 22:23: "You who fear the LORD, praise Him! All you descendants of Jacob, glorify Him, and fear Him, all you offspring of Israel!" Psalm 40:3: "He has put a new song in my mouth—praise to our God; many will see it and fear, and will trust in the LORD." Jeremiah 33:9: "Then it shall be to Me a name of joy, a praise, and an honor before all nations of the earth, who shall hear all the good that I do to them; they shall fear and tremble for all the goodness and all the prosperity that I provide for it." Philippians 2:12–13: "Therefore, my beloved, as you have always obeyed, not as in my presence only, but now much more in my absence, work out your own salvation with fear and trembling; for it is God who works in you both to will and to do for His good pleasure." Revelation 19:5: "Then a voice came from the throne, saying, 'Praise our God, all you His servants and those who fear Him, both small and great!'"

63. Hebrews 2:11; Colossians 1:18

64. Ephesians 1:20–23; Philippians 2:9

that is left for creation to do is to obey God and render unto His Son all blessing, honor, glory, and dominion forever and ever.[65]

APPROPRIATE WARNINGS

God has made this Jesus whom the nations crucified to be both Lord and Christ of all.[66] He has taken the Stone the world rejected and made Him to be the Chief Cornerstone of all His works.[67] It is an irrevocable decree. For this reason, Jesus of Nazareth will always be the Sovereign with whom men must deal.

The Scriptures teach that Jesus is a merciful and faithful high priest who has become a source of eternal salvation for all who obey Him.[68] Nevertheless, for those who reject Him, He is a stone of stumbling and a rock of offense.[69] Whoever stumbles over Christ in unbelief will be broken to pieces, and whomever Christ falls upon in judgment will be scattered like dust.[70] Jesus Christ is *the* Savior, but He is also *the* Lord. Neither of these truths should be exalted at the expense of the other, but they must be held in a biblical balance. The writer of Hebrews powerfully illustrates this: "But this Man [Christ], after He had offered one sacrifice for sins forever, sat down at the right hand of God, from that time waiting till His enemies are made His footstool."[71]

This Scripture sets forth the Christ as the Savior who sacrifices Himself to put away the sin of His enemies, and yet He is also the Lord who will subjugate His enemies who continue in rebellion and make them a footstool for His feet. Both statements are equally extreme, but they are also equally true. Men must not deceive themselves into holding to certain metaphors regarding the Son while rejecting others. While it is true that Christ is the Lamb who takes away the sins of the world, He is also the Lamb from whom the greatest and most powerful men on earth will seek

---

65. Revelation 5:13

66. Psalm 2:1; Acts 4:25–27; 2:36

67. Matthew 21:42; Luke 20:17

68. Hebrews 2:17; 5:9

69. Romans 9:32–33; 1 Peter 2:8

70. Matthew 21:44; Luke 20:18: "Whoever falls on this stone will be broken; but on whomever it falls, it will grind him to powder." This verse means that whoever takes offense at Christ and refuses to acknowledge His supremacy will be destroyed by the very judgment of God.

71. Hebrews 10:12–13

to hide themselves on the day of His appearing.[72] Finding no pity in the face of Christ, they will beg for mercy from rocks and mountains, crying out, "Fall on us and hide us from the face of Him who sits on the throne and from the wrath of the Lamb!"[73] The apostle John reports the following:

> Now I saw heaven opened, and behold, a white horse. And He who sat on him was called Faithful and True, and in righteousness He judges and makes war. His eyes were like a flame of fire, and on His head were many crowns. He had a name written that no one knew except Himself. He was clothed with a robe dipped in blood, and His name is called The Word of God. And the armies in heaven, clothed in fine linen, white and clean, followed Him on white horses. Now out of His mouth goes a sharp sword, that with it He should strike the nations. And He Himself will rule them with a rod of iron. He Himself treads the winepress of the fierceness and wrath of Almighty God. And He has on His robe and on His thigh a name written: KING OF KINGS AND LORD OF LORDS.[74]

The lordship of Jesus Christ is a blessed hope for some and a terrifying nightmare for others. However, regardless of our response, it is an unalterable reality. Regarding God, the patriarch Job declared: "He is wise in heart, and mighty in strength: who hath hardened himself against Him, and hath prospered?"[75] Without exaggeration, the same may be said of Christ. He is and will always be the Lord and Judge to whom every man will be accountable. We can be led with a shepherd's staff or we can be led by a rod of iron.[76] Either way, Christ will lead and we will be led. For this reason, we would be wise to follow David's advice and pay homage to the Son so that He may not become angry and we perish in the way. His wrath may soon be kindled, yet blessed are those who take refuge in Him.[77]

---

72. John 1:29

73. Revelation 6:16

74. Revelation 19:11–16

75. Job 9:4 KJV. The NASB reads: "Wise in heart and mighty in strength, who has defied Him without harm?"

76. Psalm 23:1–4; John 10:9–11; Psalm 2:9

77. Psalm 2:12

CHAPTER TWENTY-SIX

Christ's Ascension as the Judge of All

Truly, these times of ignorance God overlooked, but now commands all men everywhere to repent, because He has appointed a day on which He will judge the world in righteousness by the Man whom He has ordained. He has given assurance of this to all by raising Him from the dead.
—Acts 17:30–31

When the Son of Man comes in His glory, and all the holy angels with Him, then He will sit on the throne of His glory. All the nations will be gathered before Him, and He will separate them one from another, as a shepherd divides his sheep from the goats.
—Matthew 25:31–32

One of the greatest implications of the lordship of Jesus Christ is that He will judge the world. In the midst of a severe confrontation with the Jewish leaders who were seeking to kill Him, Jesus declared that the Father had given Him absolute authority to execute all judgment upon the earth.[1] The preaching and writing of the apostles repeats this radical claim over and over. In Peter's first sermon to the Gentiles at Caesarea, he declared: "God raised [Him] up on the third day, and showed Him openly, not to all the people, but to witnesses chosen before by God, even to us who ate and drank with Him after He arose from the dead. And He commanded us to preach to the people, and to testify that it is He who was ordained by God to be Judge of the living and the dead."[2]

Peter's sermon reveals three great truths that will form the outline for our discussion of Christ's exaltation to the office of judge. The first truth

---

1. John 5:22, 26
2. Acts 10:40–42

that all men must reconcile themselves to is that there will be a consummation of the world and a day of final judgment. The second truth is that on that day, Jesus Christ will preside as Lord and Judge of all. The third and final truth that demands our attention is that God has commissioned the church not only to proclaim the benefits of the gospel but also to warn men of the great and irrevocable judgment that is coming upon the world!

THE CERTAINTY AND EQUITY OF JUDGMENT

The predominant materialistic view of the universe must interpret man's existence as nothing more than a fluke, his history as nothing more than a series of random events, and his future as an absolute uncertainty with no purposeful consummation. In contrast, the Scriptures view man's existence as a purposeful, creative work of a sovereign and moral God who has revealed Himself to men through creation, His works of providence, His written Word, and finally and fully through the incarnation of His Son. Furthermore, the Scriptures teach that God will call all men to account in a final judgment at the consummation of all things. On that day, God will judge all men according to their response to the revelation that they have received.

In light of these truths, the Christian recognizes that human history is not random, or even cyclical, but linear. It had a beginning and it will have an end according to the irrevocable decree of the sovereign God who brought it into existence. To speak plainly, human history is moving, even rushing, toward a final consummation in which every man will be judged and recompensed according to what he has or has not done! The apostle Paul writes: "[God] 'will render to each one according to his deeds': eternal life to those who by patient continuance in doing good seek for glory, honor, and immortality; but to those who are self-seeking and do not obey the truth, but obey unrighteousness—indignation and wrath."[3]

To the individual or culture that judges itself by its own standards, Paul's declaration of universal judgment may seem hopeful. It is the common error of men to judge themselves as right in their own eyes. However, to those who can still hear the voice of conscience, and especially to those who know the Scriptures, these words are more than disconcerting. For it is the testimony of both Scripture and conscience

---

3. Romans 2:6–8

that all have sinned and fallen short of the glory of God.[4] There is none who has persevered in doing good and none who has sought for the glory, honor, and immortality that comes from God.[5] Instead, selfish ambition has driven all men, and all men have suppressed the truth in unrighteousness.[6] Consequently, all are subject to the wrath and indignation of a holy and righteous God.[7] It is for this reason that God intervened and sent His Son to make atonement for the sins of man. His death satisfied the justice of God and appeased the wrath of God. Now all who hear and believe in the Son will be saved. However, those who refuse the Son will be judged by Him.[8]

This declaration of universal judgment often results in questioning God's fairness: How can God judge those who have never heard the preaching of the gospel or had access to the Scriptures? To answer this question we must first stand upon Scripture's testimony regarding the righteousness of God. Although we may not be able to remove all mystery from this event, we do know the character of God and can rest in who He is. As Moses testified, whatever He does will be right: "His work is perfect; for all His ways are justice, a God of truth and without injustice; righteous and upright is He."[9]

Another truth to consider regarding the equity of God in judging the world is that Scripture declares that even the most isolated individual in the most remote area of the world has received God's revelation to some degree and will be without excuse on the day of judgment.[10] Being made in the image of God, every man has an inherent knowledge of Him.[11] Three undeniable realities further confirm this knowledge. First, God's creation testifies of His existence, invisible attributes, eternal power, and divine nature.[12] Second, the providence of God determined the appointed

---

4. Romans 3:23
5. Romans 3:12
6. Romans 1:18
7. Romans 2:8
8. John 3:18, 36
9. Deuteronomy 32:4
10. Romans 1:20. The revelation that has been given to every man through creation, divine providence, and the conscience is often referred to as general revelation, in contrast with specific revelation, which comes through the Scriptures and the preaching of the gospel.
11. Romans 1:19
12. Romans 1:20

times and the boundaries of nations and individuals so that they might seek Him and find Him, though He is not far from anyone.[13] And third, the law of God has been written upon the heart of every man and serves as a moral guide and testimony to the fact that God is a righteous God who will judge men according to their deeds.[14]

A further truth to consider regarding the equity of God in judging the world is the testimony of Scripture that men have not responded properly to the revelation they have received. In other words, they are not victims to be pitied; rather, they are rebels to be censured. They have suppressed the truth in unrighteousness.[15] Even though they knew God, they did not honor Him as God or give thanks to Him.[16] They exchanged the glory and truth of God for self-idolatry and the worship of base creatures lower than themselves.[17] They did not see fit to acknowledge God or to obey His ordinances, but they gave themselves over to every form of unrighteousness and moral depravity.[18] God can rightly judge all men everywhere because they are truly guilty. Although they have received differing degrees of revelation, they have all rebelled against the revelation that they have received.

The final truth to consider regarding the equity of God in judging the world is the testimony of Scripture that all men will be judged according to the revelation that they have received. It is a sound principle of Scripture that to whom much is given, much will be required.[19] All who have sinned against the revelation they received through creation and conscience will be judged for their disobedience. All who have sinned against the revelation of God through the Scriptures and the gospel will be judged for their sins.[20] However, the latter will be

---

13. Acts 17:26–27
14. Romans 2:14–15
15. Romans 1:18
16. Romans 1:21
17. Romans 1:23, 25
18. Romans 1:28–29, 32
19. Luke 12:47–48: "And that servant who knew his master's will, and did not prepare himself or do according to his will, shall be beaten with many stripes. But he who did not know, yet committed things deserving of stripes, shall be beaten with few. For everyone to whom much is given, from him much will be required; and to whom much has been committed, of him they will ask the more."
20. Romans 2:12: "For as many as have sinned without law will also perish without law, and as many as have sinned in the law will be judged by the law."

judged more severely than the former because of the abundant truth that they have received. In any case, we can be sure that on that final day, God's righteousness will be vindicated in judgment. As the psalmist testified: "But the LORD shall endure forever; He has prepared His throne for judgment. He shall judge the world in righteousness, and He shall administer judgment for the peoples in uprightness."[21]

THE LORD OF ALL IS JUDGE OF ALL

The second great truth that we glean from Peter's sermon is that God has appointed Jesus Christ as Judge of the living and the dead.[22] This is not an isolated claim in the Scriptures but is a frequent theme in the Gospels, the book of Acts, the Epistles, and the Apocalypse. In his sermon to the Athenians on Mars Hill, the apostle Paul declared: "Because He [God] has appointed a day on which He will judge the world in righteousness by the Man whom He has ordained. He has given assurance of this to all by raising Him from the dead."[23]

The Scriptures and the Christian church testify that every human being, without exception, will stand before Christ in judgment, and He will determine the destiny of every human being. It is an absolutely astounding truth that there is one mediator between God and men, the man Christ Jesus, and there is one judge between God and men, the man Christ Jesus.[24]

This is still another proof of the universality of Christ's reign. He is not some local deity with limited authority over a restricted area. He is not some member of a collective counsel that governs the universe or a joint tribunal that will hold court on the day of judgment. He alone is King, Lord, and Judge of all. All authority has been given to Him in heaven and on earth.[25] He alone has been seated at the right hand of God, far above all rule and authority and power and dominion, and every name that is named, not only in this age but also in the one to come.[26] The man Jesus of Nazareth, who was crucified during the reign of Pontius Pilate, will

---

21. Psalm 9:7–8
22. Acts 10:40–42
23. Acts 17:31
24. 1 Timothy 2:5
25. Matthew 28:18
26. Ephesians 1:21

not only determine the destiny of every human being who has walked this earth, but He will judge angels and demons, thrones and dominions, rulers and authorities, both in heaven and on earth, visible and invisible.[27] Furthermore, He will judge the founders of all the religions of the world who sought either to supplant Him or to diminish His glory. They will all present themselves before Him with the greatest shame and fear.

The world has one Lawgiver and Judge who is able to both save and destroy.[28] At His second coming, He will bring to light the things hidden in the darkness and disclose the motives of men's hearts.[29] Then He will render to every man according to what he has done and repay every man according to his deeds.[30] To the self-righteous, this does not seem too alarming. However, to the sensible man who has followed the ancient philosopher's advice, "Know thyself," the possibility of every thought, word, and deed being placed under the scrutiny of a perfectly righteous and omniscient Judge is the most terrifying thought that can be conceived.[31] For this reason, the apostle Paul wrote: "For we must all appear before the judgment seat of Christ, that each one may receive the things done in the body, according to what he has done, whether good or bad. Knowing, therefore, the terror of the Lord, we persuade men."[32]

Having proven time and time again that man has utterly undone himself and is without strength to gain a right standing before God, it is the greatest consolation that the one who will judge all men is the very one who died for the sins of His people.[33] If the Lord should mark our iniquities, no one could stand before Him in judgment, but forgiveness can still be found in the person and work of Christ.[34] We must turn to Him before it is too late. We must allow the reality of our sin, the fear of judgment, and Christ's willingness to save to drive us to Him without delay and to cling to Him without release. At the present, Christ stretches forth His

---

27. Colossians 1:16
28. James 4:12
29. 1 Corinthians 4:5
30. Revelation 22:12; Matthew 16:27
31. The phrase *know thyself* (*gnothi seauton*) is a popular Greek aphorism or maxim purported to be inscribed in the forecourt of the temple of Apollo at Delphi. It is written *nosce te ipsum* in Latin.
32. 2 Corinthians 5:10–11
33. Romans 5:6
34. Psalm 130:3–4

hand all day long to a disobedient and obstinate people.[35] However, we must not presume upon His patience. The Scriptures forewarn us that the Son's wrath may soon be kindled, and it is a terrifying thing to fall into the hands of a living God.[36] Therefore, let us take refuge in Him before it is too late.[37] Let us make friends with our Opponent at law while we are with Him on the way, so that we will not be judged and thrown into the eternal prison. For we will not be freed until we have paid the last cent![38]

THE CHURCH'S COMMISSION

The third and final truth that demands our attention is that the church has been commissioned not only to proclaim the benefits of the gospel but also to warn men of the great and irrevocable judgment that is coming upon the world. To the Gentiles gathered in Cornelius's home, Peter declared: "He [Christ] commanded us to preach to the people, and to testify that it is He who was ordained by God to be Judge of the living and the dead."[39] The word *ordered* comes from the Greek word *paraggéllo*, which may also be translated "command" or "charge." In this, we discover an extremely important truth: the proclamation of Christ as Judge was an essential element in the apostolic gospel. The good news preached by the early church was not limited to the pronouncement of Christ as Savior, or even Christ as Lord, but it also included His office as the Judge of all men, the living and the dead. With an uncommon boldness, they proclaimed Him to sinners and high priests, slaves and Caesars, as the One who would judge them and determine their eternal destinies. Such a claim, published by a small group of berated preachers about a Jew who was crucified in Palestine, must have seemed audacious, to say the least. It is no wonder that some mocked, others were amazed, and still others drew away with fear.[40]

In his letter to the church in Rome, the apostle Paul describes "the day when God will judge the secrets of men by Jesus Christ, according to my

---

35. Romans 10:21
36. Hebrews 10:31
37. Psalm 2:12
38. Matthew 5:25–26
39. Acts 10:42
40. 2 Peter 3:3–4; Acts 4:13. Acts 24:25: "Now as he [Paul] reasoned about righteousness, self-control, and the judgment to come, Felix was afraid and answered, 'Go away for now; when I have a convenient time I will call for you.'"

gospel."[41] Like Peter's declaration above, this is an extraordinary state-ment. Paul is telling us that the universal judgment of humanity through the man Christ Jesus was an essential, foundational truth of the gospel which he proclaimed. This is an important word for the contemporary gospel preacher who may be tempted to avoid this less palatable truth of the gospel in order to circumvent the conflict it generates. It also speaks to those ministers who believe that God has called them to preach only the more positive elements of the gospel to the exclusion of its "hard sayings."[42] According to Paul and Peter, we cannot be faithful preachers of the gospel if the proclamation of the judgment of God through Christ is absent or infrequent in our preaching. If we are to stand in that great line of gospel preachers throughout the history of the church, we must not only preach Christ as Savior, we must also proclaim Him as Judge and warn all men to prepare to meet their God![43]

It is a great truth that God did not send the Son into the world to judge the world, but that the world might be saved through Him.[44] However, He has fixed a day in which He will judge the world in righteousness through a Man whom He has appointed, having furnished proof to all men by raising Him from the dead.[45] When the Son returns for a second time, He will take up His mantle of judgment and decide the fate of all men. Peter warns us that Christ is *ready* to judge the living and the dead.[46] James declares that the Judge is standing at the door, ready to break forth once more into human history.[47] Jesus ended His revelation to John with the warning, "And behold, I am coming quickly, and My reward is with Me, to give to every one according to his work."[48] Because of these warn-ings, we must always consider and proclaim the imminence of Christ's second coming and final judgment.[49]

---

41. Romans 2:16
42. John 6:60
43. Amos 4:12
44. John 3:17
45. Acts 17:30–31; Hebrews 9:27
46. 1 Peter 4:5
47. James 5:9
48. Revelation 22:12
49. The imminence of Christ's coming is an essential article of the Christian faith. It holds Christ's coming to be imminent, or possible at any time. For this reason, the gospel call is always urgent.

The idea of a determined consummation of history and a final judgment of every moral creature by a sovereign God appears to be the stuff of myth to modern man. Nevertheless, we must not balk at the proclamation of it. The skepticism of our age is nothing new. The apostle Peter faced similar cynicism when he wrote: "Knowing this first: that scoffers will come in the last days, walking according to their own lusts, and saying, 'Where is the promise of His coming? For since the fathers fell asleep, all things continue as they were from the beginning of creation.'"[50]

Apart from a work of the Holy Spirit, fallen man will always react negatively to gospel preaching, especially when it includes a discussion of "righteousness, self-control, and the judgment to come."[51] Regardless of how thoroughly they seek to rid themselves of the God of Scripture, they will always be haunted by the fact that He is, that He has revealed His will to them, and that He will hold them accountable for their deeds. They will wear themselves out in seeking to suppress the truth and will go to any lengths to quiet the accusations of their conscience.[52] Furthermore, they will fight against any preacher who reminds them of what they choose to forget or stirs up the dread they seek to bury. They will mock his warnings of judgment as the delusions of a fanatic or the schemes of a charlatan.[53] Nevertheless, it does not change the fact that at the consummation of the age, all men will be gathered into the Valley of Decision.[54] There they will be judged, and their eternal fate will be pronounced upon them. On the Isle of Patmos, the apostle John saw that day and prophesied the following:

> Then I saw a great white throne and Him who sat on it, from whose face the earth and the heaven fled away. And there was found no place for them. And I saw the dead, small and great, standing before God, and books were opened. And another book was opened, which is the Book of Life. And the dead were judged according to their

---

50. 2 Peter 3:3–4
51. Acts 24:25
52. Romans 1:18; 2:14–15
53. Acts 26:24
54. Joel 3:11–14: "Assemble and come, all you nations, and gather together all around. Cause Your mighty ones to go down there, O LORD. 'Let the nations be wakened, and come up to the Valley of Jehoshaphat; for there I will sit to judge all the surrounding nations. Put in the sickle, for the harvest is ripe. Come, go down; for the wine press is full, the vats overflow—for their wickedness is great.' Multitudes, multitudes in the valley of decision! For the day of the LORD is near in the valley of decision."

works, by the things which were written in the books...And anyone not found written in the Book of Life was cast into the lake of fire.[55]

Our proclamation of the gospel must set forth not only the universal offer of salvation but also the universal lordship of Jesus Christ. Furthermore, we must not only proclaim the benefits of faith and obedience to Christ, but we must also give a clarion call regarding the terrifying consequences of rejecting Him, either through hostility or mere neglect. Consequently, we must also discard the idea that there is some way to preach the gospel without scandal or offense. We must keep to heart that we are not seeking a truce with the world, but we are demanding the world's allegiance to Christ. We are not begging for the world's approval, but we are giving it an ultimatum: "Now therefore, be wise, O kings; be instructed, you judges of the earth. Serve the LORD with fear, and rejoice with trembling. Kiss the Son, lest He be angry, and you perish in the way, when His wrath is kindled but a little. Blessed are all those who put their trust in Him."[56]

If we preach the gospel in this way, we will be a sign of division among our peoples. Like the apostle Paul, we are to be a fragrance of Christ among those who are being saved and among those who are perishing; to the one we will be the fragrance of life, and to the other we will be the smell of death.[57] To some we will be honored as heralds of good news and messengers of life, but to others we will be disdained as idle babblers, the scum of the world, the dregs of all things, nuisances who upset the world, men who should not be allowed to live.[58]

For this reason, the gospel preacher must prepare himself for great opposition. However, knowing the strength of our King, we should no longer fear the combined strength of the nations. We should pity them and plead for them to be reconciled. Charles Spurgeon writes:

> As Jesus is King of kings and Judge of judges, so the gospel is the teacher of the greatest and wisest. If any are so great as to spurn its admonitions, God will make little of them; and if they are so wise as to despise its teachings, their fancied wisdom shall make fools of them. The gospel takes a high tone before the rulers of the earth, and they

---

55. Revelation 20:11–12, 15
56. Psalm 2:10–12
57. 2 Corinthians 2:15–16
58. Acts 17:18; 1 Corinthians 4:13; Acts 17:6; 22:22

who preach it should, like Knox and Melville, magnify their office by bold rebukes and manly utterances even in the royal presence. A clerical sycophant is only fit to be a scullion in the devil's kitchen.[59]

God has commanded that all men everywhere repent and believe in the Son, for "He has appointed a day on which He will judge the world in righteousness" through Him.[60] There is "one God and one Mediator between God and men, the Man Christ Jesus."[61] Nor is there salvation in any other, "for there is no other name under heaven given among men by which we must be saved."[62] The eternal destiny of the entire human race depends upon its proper knowledge of the gospel, including the great judgment that is coming upon the world through its only Sovereign, the Lord Jesus Christ. These are weighty matters, and they are as urgent as they are solemn. The gospel does not deal in trivialities; rather it deals with what truly matters most within the realm of human existence: eternal life and eternal death. For this reason, we should take our direction in life, ministry, and preaching from the apostle Paul, who wrote, "Therefore we make it our aim, whether present or absent, to be well pleasing to Him. For we must all appear before the judgment seat of Christ, that each one may receive the things done in the body, according to what he has done, whether good or bad. Knowing, therefore, the terror of the Lord, we persuade men; but we are well known to God, and I also trust are well known in your consciences."[63]

With regard to ourselves, we must have a singular ambition that rises above every other passion: to be pleasing to God in every aspect of our lives. Although our highest motivation should always be the love of God, it should not be our only motivation.[64] The apostle Paul was not only constrained by God's benevolence in Christ, but he was also moved by the solemn truth that he would one day appear before the judgment seat

---

59. Spurgeon, *Treasury of David*, 1:18. A sycophant is a groveling or servile flatterer, or a person who seeks to gain the favor of another. A scullion is a servant assigned the most menial kitchen tasks. A clerical sycophant is the worst of men because he not only flatters men and grovels before them, he also denies Christ to gain their approval.

60. Acts 17:30–31

61. 1 Timothy 2:5

62. Acts 4:12

63. 2 Corinthians 5:9–11

64. 2 Corinthians 5:14

of Christ and be recompensed for every deed, whether good or bad.[65] With regard to others, we must not only proclaim the gospel to men, but we must seek to employ every biblical means at our disposal to persuade them to be reconciled to God through Christ and to live out their lives in fear and trembling.[66] In fact, as ambassadors for Christ, as though God were making an appeal through us, we should beg men, on behalf of Christ, to be reconciled to God.[67]

---

65. 2 Corinthians 5:10
66. Philippians 2:12–13
67. 2 Corinthians 5:20

Other volumes in the

Recovering the Gospel

series

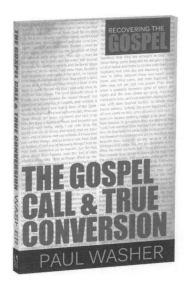

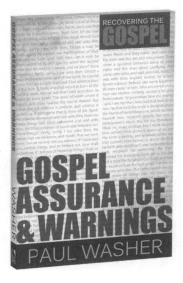